LOG

CAPTAIN'S LOG

NEW ZEALAND'S MARITIME HISTORY

ONe

livingstone
productions

GAVIN McLEAN

Hodder Moa Beckett

To Kynan Gentry
'Hey Sunshine!'

Cover

Portrait of Captain Cook by Nathaniel Dance Holland
Alexander Turnbull Library PUBL-0023-001.

Back cover images, left to right

The *Endeavour*
Alexander Turnbull Library B-011-022-

The *Crusader*
D A De Maus Collection, Alexander Turnbull Library G-2016-1/1-

The *Athenic*
Alexander Turnbull Library 1/1-001069

The *Rangatira*
G T Radcliffe Collection, Alexander Turnbull Library F-22439-1/4-.

Page i

Steamer Day was a highlight for many isolated communities well into the 20th century. This is the *Clansman* (591-tons, 1884) one of the Northern Steam Ship Company's larger and better-known ships. It lasted until 1934.
Kinnear Collection, Alexander Turnbull Library G-6197-1/1

Pages ii-iii

For decades the high cost of building breakwater ports kept Napier politicians bickering over replacing the small Inner Harbour at Port Ahuriri. When this photograph was taken, in about 1910, work had stalled on the breakwater port and cargo was still being lightered dangerously and laboriously out to Home Boats in the roadstead. The ship at the wharf is the 5777-ton trans-Tasman liner *Ulimaroa*. It was owned by the Melbourne firm Huddart Parker Ltd, originally a rival to the Union Company but later part-owned by the 'Southern Octopus'.
Auckland Star Collection, Alexander Turnbull Library G-2952-1/1-

ISBN 1-86958-881-9

© Television New Zealand Ltd and Livingstone Productions Ltd 2001
The moral rights of the author have been asserted

© 2001 Design and format — Hodder Moa Beckett Publishers Ltd

Published in 2001 by Hodder Moa Beckett Publishers Ltd
[a member of the Hodder Headline Group],
4 Whetu Place, Mairangi Bay, Auckland, New Zealand

Designed and produced by Hodder Moa Beckett Publishers Ltd
Film by Microdot, Auckland
Printed by Toppan Printing Co., Hong Kong

Contents

Acknowledgements

I owe many debts. First, I'd like to thank Johnny Givins, Gresham Bradley and the crew from Livingstone Productions for dreaming up the idea of spending summer 'messing about in boats' and for taking me along for the ride, so to speak. Thanks, too, to their researcher Margaret Dagg for her notes. I am also indebted to Hodder Moa Beckett for having the faith that, fuelled by good coffee and sauvignon blanc, I could produce a maritime history of New Zealand in three months and fewer than 60,000 words. My sincere thanks to publisher Linda Cassells, editor Diana Balham, art director Nick Turzynski and the rest of the publishing team.

Wellington Harbourmaster Mike Pryce's 'Nautical News', and his predecessor, Paddy Leahy's 'For the Record' in *New Zealand Marine News* are mines of information on the last few decades' shipping history. For the loan of photographs I would like to thank the following: Richard Jackson from the Royal New Zealand Navy, Wellington, and Fraser Meachen from the Hydrographic Office, Auckland; Frank Wall from Silver Fern Shipping; Captain David Barnes from Milburn Shipping; Captain Iain McLeod; Graham Ferguson; Captain C E Corkill; Mike Pryce; John McLeod from the New Zealand Merchant Service Guild; Terry Ryan from the NZ Waterfront Workers' Union, Auckland Branch; Merril Coke from Sealord Group Ltd; Lee Harris from Fiordland Travel Ltd; Craig Turvey from 3-D Creative Ltd; David Prendergast from Southport Ltd and Stuart Scott from Centreport Ltd.

As always, librarians have been wonderful. I would like to thank Joan McCracken and the crew at the Turnbull; Wendy Adlam from the Museum of Wellington, City & Sea; Gabor Toth from the Wellington City Archives; Chris Hurley from Archives New Zealand; Linda Tancred from the Taranaki Museum and the Victoria University Library. Finally, thanks to Kynan 'Boy Wonder' Gentry, formerly of the Wellington Public Library's New Zealand Room and now in exile in Melbourne.

A Note on Measurements

Shipping tonnages are expressed in many different ways. In this book I have generally used gross registered tonnage (GRT); this measures **volume**, not weight, and is in tons, not tonnes. For bulk carriers and tankers, deadweight (DWT), the **weight** of cargo, fuel and stores is preferred. Cargo tonnages have been converted into metric measurements, as have ship dimensions. Distances at sea are still measured in nautical miles and appear that way in this book.

Introduction

For the last thousand years or so innovation, prosperity, conflict, challenge and change have crashed relentlessly against New Zealand's coasts. They are our front door. Research has killed the myth of the Polynesian 'Great Fleet' but many fleets have surged past since — fleets of crusading colonists, fleets of 'Home' boats, the American 'Great White Fleet', the container and bulk carrier fleets of the 1970s and the Bolly-swilling America's Cup flotillas. All have left their mark.

We do not know exactly when the first Eastern Polynesian canoes shattered the long isolation of this distant archipelago but in the ensuing eight or nine hundred years since then prows and bows have been the sharp end of change in New Zealand. It took just 500 years for those first colonisers to name, settle and forever alter the islands' unique biosphere. Two hundred years ago another wave washed against the shores of Abel Tasman's 'New Land From the Sea'. Within a mere lifetime of James Cook mapping New Zealand and bestowing another layer of now familiar names, ships were discharging traders and settlers who would make New Zealand part of the global trading network.

It is ironic that globalisation became a catchword over a century after it was actually achieved, in large part through the Western sailing ship. Transformed between 1500 and the mid 1800s through cumulative micro-inventions and supported by a new science of navigation and the inquisitive/acquisitive mindset of the culture that had spawned it, the ship gave new impetus to Europe. Until then Europe had been an unimportant promontory of Asia, as often colonised as coloniser, but the marriage of canon and square-rig launched what Australian historian Frank Broeze calls 'the local expression of the exuberant energy, wealth, power and arrogance that propelled Europeans into every corner of the globe and by the mid 19th century had created a single world-wide economic and maritime system'.[1]

In 1966 another Australian historian, Geoffrey Blainey, spoke memorably of *The Tyranny of Distance*, an often quoted, if not always fully understood title.[2] New Zealand is even further from its world markets but distance has, perhaps, been overrated, or at least ameliorated more effectively than many think. Steamers slashed travelling times but, more importantly, brought reliability and regularity to commerce and communications. From 1876 the underwater telegraph cable that snaked its way across the Tasman to Sydney linked us to Britain and to Europe. By the late 1880s when James Mills and his colleagues were making the Union Steam Ship Company into a major business empire, cables permitted them to monitor fuel, steel and shipbuilding prices, competitors' activities, harvest forecasts and international events, all from

From the early 1960s onwards, RO-RO ships and bulk carriers displaced traditional coasters, along with some of the smaller ports they served. Here the *Ranginui* rests in the equally redundant Port of Kaiapoi. The 157-ton *Ranginui* had been built in 1936 and served with the Northern Company for over 20 years before being bought for the Kaiapoi trade. The old ship finished up as a venison recovery ship (note the small helipad) and a storage hulk.

– M Berthold Collection, Alexander Turnbull Library 24818–1/4–

Water Street, Dunedin. If distance was a tyranny, businessmen such as Mills and J M Ritchie felt it only lightly.

I hope that *Captain's Log* will show that seas are highways, not barriers. For most of our history, it has been cheaper and easier to move goods by sea. It still is for most commodities. More cargo moves by sea than ever, even along our 21st century 'open coast'. And, although more people now come and go through airports than seaports, imports and exports most certainly do not. As the *New Zealand Official Yearbook* earnestly reminds us, over 99 per cent of imports and more than 99 per cent of exports by volume travel by sea. The second message of the book is that the unrelenting quest for larger ships, smaller crews and cheaper cargo handling methods has drastically slashed the real cost of transport, to the advantage of every New Zealander (even if the benefits have seldom been shared equally). The steady reduction in sea freight over the last quarter of the 20th century probably did more to break down tariff barriers than political dogma or individual politicians. That has made ports very important. Think of our history in terms of digging very expensive holes in the seabed in order to improve our living standards. Only in the second part of the 20th century did any inland region centres develop (Palmerston North and Hamilton, both of which initially relied partly on riverine transport). Ports have always struggled to keep up with the larger ships required to move cargo cheaply and, as resource consents battles still show, the process remains controversial.

Ideas travel more easily than freight, but how many New Zealanders really appreciate how much they depend on the sea? We are sea-girt but not sea-savvy. Explaining that would take a book in itself, for there are many reasons. Over 40 years of flying has undoubtedly made us less conscious of commercial shipping, which in any case now comes and goes from behind distant, high security terminals. So, too, has our long dependence on foreign-owned shipping rendered us less maritime-minded. For most women, the rigid gender division aboard ships and on the wharves has also played its part. Until very recently seafaring and wharf work were almost entirely the preserve of men.

But in other ways we remain as fascinated by the sea as ever. The beach is still a favourite summer recreation space. The expensively congested marinas of Northland, Auckland and Wellington show how much we like messing about in boats. Every year we swim, scuba dive, fish, kayak, jet ski and boardsail in ever greater numbers. Most of us also passively enjoy the sea and its moods, whether we do it walking along Takapuna Beach at the height of summer or the St Clair Esplanade in the teeth of a southerly gale. Even if the Department of Conservation and regional councils no longer allow us to throw up brightly-painted cribs and baches wherever it takes our fancy, the expensive waterfront communities around the Bay of Plenty, Coromandel Peninsula and Auckland confirm that we still want to live by the sea. And we are not through with creating wealth from the sea. As I hope the last chapter shows, the new wave of waterfront development, yacht building, deep-sea fishing, eco-tourism and cruising suggests that we will continue to work as well as play within sight and sound of the sea, even if most of us are oblivious to the container ships and bulk carriers quietly going about their 'business in great waters'.

✤

CHAPTER 1
Prows and Bows
1200-1790

'*S*ATURDAY 7th. Winds NE, SE, Varble. Courses N 70° Wt. Distce sail'd miles 41. Latd in South 38°57'. Longd in West 177°54'. Gentle breezes and settled weather. At 2 PM saw land from the mast head bearing WBN, which we stood directly for, and could but just see it of the deck at sun set . . . At midnight brought too and sounded but had not ground with 170 fath: at day light made sail in for the land.'[1]

And so Captain James Cook recorded surgeon boy Nicholas Young's sighting of New Zealand's shores. Some still hoped that it was part of the fabled Great South Land but the peaks Young had glimpsed through the haze were in fact inland of Turanganui, modern Poverty Bay, so named by Cook because it afforded him little but grief. The youthful Nick, 'a son of a Bitch'[2] according to one shipmate, won a cask of rum for his alertness as well as a punning place in posterity when Cook reversed the order of his names to call a headland after him.

In the light, variable winds it took the Royal Navy bark HMS *Endeavour* until late in the afternoon of the eighth to work its way into the bay, where it anchored about a mile offshore. Cook and his men knew that they were not alone. Fortifications could be made out atop an island (Morai Island), there were canoes out on the water and smoke was rising from the beach. The shore-dwellers were almost certainly also squinting hard. At first they thought the tall-masted *Endeavour* was a floating island, then a great bird, and its colourfully garbed crew goblins from the sea.

Cook despatched boats for the shore, seeking fresh water, food and information. They landed on the east bank of the Turanganui River at a spot long since covered by port reclamation works. While scientist Joseph Banks shot birds and botanised by the Waikanae Creek, and others left nails as gifts, elsewhere along the beach the coxswain and three young men tending the yawl were approached by a party of warriors. Frightened by a challenge, they retreated to the boat and rowed frantically for the river mouth. They fired warning shots, then when a chief, Te Maro, lifted his lance and seemed about to throw, the coxswain shot him.

Next day, Cook, Banks, Solander and a party of marines landed again. A large party of warriors performed a haka, which the British terminated with a warning shot. Then their Tahitian interpreter, Tupaia, finding that he could communicate with the inhabitants, explained that they wanted food and water and were prepared to exchange iron. Through Tupaia, the locals complained about the previous day's killing. Tupaia persuaded one to come across to a rock in the shallows, where Cook also waded. They pressed noses and Cook gave gifts but the start of another haka persuaded Cook to rejoin his companions. Then things again fell apart. More armed warriors arrived and tried to exchange weapons with the British, who refused. When one man stole a short sword and waved it jubilantly in the air, Banks and William Monkhouse shot him. More shooting followed and more deaths.

Preceding pages

Warriors normally paddled a waka taua, but the canoes also carried sails, as this 1847 George French Angas painting of one passing Mt Egmont/Taranaki shows. Indeed, both could be used simultaneously (when the paddlers would also have helped keep the craft stable). Traditional sails were woven from kiekie, raupo or harakeke; the only traditional survivor, a harakeke sail, is in the British Museum.

Alexander Turnbull Library
PUBL-0014-02

M H Pryce

Although Cook visited New Zealand twice in HMS *Resolution*, the *Endeavour* has always overshadowed the later ship here. A small-scale replica cruised the country during the 1969-70 bicentennial celebrations, and when this full-scale replica visited the country's main ports in the 1990s New Zealanders trooped aboard in their tens of thousands. The ship is shown entering Wellington Harbour.

Cook took to the boats again. Unwilling to risk another landing, he intercepted two canoes returning from fishing, intending to take their occupants back to the *Endeavour*. The young fishermen resisted being kidnapped and threw stones, paddles and fish at Cook's men, who shot four of them, plucked three more from the water and took them back to the *Endeavour* where they were kept overnight. Although the earlier killings might have been an understandable reaction to ritualistic challenging they did not understand, the interception of the canoes and the violence that followed was a breach of Cook's instructions not to harm native people. As Salmond says, 'the local people must have been profoundly relieved when on the morning of 11 October, the *Endeavour* raised its anchor and sailed south out of the bay'.[3]

Cook's Landing Site Slips from Sight

T. Adams, Gisborne.   Unveiling of the Captain Cook Monument, Poverty Bay.

Port progress has been unkind to Cook's landing site (which was originally Turanganui-a-Kiwa, named after Kiwa, the navigator of the ancient Horouta canoe). In 1877 the Marine Department blasted Toka-a-Taiau, the rock where Cook met the unnamed Maori chief on 10 October 1769. A decade later the Gisborne Harbour Board reclaimed the area of the landing site. The Cook Memorial was opened in 1906, long after the damage had been done. Now the only indication of the old shoreline is a noticeable dip in the ground in front of the obelisk. Since the 1970s the Historic Places Trust has battled to retain a narrow 'cone of vision' from the memorial out to Young Nick's Head (also known as Te Kuri a Paoa).

More physically isolated than most New Zealand cities, Gisborne has struggled to keep up with the growth in ship size. This 1889 photograph of the huge steam crane used to extend the eastern breakwater indicates the investment that colonial towns were prepared to make to retain port status.

Polynesian Origins and Seafaring

Who were the people Cook encountered and how had they got there? Two hundred years of spirited debate has raged over the seafaring skills of Polynesians and how long they took to spread across the Pacific. The debate is not yet dead but in recent decades Geoffrey Irwin, Hec Busby, David Lewis, Ben Finney and others have analysed linguistic, artefactual and DNA evidence, run computer simulations and built and sailed replica craft. Just as an earlier generation sank Percy Smith's old notion of a Great Fleet bearing down on New Zealand in 1350 AD, these modern scholars and sailors have deep-sixed Andrew Sharp's theory of accidental drift voyaging.[4] Virtually everyone now agrees that the Pacific was settled through deliberate voyaging by master navigators and seafarers.

The ancestors of the modern Maori are believed to have left southern China perhaps 6000 years ago. It was not a systematic process, more a gradual diffusion 'along a line of islands that formed a kind of Milky Way across the Pacific', as Geoffrey Blainey put it. They had reached New Guinea, Tonga and Fiji by 1600 BC and Samoa by 1200 BC. By 500 AD they were at Hawaii and Easter Island. 'In distance travelled along an east-west line — the combined total of voyage after voyage made by generation after generation — it was the equivalent of a journey on land from Europe to China, spread over more than 4000 years.'[5] The first colonisers came from somewhere in Eastern Polynesia, the region that includes the Society Islands, the Marquesas and the Cooks.

Legends tell of navigator Kupe in his canoe *Matahouroa* and companion Ngahue chasing the giant bait-stealing octopus Te Wheke-o-Muturangi from the ancestral homeland, Hawaiki, to New Zealand where they killed it in Cook Strait. Along the way Kupe bestowed many names that linger still. As for actual colonisation, canoe traditions vary, with names ranging from the famous seven (*Aotea, Kurahaupo, Mataatua, Tainui, Takitimu, Te Arawa and Tokomaru*) to over 100.[6] These 14th-century canoe traditions can be contradictory. Since they usually tell of landing on already inhabited shores, Ranginui Walker calls them 'validating charters for tribal identity and ownership of land'.[7] Although some may describe arrivals in New Zealand from the tropical Pacific, most probably they refer to an internal migration from overpopulated territories; as Doug Simmonds suggested, the Hawaiki that they speak of is likely to have been Northland.

The canoes used by the early Polynesians were far more seaworthy than traditional single-hulled Maori canoes. Double-hulled Polynesian craft such as the Tahitian pahi were over 30 metres long and astonished early European explorers by literally sailing rings around their caravels. Large, fast and safe, they could carry the large quantities of people, livestock, plants and other stores needed to establish viable colonies. These double-hulled canoes could reach 14 knots and averaged eight under favourable conditions, putting in 100–150 sea miles a day, more than

This 18th-century engraving of William Hodges's 'Boats of the Friendly Isles' shows the type of double-hulled voyaging canoes used by Polynesian navigators.

any 16th-century Spanish or Portuguese ship's master might expect. Although they had a limited capacity to tack (zig-zag against the wind), they could sail comfortably as close to 75 degrees to the true wind direction.

If the boats were up to the job, so were the navigators and seafarers. The Polynesians were some of history's greatest navigators, although, as James Belich cautions, they 'are in danger of becoming deified rather than merely superhuman'.[8] Irwin argues that the Polynesians explored eastwards against the prevailing winds, using brief periods of westerlies, knowing that the easterlies would always return to get them home again if necessary. 'Practically every radiocarbon date in the remote Pacific supports the view that colonisation went first against the prevailing winds and only then across and down them.'[9] They sailed east-west along latitudes for which star signs are more useful than they are for longitude. Here observation of the skies over many generations enabled an elite group of navigators to construct star compasses of stars that were well spaced in both time and direction, to ensure that at least one or two were visible at any hour of the night. Star paths — sets of stars that rise or set in the same part of the horizon — supplemented star compasses.

Polynesian navigators used a battery of other techniques, literally feeling, seeing and sniffing their way across the sea. A skilled navigator could feel ocean swells, (which are spaced wider apart and move in a more undulating motion than the locally produced waves near land masses). He could detect reefs by the colour of the water covering them, and sense the presence of land by the effect that it had on clouds (clouds over lands appear stationary). He was always alert to the presence of land-roosting birds (which fly home every evening), phosphorescence and even the very smell of land and plant life, carried along by offshore breezes.[10] It is quite possible that the first colonists may have followed migrating birds such as the long-tailed cuckoo and the shearwater, whose spring departures for the south would have suggested the probability of land in that direction.[11]

New Zealand, like Easter Island and Hawaii, marked the outer limits of this Polynesian triangle. It was the last significant landmass in the world to be settled by people. It was probably also the outer limit of Polynesian maritime capacity. On the basis of current knowledge, the absence of New Zealand artefacts in tropical Polynesia and the lack of pigs (Polynesia's most highly prized domestic animal) here makes it unlikely that these first New Zealanders made return voyages or that there were multiple waves of colonisation. They certainly colonised the Chatham Islands in about 1400 and may even have settled Norfolk Island and the Kermadecs. Nevertheless, these are 'in the neighbourhood' and the long isolation of the Moriori in the Chathams, just 860km away, is significant.

Raiders of the Lost Ark

Just when the first Polynesian foot stepped onto a New Zealand beach remains a keen topic of discussion and debate by disputatious archaeologists, armed with radio-carbon data, artefacts and theories about rats. In the 21st century, as in the 19th and 20th, there is no consensus and even the most widely shared opinion is hedged about with qualifications about the need for further research. The shifting sands of this debate are likely to remain as unsettled as the coastal sites the archaeologists probe. Some have suggested that people may have brought rats here as long as 2500 years ago but, even if that is so, first contact and continuous settlement are probably very different things. In the early 1990s Atholl Anderson drew a new line in this scholarly sandpit by bringing forward the date for ongoing settlement to about 850 years ago (although not ruling out earlier visits). That will do for now. The site of the Polynesian Plymouth Rock is just as contentious. Northland has long been the preferred place, although some have suggested the South Island. Wherever the first seafarers fetched up, it is likely that they soon moved north along the coast in order to save tropical plants such as taro, yam, aute and ti that would never have survived southern frosts.

What is certain is that once these Polynesians put down permanent roots, they remained dependent on the sea as a source of food. In all likelihood their settlement pattern was what is called 'chaotic expansion', undertaking extensive coastal exploration in the early period, just as the 19th-century European colonists would use ports as staging posts for further settlement. They also continued to use the sea and the rivers as a highway for trade and warfare, although they lost either the inclination or the ability to undertake the oceanic journeys of their ancestors. This is not surprising. The landmass of New Zealand exceeds that of all the other islands of Polynesia, making it big enough to absorb the energies of a small colonising population.

Still, Maori remained intimate with the sea and its ways. In the South Island, in particular, the population was almost entirely coastal, venturing inland only seasonally, or hugging the shores of rivers and lakes. Unlike most Europeans of the time, most could swim. They made extensive use of coastal and riverine food resources, in some instances too much. They devastated populations of the southern fur seal, once abundant from the Far North to Stewart Island, leaving only remnants along the rugged shores of Murihiku, southern New Zealand.[12]

The voyaging canoes had vanished by the time that Europeans reached New Zealand. While early reports occasionally mentioned outriggers or two canoes lashed clumsily together, single-hulled craft were the norm in New Zealand. They were adequate for the coast-hugging done here, and more suitable for being portaged across isthmuses and shingle banks in rivers and paddled or poled up narrow, shallow rivers. There was some regional specialisation, mainly in decorative styles but canoes used to cross the rough Hokianga bar had higher and wider bows.[13]

There were three basic types, the waka taua (war canoes), waka tere (fishing canoes) and waka tiwai (river canoes). With the exception of the reed and flax stalk boats, all were dugouts. Almost all craft were narrow-hulled, adzed from single trees. These craft were paddled, although at sea and on lakes a mat sail could sometimes be used within the limitations of stability imposed by the single narrow hull. On rivers poling supplemented paddling, especially across rapids and shallows.

The iconic Maori craft is the waka taua. Up to about 25 metres long and capable of carrying a hundred or more paddlers, waka taua were built of kauri or totara. Just like the European ships of the time, they were both warships and expressions of tribal pride, and they represented a considerable

Sydney Parkinson, an artist aboard the *Endeavour*, painted this magnificently decorated waka taua off Gable End Foreland in 1770. A craft of this size represented an enormous investment of tribal resources and would usually be stored under a special shelter. Although the use of waka taua was not restricted to fighting, for everyday work the simpler, less manpower-intensive waka tere was preferred.

investment of time and tribal resources. Guided by tohunga tarai waka (canoe-making experts), experienced carvers worked under strict ceremonial conditions. The forest god, Tane Mahuta, was propitiated before a tree was felled. Women and children were not allowed near a work site, nor was food, and the men wore special garments while working on the hull. Once the tree had been felled, branches were removed and fire and adzes hollowed it out and lightened it to make it easier to drag to a river for seasoning in water or mud. This could take several months. Then the hull was finished, the top-strake was added (to build up the sides), the interior fittings, decorated prow (tauihu) and stern-piece (taurapa) were added and the hull was painted (usually dark red, with a mixture of shark-liver oil and either kokowai or burnt karamea clay). The entire process, from selecting the tree to completing the boat, might take up to two years.

Waka tere may have lacked the fine carving of the waka taua, but they were far more numerous. They were smaller (averaging 15 metres), but shared the same construction technique of adding top-strakes (planks) to the sides of dugout logs to build them up. Their prows and stern-pieces were simpler and not decorated with feathers. Waka tere were used for coastal voyages and for line fishing. Even more common were the waka tiwai, especially on rivers. They were simple dugouts, without topsides and much or any ornamentation and on average were about nine metres long. They were used for fishing, food-gathering and transportation. Usually waka tiwai were poled as well as paddled on rivers.

Two more specialised craft were the reed and flax stalk craft. In the remote Chathams where large trees did not grow, korari, the so-called wash-through canoes, replaced large dugout canoes. The largest, waka pahi, were up to 15 metres long and could carry 50 or more people between Chatham Island and Pitt Island. With their base of inflated kelp for buoyancy and their reed floor and sides, korari looked ungainly but they were stable and well suited to conditions around the islands.[14] More ubiquitous in New Zealand, and the South Island in particular, were the flax stalk craft such as mokihi. Usually throwaway craft, mokihi were usually made from bundles of raupo that grew near waterways. Their weight when saturated made them stable and ideal for travelling down rough rivers.[15]

Samuel Head Collection, Alexander Turnbull Library G-72951/1

On sheltered harbours and inland waterways the simple waka tiwai remained in everyday use well into the colonial period. These craft are on Lake Taupo.

These canoes and rafts were widely used for transportation, trading and warfare. They transported small quantities of stone material hundreds of miles, although there is a suggestion that the stormy seas off the West Coast led to considerable reliance on land trails. Beaches were widely used as highways. James Watson observes that 'the fragmentation of Maori society into numerous hapu can also be seen as at least partly a product of transportation limitations'.[16] With hunting and gathering providing a major part of the diet in many parts of New Zealand and without rapid means of transport, foraging had to operate over short distances and could therefore support only small populations. Canoe limitations and the importance of seafood led to concentration in sheltered coastal areas such as the harbours of Northland, the Hauraki Gulf and the Marlborough Sounds, lakes and along major river systems.

Europe's Global Economy

By the 18th century Maori had long since turned their backs on oceanic navigation but Europeans, formerly coastal voyagers, were laying the foundations for a new global civilisation based on maritime commerce and naval mastery. Through cumulative micro-inventions over several centuries they had improved their shipbuilding and navigational skills. One important early step was the invention of carvel shipbuilding techniques by northern European shipbuilders. Carvel-built ships have their hull boards placed edge-to-edge along a skeleton of beams and caulking between the planks ensures watertightness. This used less wood than the old clinker technique (based on overlapping planking) and enabled European shipbuilders to make their craft lighter, larger, faster and cheaper. Their combination of square rig and fore-and-aft sails brought new flexibility. By 1400 a few ships exceeded 1000 tons, although smaller ones would remain the norm for another 450 years.

In the late 16th century the Dutch developed the fluytschip, the 'fluyt'.[17] Cheap to build and to operate, these fluyts soon had the British and French dancing to their tune by undercutting freight rates by 30–50 per cent. Other maritime powers absorbed the lesson and developed their own increasingly specialised craft. It says much for the strength and adaptability of the 18th-century sailing ship that Cook's *Endeavour*, which would circumnavigate the globe during a voyage of over two years, was a mere coaster, a Whitby bark designed for the North Sea collier trade.

Western seafarers also sharpened up their navigation along with their shipbuilding. The masters of Greek and Roman ships had watched the stars and had hugged the coasts as closely as possible, as had even the Vikings. In the closing centuries of the Middle Ages, however, the compass (invented simultaneously in China) enabled navigators to venture further and with greater confidence. At first

Livingstone Productions

Livingstone Productions

little more than a magnetised needle floating in a bowl of water, by 1300 the compass had become recognisably modern — a self-contained unit complete with the wind rose (a rose diagram indicating the relative frequency and strength of the wind). From about 1280 the Mediterranean, formerly closed to navigation in the winter months, was being used year-round by shipping.[18] From the 15th century Portuguese navigators began adapting Greek and Islamic knowledge to produce the astrolabe, a device that measured the altitude of the Polar Star, thus indicating the observer's latitude (the distance of a position north or south of the equator). It was simplified for navigational purposes as the quadrant and then the sextant.

Quadrants and astrolabes gave only part of the picture. What was missing was a reliable means of determining longitude, the position on an east-west line.[19] This was the Holy Grail of navigation. If longitude could be mapped as accurately, mariners would be able to find their way anywhere in the world by cross-referencing against grids made up of co-ordinates from latitude and longitude. Latitude they could get easily enough with the help of the compass, which they learned to adjust according to their location on the globe and by sightings of the sun. Dead-reckoning, however, gave a far less accurate measure of longitude. Solving the 'longitude problem' would save thousands of lives. It occupied many great scientific minds, including Sir Isaac Newton's, until an obscure English clockmaker, John Harrison, devised 'The Watch', a highly accurate clock that kept time at sea. H-4, as it was called, was a 127-mm diameter, 1.5kg, finely jewelled watch that kept near-perfect time, certainly accurate enough for navigational purposes. In its own way H-4 was every bit as world-changing as the first microchip. In time the combination of the chronometer and the sextant would let seafarers fix their position anywhere with unprecedented accuracy.

This was also the start of the great age of cartography as Europeans vastly improved their knowledge of the globe. In a sense they had travelled here already. For centuries Westerners had been constructing conceptual maps of southern lands and tropical maidens, making them pre-silicon chip 'virtual travellers'. Many

Waka have played an important part in Waitangi celebrations for decades. Interest in these traditional craft intensified after the 1990 celebrations and several now take to the water every year. These photographs were taken at Waitangi in 2001.

By the end of the 18th century the Western sailing ship could circle the globe, even a little 'cat-built' coastal collier like the *Endeavour*. Apart from the need to replenish stores and water, it was practically a self-contained unit. It could voyage for several years at a time, conducting most running repairs at sea or in sheltered inlets. This 1920s sketch by Francis Bayldon shows the *Endeavour* under the Red Ensign. The ship was tiny by modern standards, just 368 tons burthen, 32.3 metres long and 8.9 metres at the broadest point. Into this cramped wooden world squeezed 94 people, four pigs, three cats, two dogs, a goat, several dozen fowl and stores for 18 months.

clung to the old notion of Terra Australis, a mysterious great southern continent that was thought necessary to balance the landmasses of the Northern Hemisphere, and the long search for the 'Great South Land' played a part in New Zealand's 'discovery' by men such as Tasman and Cook. In 1756 Charles de Brosses divided the still unmapped southern lands into Magellanic, Australasia and Polynesia. From offices in London, Paris or Lisbon European cartographers bestowed new names, and sorted lands, people, animals and plants into new taxonomies. Mapmaking improved immeasurably during the 18th century as explorers filled in the missing gaps and as improvements in navigation enabled explorers such as James Cook to chart with unprecedented accuracy.

Cook was not the first European to glass New Zealand's shores. Romantics dream of Tamil bells and Spanish helmets but the first known European explorer here was a Dutchman, Commander Abel Janszoon Tasman. By the 17th century the Dutch Republic had become a major maritime power. In 1642 Anthony van Diemen, the Governor-General of the Dutch East Indies, sent Tasman, merchant Isaac Gilsemans and pilot

Jacobszoon Visscher off in the war yacht *Heemskerck* and the fluyt *Zeehaen* to hunt the fabled 'Great South Land' that Europeans had long hoped lay in the Pacific.[20] Neither vessel was very big; the *Heemskerck* was 120 tons and the *Zeehaen* just 50 tons.

After skirting 'New Holland' (modern Australia), the Dutch ships sighted a 'land, uplifted high', the South Island's West Coast, on 13 December 1642. Five days later they anchored in what is now Golden Bay. Unfortunately their timing was bad. Local politics were tense, the result of resource depletion and the effects of the Little Ice Age making the bay a contested zone. Two canoes paddled out to initiate an unintelligible musical exchange, a Dutch trumpeter responding to Ngati Tumata Kokiri's ritual shell trumpet challenge. This seems to have encouraged the Maori to treat their visitors as hostile, because next day they rammed a cockboat crossing from the *Heemskerck* to the *Zeehaen*, killing four Dutchmen.[21] After firing at more canoes bearing down on them, Tasman's ships hurried away from the bay, leaving behind one body and a new name for the bay, Murderers'.

Tasman and his colleagues also gave a name to the unnamed archipelago, Staten Landt, which a Dutch mapmaker later named Nieuw Zeeland, the highly appropriate 'New Land From the Sea'. The name they made for themselves has been equally fluid. The traditional consensus has been that Tasman and Visscher's 5000-mile voyage was 'a splendid failure'.[22] They had circumnavigated Australia without seeing it, had missed New Guinea entirely and had left the outline of part of New Zealand hanging off the map like a big question mark. Belich suggests that this negativity may be because Tasman was not British, a point picked up by Grahame Anderson in his spirited 2001 defence of the expedition, *The Merchant of the Zeehaen*.[23]

James Cook was English and he not only filled in the gaps left by Tasman, he also took pride of place in the settler Historical Hall of Fame. Cook was born in 1728 at Marton-in-Cleveland, in Yorkshire, the second son of a Scottish day labourer. After training in the merchant marine, he transferred to the Royal Navy, where he rose through sheer professionalism in an institution not much fussed about advancement on merit. He remains a controversial figure in a land groaning with Cook place names and Cook statues and markers. Early 20th-century settler hagiography presented Cook as a seagoing Christ with spyglass but in recent attacks of the post-modern, post-colonial vapours some scholars have dynamited the pedestal from underneath the Great Navigator. More faecal than fecund, the worst excesses of dreary deconstructionism have nevertheless provided a counterweight to the earlier extremes. The Cook that emerges is still a great man but one who sometimes made mistakes in his dealings with indigenous peoples and who by the time of his third great voyage was showing signs of burnout. The *Dictionary of New Zealand Biography* entry describes him as 'a genius of the matter of fact: a systematic, professional and thorough explorer, who knew just how far to take his ships and his men . . . In his relations with indigenous peoples he was essentially a creature of his time, carrying to the Pacific a compassionate version of British concepts of justice, which he endeavoured to adapt to new circumstances.'[24]

Cook made three great circumnavigations of the globe. The first, launched to observe the transit of Venus, mapped Australia and New Zealand. As we have seen, it began with the killings at Poverty Bay. After leaving that place, Cook anchored in a bay he called Hawke's. There Maori turned the tables on him, trying to kidnap Taiata, Tupaia's servant. After making reconnaissance southwards, the *Endeavour* anchored at Anaura and Uawa bays (Tolaga Bay). At Cook's Cove they replenished their water supplies, took on board wood and some 'Sellery and Scurvy grass', the wild celery which Cook boiled with other food every morning to prevent scurvy.[25] While they did that Banks and the scientists observed and took samples. Cook moved north, stopping at the places forever associated with him, Mercury Bay and the Bay of Islands, before rounding North Cape and sailing southwards down the west coast of the North Island. He found Cook Strait (which Banks named after him), then anchored in Queen Charlotte Sound, a place he would return to on his later voyages. For the next two months he sailed around the South Island, finally heading off for New Holland on 31 March 1770. He had shown that New Zealand was a set of islands and not a Great South Land. Cook made a few mistakes — he thought that Banks Peninsula was an island and he made Stewart Island part of the mainland — but his charts were an extraordinary achievement by the standards of the time. Oddly enough, Cook at first reaped little benefit from this. Society lionised the well-heeled and well-connected Joseph Banks and Cook's importance was not fully appreciated until his journal was published.

Cook made two more voyages, both virtually entirely South Island affairs, basing himself at Dusky Sound and at Queen Charlotte Sound. Though the second voyage (1772–75) is not so celebrated in New Zealand, it was considerably more important and is probably the greatest voyage in history. This time Cook had two converted colliers, HMS *Resolution* and HMS *Adventure*. In four very productive years he successfully tested a copy of H-4, Harrison's chronometer, and torpedoed forever the notion of a habitable 'Great South Land'. His explorations took him across the Antarctic Circle, the first time anyone had done this. Above all, Cook's charts, produced with the help of the chronometer and the persistence that was his trademark, threw new light on the Pacific. The third voyage (1776–80) again used the *Resolution*, accompanied by HMS *Discovery*. In his last contact with New Zealand, Cook again called in at Ship Cove on his way to search for the North-West Passage. His judgment was less acute by now and he paid the price for his mistake at Kealakekua Bay in February 1779 when Hawaiians attacked and killed him.

Cook still overshadows the other European explorers who left their calling

Cook and Banks

CAPTAIN COOK

London Published as the Act directs Sept 20 1800 by J.Wilkes

James Cook (1728–79), the greatest navigator in history, was a Yorkshireman who rose to prominence through determination and intelligence. This portrait was issued after Cook's death (see vignette) and is based on the painting by Nathaniel Dance made after Cook's second circumnavigation.

Joseph Banks (1743–1820) came from a very different social background to Cook. His entourage included two family retainers, two black servants and an aristocratic greyhound. This Benjamin West portrait shows the young Banks fresh from the first circumnavigation, proudly wearing his laurel leaves, in this case a Maori flax cloak. The archetypal gentleman scholar, Banks was later knighted and served as President of the prestigious Royal Society.

SIR JOSEPH BANKS B.

Cook's Map of New Zealand

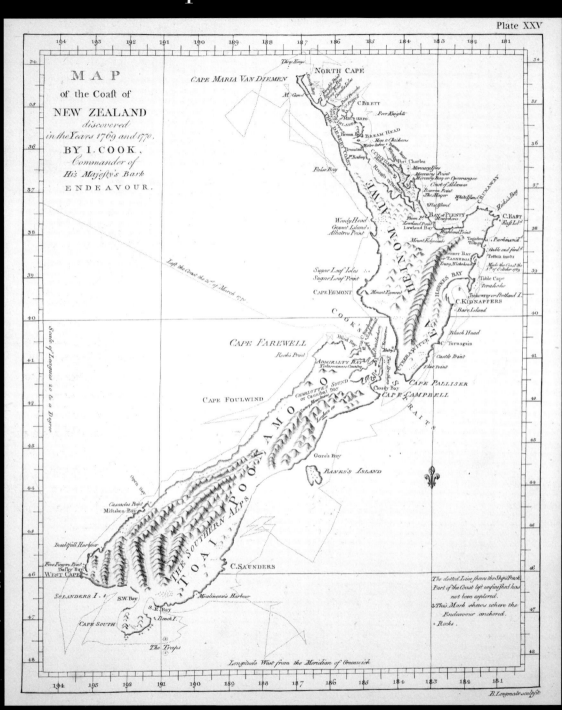

Plate XXV

Map-making had great strategic as well as commercial significance and if Tasman left New Zealand looking like a question mark hanging in space, Cook, doyen of hydrographers, put the islands on the map. In *This Stern Coast*, his 1969 history of charting the New Zealand coast, Rear Admiral John O'C Ross, recorded that a young navigating officer of the radar and satellite era navy felt that he could still take a ship around the coast with Cook's chart.

Alexander Turnbull Library B-043-018

Our Anglophile historiography under-represents the contribution made by the French in our pre-colonial and early colonial history. Dumont d'Urville, like Cook, made three voyages to New Zealand. Here we see his ships *Astrolabe* and *Zélée* at the delightfully named Bay of Sarah's Bosom in the remote Auckland Islands, in May 1840. The French added much to Western scientific knowledge and sometimes also enjoyed better relations with Maori than their British counterparts. French trade also followed the explorers. French whalers were numerous not just at Akaroa, but also the Bay of Islands and for much of the 1840s the French warships stationed at the small French settlement at Akaroa were a welcome presence to many settlers.

cards on New Zealand's shores. The French, Britain's great continental rivals, were also pushing the geographical boundaries of the Enlightenment and in December 1769 Jean-François de Surville and Cook actually passed within 50 miles of each other as they each rounded Northland's opposite coasts. De Surville had read Tasman's bad press about New Zealand but had too many crew sick to be fussy. On 17 December he anchored in Doubtless Bay (which he named Lauriston Bay) and had a relatively peaceful stay, marred only by the theft of a dinghy and bloodless French retaliation. Three years later another Frenchman, Marc-Joseph Marion du Fresne, entered the Bay of Islands, where he and 26 other officers and men would be killed for violating a fishing tapu. French utu left 250 Maori dead. Later French visitors included Chevalier d'Entrecasteaux (1793), Louis Duperry (1824), Dumont d'Urville (1827 and 1840), Cyrille-Pierre-Théodore Laplace (1831) and C F Lavaud (1840–43), supplemented by Spaniard Alessandro Malaspina's 1793 expedition, later British ones by George Vancouver (1791), Robert FitzRoy (1835) and James Clark Ross (1840) and the Russian, Fabian Gottlieb Benjamin von Bellingshausen (1820). Even Austria would later send a scientific expedition. Belich wrote memorably of the Dutch Republic grasping the world's trade and sending out its farthest outstretched finger to New Zealand in 1642 where it was pricked and recoiled. As the long list of explorers, scientists and naval officers recited above shows, however, Western Europe was getting better at grasping and at smacking when necessary. And, as we shall see, there was no shortage of Maori willing to reach out and to discover Europe as well.

✳

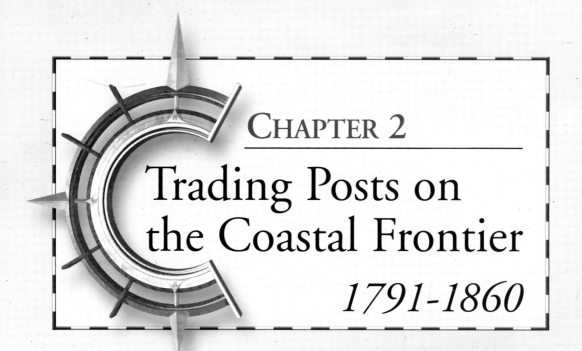

CHAPTER 2

Trading Posts on the Coastal Frontier

1791-1860

A fter 1500 'Europe could now plant itself anywhere on the surface of the globe within reach of naval cannon'.[1] No European nation was better placed than Britain, whose flourishing merchant marine enabled its entrepreneurs to reach across the globe to trade economically even in low-value bulk cargoes. They made pre-1840 New Zealand 'essentially a mine with several natural products'.[2] From New South Wales a mixed bag of colonial entrepreneurs, sealers and stowaways, aided by Maori, formed the scruffy advance guard of what Alan Grey calls 'a Robber Economy' and Belich terms 'Old New Zealand'.[3] It was an unconscionable time a-dying. Whaling did not finally end until 1964 and the extractive industries of 'Old New Zealand' kept Northern New Zealand timber mills buzzing until well into the early 20th century. Nevertheless, from 1840 onwards, when Lieutenant-Governor Hobson proclaimed British sovereignty over the islands and the New Zealand Company planted its controversial settlements around Cook Strait, more permanent roots were also being grafted on Old New Zealand.

Preceding pages
Early New Zealand colonial shipbuilders made good use of skilled labour and plentiful timber supplies. As this 1863 photograph of the schooner *Lotus* nearing completion at Wakatiwai near Kaukapakapa on the Kaipara shows, they worked almost anywhere. Completed next year by William Bonar, the 81-ton *Lotus* was the pride of the Kaipara during its extraordinarily short life. Just a few months later, on 13 August 1864, the vessel was lost while trying to cross the Kaipara bar with a load of timber. Heavy seas drove the schooner onto first the south and then the north spits before tearing it apart.

D M Beere Collection, Alexander Turnbull Library G-096079-½

The Robber Economy – Sealing, Timber and Whaling

Contrary to popular belief, European commerce began not in the Far North, but in the Deep South. In November 1791 George Vancouver called at Dusky Sound in HMS *Discovery* and HMS *Chatham*. At Cook's old anchorage in Pickersgill Cove, they 'drank a cheerful glass to the memory of Capt Cook, whose steps we were now pursuing', and fossicked for signs of his presence in the regenerating bush.[4] The rest of the time they blasted the biota, taking fish, birds and seals. Their reports of rich fur seal rookeries were music to the ears of the New South Wales 'pursuers of peltry' who had just about exhausted the Bass Strait grounds. A year later the British ship *Britannia* left Sydney and deposited a sealing party in Fiordland. So, in this low-key and almost forgotten way, Murihiku (the southern South Island), began totting up a list of firsts: the first wreck of a European-style ship in New Zealand waters, the first European-style ships built there, the first European-style house and the largest settlement of Europeans until the 1830s.

This first settlement was, Belich reminds us, more interested in getting out than in getting on. It came about by accident in September 1795 when the unseaworthy ship *Endeavour* (qv) limped into Facile Harbour, accompanied by the 150-ton *Fancy*.[5] Captain William Wright Bampton had planned to complete an unfinished schooner left there by the *Britannia*'s sealing party and load all three ships with spar timber for sale in India but his plans came unstuck when the *Endeavour*'s hull did. When the *Endeavour* was found to be beyond repair a motley assortment of 244 people, sailors, sealers and convict stowaways, found themselves stranded. The Facile Harbour detainees were not happy campers. The chief officer resigned, the new first officer and a passenger traded insults and a challenge was issued. When the officer refused, the passenger called him 'a Coward, a Dastardly Coward!' and threatened to publish the accusation in India. They did not speak again.[6]

Sealing, the industry that drew them to Facile Harbour, was spawned by a peculiar trade triangle. European women wanted fur hats and Australians cups of tea. To support their caffeine fix, New South Wales merchants turned Murihiku into the bloody fringe of the Australian frontier.[7] For three months at a time gangs of 30-40 men lived ashore, fending off hostile Maori and praying that their ship had not sunk or been diverted elsewhere. Even when things went smoothly, the work itself was thoroughly unpleasant. John Boultbee, a gent slumming with sealers in Murihiku, fought Maori, but remembered that 'the most dangerous part of a Sealer's employment is in landing on rocks, when there are heavy surfs, & I have been a quarter of an hour, waiting for a smooth to land, & then could not succeed'.[8]

It was a brutal, brutalising life and most reports described sealers as a rough, violent and drunken lot. The sealers Boultbee met hated 'scholards', 'swells' and gentlemen but reportedly saw themselves as middle class. It would be difficult to extend that description to the largest of these larger-than-life characters, Thomas Chaseland. The illiterate son of an Australian settler and an Aborigine, Chaseland possessed legendary size and strength.[9] Genial, 'at least when sober', he was feared and respected by European and Maori alike, because he spoke the language of utu. When avenging an attack on a sealing party, Chaseland shot Maori from a boat, stormed into the kainga like a Regency-era Rambo and slaughtered anyone who got in his way. 'Among his other acts he seized a child . . . and dashed her head on a rock'.[10]

Using clubs, lances and knives, the sealers had almost wiped out the fur seals of Murihiku by 1810.[11] Hardly surprising, considering that in just one week that year they landed £100,000 worth of seal skins at Sydney! The discovery of the sub-Antarctic rookeries in 1810 sent the sealers down to these icy waters. Although sealing lingered on as an adjunct to other activities, and even staged a minor revival in the 1820s, over-culling and changing hat fashions in London killed it.[12] The scorecard for race relations was marginally better. Despite ravaging a major food resource for southern Maori, the sealers recompensed them by introducing white potatoes and providing a commercial crop, thereby opening up Foveaux Strait for periodic or permanent occupation by Ngai Tahu.[13]

Timber cutting began about the same time as seal culling, although mostly in the north. Late in 1794 Edgar Dell took the 150-ton brig *Fancy* to Doubtless Bay, in Northland, then sailed down to 'the River Thames', the Firth of Thames, for the stands of timber mentioned by Cook and Banks. Dell's men spent several months cutting and dressing timber for spars and planks for East India Company ships. After 1798 ships visited the Coromandel Peninsula and then Northland for the spar trade. It met both entrepreneurial and strategic requirements. The entrepreneurial impulse came from New South Wales merchants, who largely ignored the East India Company's theoretical trading monopoly. The strategic impulse came from the Royal Navy, which sent the store ships HMS *Dromedary* and HMS *Coromandel* to New Zealand in 1820 to collect timber. They paid Maori an axe for a tree, but the voyage was a mixed success.[14] Kahikatea made poor spars and kauri cost more than Virginia spars; nevertheless, Admiralty contracts kept New South Wales merchants Thomas McDonnell and Dacre Brown busy before the navy returned with HMS *Buffalo*.

The timber and the flax processing industries required the permanent presence of Europeans. As Duncan Mackay notes, 'Control was particularly vital in the flax and timber industries because flax, masts and spars had to be prepared to the exacting standards of European shipyards and be ready in time for the schedules of trading ships.'[15] Between 50 and 100 flax and timber ports sprang up around New Zealand in the late 1820s and the 1830s, clustered in Northland, Hauraki/Bay of Plenty, the Wellington region, Cloudy Bay, Banks Peninsula and the Otago/Southland coasts. Most had just a single European resident or two, but in the Bay of Islands, the Hokianga and at the bigger southern whaling stations, larger groups could be found.

Hokianga, located on the north-western coast of New Zealand, was accessible to Sydney and had a large Maori workforce keen to earn firearms. Chief Patuone, an early Ngatihao

The Kaipara, New Zealand's largest harbour, is the confluence of eight rivers. In the 19th century it was navigable for about 100km of its length, from Dargaville in the north to Helensville in the south. Its entrance is one of the more challenging in the country. During the steam sawmilling era the Kaipara's rivers were dotted with 'sawdust towns', each of them with its own jetties and ships. This 1863 photograph shows a small trading vessel at McLeod's sawmill, which was near the junction of the Kaipara and Awaroa rivers. Helensville got its name from John McLeod's wife, Helen.

D M Beere Collection, Alexander Turnbull Library G-09608o-½

entrepreneur, visited Sydney in 1826 to promote the harbour as a trading base and returned with the agent of Sydney firm, Raine and Ramsay, to sell land at Horeke.[16] In August 1827 the *Sydney Gazette* reported that about 50 Britons were there, sawing timber and instructing Maori in shipbuilding [q.v.]. Augustus Earle, who passed through 'Deptford', as it was called, reported 'store-houses, dwelling-houses and various offices for mechanics'.[17] By the early 1830s sawpits dotted the Hokianga Harbour and John Martin was running a regular pilot service. Throughout most of the North forests were being exploited. In 1833 timber exports exceeded those of flax fibre and by the 1840s 'the kauri forests had been cleared well back of the coasts of the Bay of Islands, Whangaroa and Hokianga'.[18]

But the whaling industry was of even greater significance. 'Ocean whaling "was the eighteenth-century equivalent of today's petroleum industry" — Moby Dallas'.[19] Whale oil was used for lighting, cooking and in industrialising Britain, for lubricants. Sperm oil, worth three times as much as other oil, was prized as an agent in leather tanning. The sperm whale was a seagoing treasure chest. Spermaceti, the very light oil in the sperm whale's head, earned a premium, as did ambergris, a valuable fixative for perfume. The meat was seldom consumed, but baleen — whalebone — strengthened chair-seats and corsets and made fine buggy whips.

There were two types of whaling, pelagic or ocean whaling from ships and shore whaling.[20] The two overlapped, but pelagic whaling began in the mid 1790s and shore whaling began in the late 1820s to exploit the southern right whales that swam seasonally through Cook and Foveaux Straits and calved in bays along New Zealand's east coasts. Although whalers usually took whatever they could, in New Zealand they had two main prey. The favoured whale was the southern right whale, which was large, docile and slow and floated when dead. The shore stations hunted it almost exclusively. Pelagic whalers hunted the faster, square-headed sperm whale, and the more aggressive humpback.

Once again, New South Wales provided the jumping-off point for mining New Zealand resources. Some of the transports used to take prisoners to the New South Wales penal colony were whaleships and by 1791 five British vessels were whaling in the Tasman Sea. Most were ship and barque-rigged, usually about 250–400 tons, blunt-bowed, square-sterned and round-bodied, 'built by the mile and cut off in lengths as you want 'em', as one whaler put it.[21] Short and stubby, they pitched and tossed so badly that a passenger once claimed that her ship had done 20 knots in a storm, 'ten straight ahead and ten up and down'.[22] Never things of beauty, their marks of distinction were the half-dozen or more whaleboats that hung from davits at the ship's side and the chimneys and tops of the try-works. If the wind was blowing right, they trailed another signature, the stench of boiled whale blubber that hung about them in a miasmic fug. Still, as Morton says, 'The smell of whales, alive or dead, was the smell of money.'[23]

Whaling

Whaleships were solid-looking vessels, always readily distinguishable by the generous outfit of whaleboats hanging from ships' davits. Pelagic whaling was waning by the 1850s but ships kept calling in odd numbers for the rest of the century. New Zealanders also kept a few going until late Victorian times, making them as hardy survivors as the Americans. Two famous locally owned ships were Bluff's *Chance* and Dunedin's *Splendid* (above). On one occasion the *Splendid* did too well; a lump of ambergris taken from a sperm whale was so large that it depressed world prices, earning only £25,000 instead of the £89,000 that might have been expected.

THE WHALE STARTED OFF TO WINDWARD WITH US AT A TREMENDOUS RATE,

Once the harpoon struck the whale, the danger increased. This 1899 engraving from Frank Bullen's classic book, *The Cruise of the Cachalot*, based on a voyage aboard the New Zealand whaleship *Chance*, skippered by Paddy Gilroy, shows the famous 'Nantucket sleigh ride'. A powerful whale could tow a boat for several miles.

At the sound of the lookout's call 'there she blows!' the men would rush to lower the whaleboats. These were the business end of whaling. Eight or nine metres long, clinker-built (each plank overlapping the one below) and double-ended, these light, manoeuvrable boats sliced through the water under either sail or oars. Sail was preferred — it was quieter and easier — but more often than not the men had to row. And row. The boats carried six men, the steersman, the harpooner and four oarsmen. If the harpooner lodged one or more harpoons in the whale, it could run for a long distance, often pulling the boat along in the hair-raising 'Nantucket sleigh ride'. If the harpoon held, if the line did not break, and if the boat was not overturned or dragged under, the whale would eventually tire and it was time to make the kill. The steerer, an officer who changed places with the harpooner to lance the whale at close quarters, usually did this tricky task. This was the most dangerous moment, when the men ran the greatest risk of a fluke smashing the boat. As the old whaler's cry went, 'A dead whale or a stove boat.'

Once the whale was dead and made fast, it had to be taken to the whaleship for processing. If the boat crew was lucky, and if the wind was co-operative, the ship would sail to them. If, however, it was busy with another boat or the wind was blowing from the wrong quarter, the men would have to row, towing a carcass of 60 to 100 tonnes tail-first behind them. It could be a very long row. Once alongside the crew began cutting-in, stripping the blubber from the carcass, which revolved grotesquely in the shark-infested water as the heavy strips were pulled off and hoisted aboard. When the blubber was lowered to the deck it was sliced into chunks and tossed into the great iron pots of the try-works. The oil was poured into barrels, whalebone was stored in the holds and specialised oils were packed separately. It was filthy, dangerous work. Dense greasy smoke smudged sails, hulls, clothes and men alike. The very qualities that made whale oil a good lubricant made walking across the decks hazardous, even in calm weather; when the ship was rolling the safest way to move around was to slide on the seat of one's pants.

The risks were monetary as well as physical. Like authors, crews were paid a 'lay' or share of the value of the catch. On a typical Australian vessel of 1832, the captain received 10 per cent, the second mate 1/70th, the cooper and carpenter 1/95th each, a harpooner 1/140th, an able seaman 1/140th, and an ordinary seaman 1/200th. But few men made much money. When Burr Osborn, 'Yankee Jack', signed on the whaler *Tenedos* in the 1840s, crewmen were told they would receive the 'two hundredth lay', one barrel out of every 200. A 3000-barrel catch would, therefore, earn each man about $300 for a voyage of three or four years. But there was a catch and a modern meaning of the word 'lay' probably better describes how the owners saw their crewmen. 'We were charged one hundred and fifty dollars for our outfit, which was actually worth about twelve dollars,' Osborn remembered, 'and the men were expected to make up the balance due to them.'[24]

Between November and April the whaleships crowded New Zealand waters. They called at many ports, in the Far North, around Cook Strait and Banks Peninsula and Murihiku, but they congregated most heavily at the Bay of Islands. Ships are thought to have begun calling there in 1794 and by the turn of the century it was well-known as an important anchorage. There British, American, Australian, French, Dutch, German, Portuguese, Danish and Canadian whaleships could be found, drawn by water, wood, food and sex. British ships were the most numerous in the early period, but by the 1830s the Americans had taken the lead. In that decade an average of 118 whaleships a year called.

With 20–30 men aboard each ship, that meant 3000 European visitors.[25] These were the hell-raising tourists who made the Bay's main town, Kororareka, 'the Hell-hole of the Pacific'. Mission printer William Colenso said that it was 'notorious for containing a greater number of rogues than any other spot of equal size in the universe', while John Dunmore Lang labelled its residents 'the veriest scum of civilised society'.[26] By then it had five hotels, 50 grog shops, brothels, several billiard halls and bowling alleys and a theatre. The place undoubtedly rocked whenever seamen flooded ashore after months at sea.

They sought two commodities, alcohol and women. The rum was so bad that it was termed fighting rum, for that is what often happened after enough had been consumed. The women were Maori, who had a tradition of sexual hospitality. Although chiefs acted as procurers, the sex industry paid women more than they could earn working the land, and far from degrading Maori women, as twitchy modern descendants sometimes claim, it increased the status of women and reduced female infanticide. No wonder a woman named Mary 'harangued [missionary Samuel] Marsden for forbidding, with mixed success, intercourse with the crew of the *Active*'.[27] By 1836 there was a temperance society, but the town had a grog shop for every wowser and it knew how to treat those who represented authority — a Sydney debt-collector was tarred and feathered. Not everyone shared the missionaries' views. John Knights, an American trader, preferred the 'barefaced villains' to the 'respectable' merchants and the missionary traders, whom he thought 'the greatest sharpers and [who] descend into the meanest and lowest subterfuges of any men I ever before fell in with'.[28]

In any society, sex, gunpowder and money make an explosive mix, so it is remarkable how well Maori and Europeans got on in this rough frontier society. It helped that they wanted different things — Maori and Europeans competed for seals, but not whales, timber, or flax — but it also helped that each usually preferred to trade rather than take. Of course the record was not unblemished. Maori captured the brig *Venus* at the Bay in June 1806, slaughtered all but one of the crew and stole everything. Its ragged crew of mutineers, convicts and crewmen, egged on by the grossly corpulent pirate

Charlotte Badger, had brought this upon themselves by kidnapping Maori women. Two years later the crew of the schooner *Parramatta* paid dearly for wounding three Maori and trying to leave without paying for a cargo. A wind of cruelly ill fortune blew the Parramatta back onto the rocks near Cape Brett, where all were massacred.

The most notorious incident, the burning of the *Boyd*, has been the subject of books and television documentaries.[29] The subtitle of Wade Doak's book, 'A Saga of Culture Clash', best sums up a confusing series of incidents that cast a pall over European-Maori trading relationships for several years. Until then things had been developing promisingly, thanks largely to two adventurous cross-cultural travellers, Governor Philip King of New South Wales and Hikutu chief Te Pahi. King had been fascinated by New Zealand and wanted to establish a whaling and trading base there. Te Pahi wanted European technology and knowledge and visited Norfolk Island and Sydney in 1805 to see things for himself. This may not have found favour with rival Whangaroa Maori, who in 1808 believed that Captain James Ceroni from the *City of Edinburgh* had placed a curse on their little-used harbour after disease struck. They would not be so welcoming to the next ship to call, the *Boyd*. To make matters worse, this brig was carrying a Ngati Uru chief, Te Ara, whom Captain John Thompson had treated badly. The indignant Te Ara lured Thompson and some of the men ashore and murdered them. That night, dressed in the dead sailors' clothes, they boarded the brig and killed almost all the passengers and crew. In the confusion a Maori lit a flintlock over the *Boyd*, blowing it to smithereens. He also blew apart the trading gains that Te Pahi had worked so hard to achieve. The chief tried ineffectively to rescue some of the survivors but was rewarded by being mistakenly blamed as the villain. Sailors raided Te Puna, killing many of his people, and he died months later in an inter-tribal skirmish. This setback lasted for almost half a decade. Missionaries were kept away from the Bay until 1814 and shipping arrivals would not exceed the 1810 figure until 1815. Sydney merchants depending on New Zealand raw materials fell on hard times.

One of the last major pre-colonial clashes took place in Taranaki in 1834. Te Awaiti whaler John 'Jacky' Guard and his family were returning from a visit to Sydney when their barque blew ashore near Cape Egmont in a gale.[30] Everyone made it ashore safely but then Maori attacked, killing several sailors and capturing the rest. They released Jacky Guard and several companions to get a cask of gunpowder to ransom Betty Guard, her children and the others. At Sydney, however, Guard persuaded Governor Richard Bourke that gunboat diplomacy was better than gunpowder donations. He returned with HMS *Alligator*, the colonial schooner *Isabella* and part of the Sydney garrison. The naval commander shot and shelled his way through Maori resistance to recover all the prisoners.

Guard was one of the new breed of shore whalers. Shore whaling took place during the autumn and early winter and at its peak it employed 500–700

S Williams Collection, Alexander Turnbull Library PAColl-0435-1

Te Awaiti, founded by Jacky Guard, was the first shore station but it was also home to other major stations. This photograph was taken about 1900 and, as the stares on the faces of the crews show, it was obviously staged for the camera in the placid shallows off the beach. Nevertheless, the station itself and the boats look much as they would have 50 years earlier, with thatched cottages and whale rib fence posts. The sleek boats are believed to be the *Alabama* and the *Swiftsure*.

Europeans, a third of the 2000 estimated to be living here by the end of the 1830s. The stations were concentrated around the Kapiti Coast/Cook Strait region and the eastern and southern coasts of the South Island. Like the ships, the stations stank of boiling blubber and had few of the comforts of home. Most whalers lived in crude wooden or thatched huts and ate a simple, monotonous diet of pork, potatoes, flour, sugar and tea. Visitors often mentioned fleas and rats.

The shore stations were a cheap alternative to ships, since they cost just £1500–2000 to set up compared to £10,000 for a new ship. Because of this Sydney merchants or local syndicates, who amalgamated ownerships to achieve economies of scale in supply, owned most. The first seems to have been set up at Te Awaiti by John Guard in 1827, although the venture was not fully operational until 1830 or 1831; the area would support commercial whaling under the Peranos until 1964. Other well-known shore whalers were Dicky Barrett, from Te Awaiti, Joseph Thoms from Marlborough and later Porirua, the Wellers — George and Edward — at Otago, Purakanui and Taieri Island, Johnny Jones at Waikouaiti, John Hughes at Moeraki and Thomas Howell from Riverton.

The men spoke a distinctive slang and went by nicknames such as 'Geordie Bolts', 'Flash Bill', 'Fat Jackson' and 'Black Peter', as the old whaling song 'The

Beautiful Coast of New Zealand' went:

Peter Shavatt [Chevatt] has a shocking bad hat.
And old John Hughes with his shocking bad shoes:
But for all that they are having some chat –
On the beautiful coast of New Zealand.[31]

They worked and played hard and they certainly sometimes worried those who took outward displays of piety seriously. 'Casks of rum, usually of such foul quality that it was said to smell worse than the decaying whale scraps, assumed equal importance to casks of meat in the station supplies,' but, as Morton notes, most reports also described the stations as well run.[32] There was a working season and a drinking season and most shore whalers kept the two separate.

As Anderson says, 'Bishop Selwyn, more thoughtful than his colleagues, observed that "the whalefishers impart a considerable amount of civilisation to the natives", more so than the towns or the mission stations.'[33] Selwyn praised the men's love for their children, the half-caste, bilingual youngsters, who daily bridged the cultural divide. While whaling lasted, the Maori population divided its settlement patterns. The men, older women and some of the marriageable women kept to their traditional sites and maintained recognisably traditional patterns of authority and community life. Many of the younger women lived at the stations with the whalers and when whaling declined, 'followed the retired whalers to small "shagroon" colonies scattered about the coast, where the men took up boatbuilding, fishing, and subsistence farming'.[34] And some did better than merely subsist. The former Sydney waterman Johnny Jones owned a string of southern whaling stations and supply craft before turning coloniser. In 1840 Jones sent immigrants and livestock across to his Waikouaiti station, where he moved three years later. Visitors reported the sound of piano music coming from his house. Jones's farms prospered and he was nicely positioned to add to his wealth when the first Free Church settlers waded through the mud and sand to found Dunedin in 1848.

James and Te Wai Heberley exemplify the solid partnership between the races that the shore whalers created. James, nicknamed 'Worser Heberley' because of the frequency with which he predicted 'worser' weather, was also known as Tangata Whata to the Maori. He arrived at Guard's Te Awaiti station in 1830 and 'bought' Te Wai for a blanket. In a long and colourful career, Worser whaled and was later Wellington's first pilot (Worser Bay is named after him). Although he frequently crossed Cook Strait in an undecked 4.2-metre boat, he is said to have drowned in a few centimetres of water in Picton Harbour in 1899.

J Heberley Collection, Alexander Turnbull Library F-49177-½

Many shore whalers went on to become traders, shipowners or harbour pilots but Johnny Jones (1808–69) was in a league of his own. Already the founder of his own small colony at Waikouaiti, Jones got rich supplying the early needs of Dunedin. He dominated the province's early shipping history with ships like the brig *Thomas and Henry* and the paddle steamer *Geelong*. His Harbour Steam Navigation Company would form the nucleus of the Union Steam Ship Company after his death. Here he poses, in the London Portrait Rooms, Dunedin, in 1866: the very image of respectability.

Alexander Turnbull Library F-103950-1/2

1840 and All That

The shagroon colonies and the whaler/traders of early New Zealand had lived more or less on good terms with Maori New Zealand. Maori had spoken of 'their Pakeha' and had competed to obtain trophy Europeans who would attract ships, muskets and other trade goods. 'Traders, ship-captains, labourers, employers of labour, these were to be honoured, cherished, caressed, protected and plucked,' Frederick Maning wrote in *Old New Zealand*. 'Plucked judiciously . . . so that the feathers might grow again.'[35] Important traders married women of chiefly status, workers women of lesser rank. These trophy Europeans were, the chiefs hoped, the portal for muskets and other trade goods. They married into the local real estate, offered technical and business advice and they sometimes offered military assistance against tribal enemies.

The organised settlers whom arrived from 1840 onwards were completely different to these rough self-made men and their Maori wives. The settlers recruited in the thousands by the New Zealand Company and its offspring, 'did not want to live in a Maori world, even one transforming itself while dancing an odd tango with early nineteenth century capitalist Europe and America. The settlers — or their leaders anyway — wanted to recreate Britain anew in the Southern Hemisphere.'[36] At first Maori thought that they could contain and control the newcomers. At Wellington, Te Ati Awa, occupying the harbour but fearful of Ngati Toa, thought that they could use the New Zealand Company to prop up their mana. Te Wharepouri expected only 10 or so white faces and was white-faced when 1000 land-hungry Britons spilled out around the beaches of Port Nicholson in just a few weeks. It was like a demographic and cultural earthquake, the European plate crashing across the Polynesian one.

The impetus for organised settlement came from Edward Gibbon Wakefield. Outside New Zealand he is regarded as one of the more influential thinkers of the 19th century. He was at the forefront of the systematic colonisation movement. Its true believers felt that Britain had too much capital and labour and needed to export the surplus to new colonies. At the heart of Wakefield's theory of 'sufficient price' was the idea of using land pricing to transfer a hierarchical slice of British society to the antipodes. In practice it meant buying land cheap from Maori and selling it at an inflated price to settlers, using the profits to pay for settlement costs and to enrich shareholders. To do this, however, the New Zealand Company had to beat the Crown to New Zealand, getting in before it regulated land sales. Late in 1839, therefore, and without having bought a single hectare of land with the funds obtained by selling purchase orders, the company directors despatched the ship *Tory* with an advance party. Close behind followed the surveyors in the *Cuba*, and just a few weeks behind them, the main body of emigrants in six ships. It was a thoroughly reckless gamble. Had Wakefield been unable to buy land, had the *Tory* or the *Cuba* been lost, all would have been more chaotic than the shambles that they only just muddled through in the early 1840s.

Then, as now, Auckland remained an exception, more focused on Australia. It alone of the main centres was not settled

All companies engaged in propaganda to attract migrants and investment. The Wakefields were masters of this. When the main fleet of migrant ships gathered in Port Nicholson on 8 March 1840 land was in dispute, it had not been surveyed properly and the steep terrain was very definitely not what many migrants had been led to believe. William Wakefield, however, fired off gun salutes and pretended all was well. When the *Auckland Weekly News* published this engraving 'as described by E J Wakefield' in 1899, pioneer mythology was flourishing.

Alexander Turnbull Library C-033-005

SETTLEMENT OF WELLINGTON BY THE NEW ZEALAND COMPANY.

by a Wakefield-style company. To the Company's chagrin, Lieutenant-Governor Hobson selected the Waitemata Harbour for the site of his new capital instead of Wellington. There officialdom pitched its tents while the capital was shipped down from the Bay of Islands. On 18 September 1840 the necessary official ceremonies were observed — the British flag was hoisted and a 21-gun salute was fired — but Aucklanders being Aucklanders, they celebrated with boat races. In an era before corporate boxes, they divided the races into three categories. The gentlemen raced each other (the Surveyor-General's gig against the Captain's), the sailors against the harbourmaster and the Maori against each other. The sailors competed for a purse of £5 but the Maori had just a half a kilo of tobacco. Nevertheless, despite the magnificence of the Waitemata, Auckland's port facilities were modest; a handcart in front of the government store and harbourmaster Captain David Rough's boat were the only ways of unloading a ship.

The Wakefield settlements — Wellington (1840), Nelson (1841), New Plymouth (1841), Otago (1848) and Canterbury (1850) — all owed more to Australian settlers, merchants and other non-systematic colonists than the New Zealand Company ever admitted, but they were products of 'the Dishonourable Company'. There was, it must be admitted, an element of 'the New Zealand Bubble' about the process. Nevertheless, there was also what Belich calls the 'Colonising Crusade', 'a genuine crusading zeal, which converted numerous enthusiastic disciples, some with no possible self-interest, and brought hundreds

This view of Official Bay shows Wynyard Pier picking its delicate way across the mudflats during the 1850s. In the distance in Mechanics Bay, small coasters await the return of the tide.

Alexander Turnbull Library B-043-018

The New Zealand Company liked patriotic names for its settlements. Nelson followed Wellington in 1841. Company artist/propagandist Charles Heaphy's watercolour, 'Astrolabe Roads, Tasman's Gulf' depicts the ships *Arrow* and *Whitby* in the roadstead, with Fisherman Island in the background. Nelson was for a while one of the 'Big Five' centres in early colonial New Zealand, but gradually fell behind the others because of its isolated position and the limitations of its harbour.

of thousands to the Holy Land'.[37] If the Company was often long on promises and short on performance, there can be no doubt that it put on quite a show. In the 1840s it had 15 staff in its London office, just 10 fewer than the Colonial Office needed to run the entire British Empire.

They had to work hard, for while Britons — especially the Irish — were accustomed to emigration, it was to North America and not the distant antipodes. The voyage out here was so lengthy, dangerous and expensive — even with an assisted passage — that it was almost certainly one-way for all but the very richest. That is why 'Crusader literature' painted unrealistic portraits of bananas growing in Wellington and a Thames-like navigable river flowing happily through a verdant, flat Hutt Valley landscape. It also tried to portray the voyage out as a long holiday, fed gluttonously from the Company's groaning table. The reality was different. The ships of the 1840s and the 1850s were smaller, squatter and slower than the 'colonial clippers' of the 1860s and the 1870s. The *Aurora*, a ship of 550 tons, took 126 days to reach Wellington; the 540-ton *Bolton* took 154 days — nearly four months — to get its 232 people to the dubious comforts of 'Bolton Row', the row of shanties on Thorndon Beach.

Just as the Seven Canoes of Maori legend live on in modern landscapes and bloodlines, each Wakefield township still celebrates its 'first ships' in the names of its street and buildings. Wellington has its Tory, Cuba and Roxburgh streets, Aurora and Glenbervie terraces, Oriental Bay and a concrete model of the *Aurora*'s bow projects from the 1940 Centennial project, the Petone Settlers' museum. One of the ugliest modern buildings in Dunedin's splendid Victorian townscape is John Wickliffe House, a structure as invasive as the settlers had been in 1848. Ocean-going trawlers called *Will Watch*, *Arrow* and *Whitby* fish out of Nelson's modern port and in Canterbury some people still spend an unhealthy amount of time tracing connections to the 'First Four Ships', the *Charlotte Jane*, the *Randolph*, the *Sir George Seymour* and the *Cressy*.

Ports — Colonisation's Beachheads

Coastal shipping was the lifeline of the new settlements, which expanded by sea, establishing out-settlements linked by ketches, cutters and schooners rather than roads and bridges. 'Auckland ruled by sea and credit over an archipelago of Pakeha settlement and extraction, in Northland, Thames, Coromandel and the Bay of Plenty, like the early Maori colonies.'[38] Wellington colonised Wanganui, the Wairarapa and Marlborough during the 1840s. Nelson also expanded into Marlborough after 1847 and Buller in the 1860s. Dunedin sent out small ships that inevitably mixed exploration with commerce. In September 1849, for example, the *Twins* took a cargo of biscuits, flour, tea, paint, oil, chairs, slops and two ploughs to Moeraki. Next month the schooner *Dolphin* took another cargo there and returned with potatoes. That month the schooner *Otago* brought potatoes, goats, geese, cattle, flour, kegs of butter and bags of feathers up from Jacob's River (Riverton), at the other end of the province.

In time each new settlement would form its own harbour board, shipping agents and sometimes shipping lines. In the meantime, though, they depended utterly on passing traders, whaleships and the embryonic coastal fleets based at the main ports. During the 1850s the provincial councils took over from the New Zealand Company administrations and cobbled together what infrastructure they could: pilot services, jetties, buoys and beacons for the favoured few and landing services for the rest. It was never enough. William Thomson, Otago's first provincial harbourmaster (1859), had not only to satisfy the conflicting demands of Dunedin and Port Chalmers, but also Port Molyneux, Taieri Mouth, Purakanui, Shag Point, Waikouaiti, Moeraki, Kakanui and Oamaru. With so many snouts in the provincial pork barrel, it was inevitable that none got all it wanted.

In fact, before the large population increases of the 1860s and the 1870s, even the major ports struggled. Take Lyttelton and Otago Harbour. In both cases the harbours determined the provinces' selection, but neither was perfect. Lyttelton had deep, sheltered water, but little flat land, and was cut off from Christchurch by the Port Hills. To get to the swampy, dismal site of Christchurch, passengers from the 'First Four' plodded their weary way up and over the tortuous Bridle Path. With its gradient of one in five, the Bridle Path was really only suitable for light loads. Until the rail tunnel opened in 1867, the only way of moving heavy goods was by sea, across the dangerous Sumner

Making New Zealand Collection, Alexander Turnbull Library F-1501-½-MNZ

bar and up to the Bricks Wharf in the Avon. At 30 shillings a tonne, it cost half as much to move freight from Lyttelton as it cost to bring it from Britain. Little boats such as George Day's *Flirt*, the *Fanny* and the 24-ton *Phoebe*, made their slow and costly way to Sumner, where the smaller craft and a flotilla of whaleboats and punts went up to Bricks Wharf. The Heathcote River, the other river flowing into the Estuary, was more heavily used than the Avon and remained an artery for cargo for several decades.[39]

Otago also had its problems. Organised settlement began in March 1848 when former whaler Richard Driver piloted the 662-ton ship *John Wickliffe* up a crudely buoyed channel to Port Chalmers. There the 547-ton *Philip Laing* joined it a few weeks later. Port Chalmers was indeed a charming place, with deep water, but it lacked flat land, so the settlers had to take small boats up a narrow channel to Dunedin, where the township site had been surveyed. The surveyors had built a jetty at Pelichet Bay, but as few chose sections there, they built 'Wickliffe Pier', a straggling manuka pier that was really only useable at high tide, when water covered the long tidal flats. 'There, on fine summer afternoons in the spring of 1848, might be seen the Rev. Thomas Burns and Captain Cargill, the company's resident agent, strolling to and fro, discussing matters of state and, probably, harbour improvements.'[40] Right from the start citizens argued over where the port should be — Port Chalmers or Dunedin. They would still be doing it 120 years later before the container age settled it once and for all.

Before getting tied up in the details of that debate, however, we should step back and ask why it mattered so much to people. The first point to note is that 19th-century and early 20th-century New Zealand had a whiff of the seabreeze about it. Every European New Zealander had travelled by sea to get there and

A shallow harbour was better than no harbour at all. The early colonists at New Plymouth, like those of Oamaru and Timaru on equally exposed coasts, had to endure wild rides through the open surf in surf boats. When photographer William Collis photographed this boat at New Plymouth in 1884, the port still had its problems but the boat was already a relic.

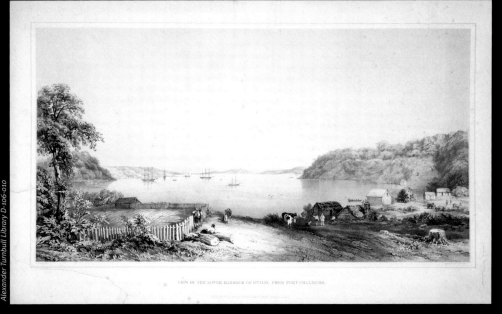

VIEW OF THE LOWER HARBOUR OF OTAGO, FROM PORT CHALMERS.

Otago Harbour has two ports. Port Chalmers, in the lower harbour, nearer to the entrance than Dunedin, has deeper water, but lacks the flat land for a major settlement. Charles Kettle's tranquil 1849 picture shows it just months after the arrival of the Otago Company's first ships.

Dunedin had more flat land but the water in the upper harbour, deceptively broad at high tide, was very shallow. Only the smallest coasting craft could come near the shoreline. Even with expensive modern dredging, the upper harbour channel depths are eight metres, compared to nearly 12 metres at Port Chalmers.

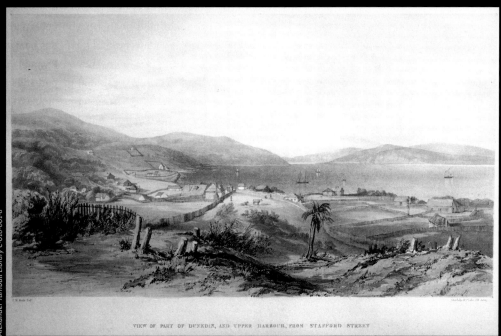

VIEW OF PART OF DUNEDIN, AND UPPER HARBOUR, FROM STAFFORD STREET

everyone else moved about by it. They knew ships, people and the moods of the sea. It was a highway, not a barrier, their gateway. Inside the little settlements, everyone kept a weather eye on the harbour. The sight of a sail would turn heads and unstop tongues. Was it a whaleship, a warship or did it bear friends, business partners, settlers, mail, urgently needed goods and gossip? The little four-page newspapers were crammed with advertisements that spoke the language of ships, shipping and the sea: agents' advertisements, promising speedy voyages on first-class ships, merchants announcing that they had unpacked the latest London fashions just delivered by a named ship, reports of shipping movements and accidents, and the voyage reports of the latest migrant ships.

Everyone went by sea, whether it was across and around the larger harbours, or up and down the coast. Surface transport was either physically or economically impossible in early colonial New Zealand. Even in the townships themselves, roads were mere tracks or bridle paths, dusty in summer and muddy quagmires in winter. For its first decade the wags called Dunedin 'Mud-edin'. Wellington did not have such extensive tidal flats, but its steep hills and limited flat land made life just as difficult. Everyone relied on bullocks (horses were only for the wealthy). A ride in a springless bullock cart was bone-jarring torture, but these animals had the traction to cope with the terrain and they could move what the human back could not. Nevertheless, they could carry only a fraction of the load of the smallest cutter and were, therefore, expensive.

Settlers used water transport wherever possible, navigating even the smallest creeks and rivers and reclaiming land for wharves and warehouses alongside deep water. Wellington began its 120-year history of reclamation at the south-west corner of Thorndon in 1852. When that began the hulk of the ship *Inconstant*, beached in 1850 by John Plimmer to act as a warehouse at Clay Point, at the southern end of Lambton Quay, was at the water's edge. In time, though, a dense network of streets and buildings grew up around 'Plimmers Ark' as the wharves marched further out into Lambton Harbour. Twice the Ark and its encumbering warehouse were cut down as new buildings appeared on the land-locked Quay and it was again unearthed in the 1990s during conservation work on the Victorian/Edwardian buildings.

The high cost of reclamation meant that for the first decade or so the small settlements had to live with their scrawny little jetties and those annoying tidal mudflats. Progress was literally measured in centimetres in Dunedin, which felt pathetically proud on 1 March 1856 when the 175-ton brig *Gil Blas* inched its way up the Eastern Channel to drop its pick within sight of (but not alongside) the jetty. Even at high water, though, the channel offered barely more than three metres of water. Long-term solutions to the port's problems, reclaiming out into the bay and dredging a deeper channel up from Port Chalmers, would require more people and money than were available before the mid 1860s.

Hulks

'Plimmer's Ark', the former ship *Inconstant*, was a prominent feature of early colonial Wellington, where it served as a water's edge shop, warehouse and offices for John Plimmer. This computer reconstruction was created by 3D Creative for the Wellington City Council. A large section of the ship has been put on display on Queen's Wharf and part of the bow section can be viewed under the former BNZ buildings on Lambton Quay, the old 'beach' of the 1840s.

Most hulks served less glamorously as floating gear stores or coal hulks for steamers. In the major ports they could be seen in almost any port scene. Port Chalmers had many, and redundant hulks were abandoned all around Otago Harbour. The *Don Juan, Esk* and *California* were curiosities even when Muir & Moodie published this old postcard. Traces of them can still (2001) be made out at low tide in Deborah Bay, near Port Chalmers.

14 R.   Port Chalmers N. Z. "Lifes journey O'er."   Muir & Moodie
The remains of the once noted Blockade-runners "Don Juan", "Esk" & "California".

Maori Maritime Enterprise

Almost any watercolour of an 1840s New Zealand town will show them —
Maori canoes drawn up on the beach or else threading their way among the
settlers' ships. Some of this was artistic convention, a touch of 'the other' to
fascinate Old World viewers, but it also showed how much the shaky new
settlements depended on Maori for food, fuel and other basics. The 1840s were
a time of prosperity for many coastal Maori communities as they used their
land to grow crops for European settlers and traders. In all but Wellington and
the sparsely populated South Island, they kept the upper hand.

The canoe trade went on for a couple of decades at Auckland, fed through
two routes. Waikato suppliers sent waka up the West Coast via the Manukau
Harbour and Hauraki Maori went direct to the Waitemata. They moved
prodigious quantities of material. The canoe trade to Auckland and Onehunga
for 1852 included 1200 tonnes of wood via the Waitemata and 360 via
Onehunga, 45 tonnes and 7 tonnes of fish respectively, as well as quantities of
flax, grain, fruit, potatoes, vegetables, and livestock and poultry.[41] 'Fleets of
their canoes entered the Waitemata laden with pigs, fish, potatoes and maize
and left riding high, carrying clothing and other English goods,' Paul Monin
noted. 'Not only were they doing much to feed the town, but also to consume
the surplus stock of its merchants and thereby to contribute through the
payment of customs duties to the colonial exchequer'.[42] In January 1853 *The
New Zealander* reported 33 of the schooners and cutters trading to the
Waitemata as 'native craft'. Wellington was supplied by sea from both
Wanganui and Poverty Bay.

Alexander Turnbull Library F-2749-½

This old photograph, labelled 'Stand by to take the bar' by the photographer, shows the basic improvements that improved the safety of harbours such as Hokianga — a signal station and steam towage. Many colonial ports knew nothing more sophisticated.

Waka continued to be important for many years, but in the south in particular, Maori quickly switched to European boats. In the 1820s Ngai Tahu had fitted oars and square sails to waka. 'The large canoes, however, including both the war canoe and the double-hulled canoe, were poorly adapted to the difficult sea conditions of southern New Zealand and could not be easily improved, despite some attempts to do so', Atholl Anderson notes.[43] 'As soon as the whaleboat and sealboat became available, their manifest superiority in sailing and sea-keeping qualities was recognised'.[44] Harry Evison fingers depopulation because whaleboats required fewer crew and could carry more cargo and passengers. 'The modern boats were more easily handled in the surf, making both launching and landing safer, and they made coastal travel easier and faster'.[45] By the time of the 1839–40 fighting season European boats had entirely replaced the southerners' waka taua.

In the calmer northern waters, waka lingered much longer and in some shallow river trades such as the upper Wanganui, settlers even commissioned motorised waka tiwai. Nevertheless, Maori also invested heavily in European schooners and cutters. Paul Monin, who studied the Maori economy of Hauraki between 1840 and 1880, characterises the 1840s as a time of vigorous commercial production, to be followed in the 1860s by

Charles Heaphy's 1850s watercolour looks out across the tranquil Waitemata harbour to Browns Island and in the background, Rangitoto Island. It is idealised but it nevertheless shows a typical mix of water traffic, two sailing ships, a raft of cut timber and Maori waka. These brought significant quantities of fish, vegetables and firewood into the town and transported manufactured goods back to the hinterland.

dislocation and growth in reliance on non-work-derived wealth.[46] In the 1840s and the 1850s Maori invested heavily — too heavily, he argues — in major capital items such as schooners and flourmills. By 1847 Hauraki hapu owned 15 schooners, far in excess of their commercial requirements, especially since canoes were still conducting much of the Auckland supply run.[47] A decade later East Coast Maori owned 43 such craft.[48]

The schooner mania, as Monin calls it, became an extension of traditional inter-hapu rivalry and a source of profit to European shipbuilders, as Opotiki shows. Records are sketchy, but Maori ownership may have begun in 1846 when Paora Taia bought a part-share in the 16-ton cutter *Providence*, built at Opotiki by Thomas Wilkinson and William Webb. In 1849 Ngatai bought half the cutter *Napi* (17 tons); in 1851 Hakariah bought the schooner *Mary Paul*, Ko Makao the 15-ton *Mana of the Queen* and Gangaria Tenaka the 23-ton *Louisa*. Others followed, although the boom was brief and by 1859 it seems that Opotiki Maori no longer owned any trading craft.[49] Opotiki shipbuilders did well out of this. Hezekiah Hunt built the *Hera* and *Hera Puhi* and Lovett Thoroughgood the *Mary Paul*, the *Hope* and the *Mana of the Queen*. They were expensive to buy, costly to maintain and, for all the mana that ownership brought, they were risky investments. And once European-owned steamers entered the short coastal routes, Maori-owned shipping fell further behind. Indeed, in the entire 20th century era of conventional shipping, only two full-blooded Maori (to use the language of the day), Captain Te Waari Kahukura (Ward) Whaitiri and Captain Albert Moko Moko, would command large trading vessels.[50]

This circa 1860 view shows Waipapa, the canoe reserve at Mechanics Bay (Te Toangaroa) left after Auckland was sold. In the early decades of settlement Maori used it to bring in potatoes, fruit and wheat to early Auckland.

Auckland War Memorial Museum Neg C7516

Shipbuilding

European shipbuilding predated the colonial era. The first such ship built here was in the far south, a 65-ton schooner, begun at Luncheon Cove, Facile Harbour, in Dusky Sound in November 1792 by the *Britannia* sealers William Leith and Thomas Moore.[51] Not expeditiously, it must be said, for the sealers were recalled before they could complete the job and the unnamed craft was left to weather on its lonely stocks, mysterious to local Maori 'and potent with supernatural power'.[52] There it still lay three years later when, as we saw earlier, the *Endeavour* limped into the harbour and quietly expired.[53] With their ship gone, the *Endeavour*'s men depended more than ever on the *Britannia*'s schooner. 'Some of the planks of ye vessell had shrunk and a plank or two on the bows at the wooden ends had rent,' third officer Robert Murry recalled, but the *Providence*, as they named it, would ferry 90 passengers to Norfolk Island, in safety if not comfort.[54] Shipwright James Heatherly also lengthened and decked over one of the *Endeavour*'s boats. The tiny *Assistance* sailed into Sydney in March 1796, carrying 55 people and news of the 35 Dusky Sound castaways still awaiting rescue.

New Zealand's timber attracted shipbuilders. Duncan Mackay notes the interchangeability of bushmen and sailors during the 19th century. Sailors handled timber during the years of the mast and spar trade, and equipment used in the bush to move logs had been adapted from the gear used on ships to move heavy pieces of timber.[55] The hard work of pitsawing the timber

William Bambridge drew this early colonial shipbuilding scene in December 1847 when he visited Captain Nagle's residence on Great Barrier Island. The island provided good timber and deep water, both attractions to early colonial shipbuilders.

Alexander Turnbull Library A-090-018

slowed early construction times but small craft were in plentiful demand and by the late 1820s Raine and Ramsey were operating a shipyard on the Hokianga. In 1827 they completed the schooner *Enterprise*, following with the 150-ton brig *New Zealander* in 1828. In 1830 Raine and new partner Gordon Browne completed the 394-ton barque *Sir George Murray*, a very large craft for the time. It played a bit part in the road to Waitangi in 1840. From 1829 New Zealand-built ships could not be registered as British ships. In the absence of a recognised national flag, they were vulnerable to seizure, as happened to the *Sir George Murray* on its first visit to Port Jackson (although this was probably just a pretext by Raine's bank, which had foreclosed on him). New Horeke owner Thomas MacDonnell's 'Maori Register' failed to prevent other arrests, which probably contributed to shipbuilding ceasing at Horeke. It also inspired the newly appointed British Resident, James Busby, to persuade the Northern chiefs in 1834 to design a 'national' flag and sign a Declaration of Independence. New Zealand ships still did not have a New Zealand register but the Admiralty accepted the new flag and Australian ports honoured Busby's 'certificates of registration'.[56]

At the other end of the country, at Port Pegasus, in southern Stewart Island, shipbuilders launched the 49-ton schooner *Joseph Weller* in 1833. At first fittings such as blocks were obtained from Sydney, along with ropes and sails, but local shipwrights learned to improvise. When David Carey and Charles

Regattas and water carnivals featured prominently in all early colonial calendars. None has been more successful than Auckland's Anniversary Day Regatta. These Aucklanders gathered at the foot of Hobson Street in 1864 are looking out over Queens Wharf to the harbour, where small racing craft pick their way among the commercial shipping anchored off the township. Note the small coaster under construction in the foreground.

D M Beere Collection, Alexander Turnbull Library G-096101

Roebuck built the ketch *Mercury* at Otakou on Otago Harbour in the 1840s, they fashioned the ironwork from old harpoons and scrap iron, and the sails were made from blue dungaree cloth. The 'Jumping Jackass', as the *Mercury* was nicknamed, was lively in a seaway but served several pioneer trades well. In 1842 colonial shipbuilders launched 42 craft, averaging 20 tons.

Auckland soon established itself as the centre of wooden shipbuilding in the colony. Men with skills and modest capital could build their way to success, as Henry Niccol did. After arriving in October 1842 with his family and shipwright William Garrick, Niccol moved to Waiheke Island, where he built the 16-ton schooner *Thistle*. Back at Auckland again, he built three pleasure craft on the foreshore before a government contract for the brig *Victoria* literally set him on his feet, at Mechanics Bay, where with a little private reclamation he enlarged the yard to make it dry at all stages of the tide. Niccol stayed there until 1872.[57]

The first New Zealand-built steamer, the *Governor Wynyard*, took to the water at Freeman's Bay, Auckland, in 1851. Since no one in Auckland knew how to build a boiler, the sponsors were lucky that an American named Brown showed up. 'He made a mould of hard clay to the shapes required on which he beat the plates after heating them; old-age pensioners and discharged soldiers were employed to work the bellows, and when it came to punching the rivet holes, he put out a call for the strongest man in Auckland,' W W Stewart recorded.[58] In service, though, the ship performed more like those pensioners than the Auckland Hercules. It made a few harbour trips and fussed about dispensing refreshments at the 1852 Anniversary Day Regatta, but like most steamers of its day, it could not compete with the cheaper schooners and cutters. Months later its owners removed the funnel and paddle boxes, rigged it as a schooner and sailed the *Governor Wynyard* off to Melbourne to find the buyer that eluded them in Auckland.

Voyages in Early Coasters

In early colonial times shipowning was an adjunct of other activities and not a specialised business in its own right. The cutters and schooners of the 1840s were small craft, often built by farmers and merchants as much to ensure access to markets as for profit in their own right. A good example was the 27-ton schooner *Agnes Hay*, begun at Pigeon Bay, Banks Peninsula, in 1846 by John Hay and partners. Although the small cluster of Pigeon Bay settlers traded with passing whaleships, they knew that they would have to build their own ships if they wanted to trade with Wellington reliably. Captain Sinclair and his sons had already completed a 10-ton cutter, the *Jessie Millar*, and it was taking the bay's produce to Wellington when it went down with Sinclair, Hay and others. The destitute Eliza Hay sold the incomplete schooner to Captain James Daymond, who finished the vessel at Pigeon Bay early in 1847 and named it

Agnes Hay in tribute to the family.[59] For the next 18 months Daymond ran it between Wellington and Port Cooper, Pigeon Bay and Akaroa, with occasional diversions elsewhere. In 1848 the *Agnes Hay* made three trips to Otago and was nearly lost on Banks Peninsula while returning from one of them in October. It was recovered, repaired and put into the Wellington–East Coast trade. The schooner's end came in July 1850 when it was blown ashore at Hawke's Bay in a violent gale. The crew had refloated the vessel when the gale subsided but another struck before they could get away and completely wrecked the *Agnes Hay*.[60] A life of just three years was not unusual then.

'A voyage in a New Zealand coaster . . . must be experienced to be understood,' 17-year-old Charles Rous-Marten wrote in his diary in 1858. He was sailing southern waters aboard the 40-ton schooner *Shepherdess*:

> *I sleep on one of the lower shelves, which is constructed near the bottom of the vessel and therefore accommodated to the slope of the same; if it were not for the ledge I should have as much difficulty to keep in bed as anyone taking his nights rest on a slated house top would have in preventing himself from slipping off. I may add that there being a ledge at the top as well as the bottom I have to twist and turn in a most ludicrous and ungraceful manner to get into my shell and when in it needs considerable skill and experience to get out. Of course sitting up is out of the question, it is as much as I can do to turn over. Our ablutions we perform on deck. During the severe gale of April 18,19 and 20 I had great difficulty in keeping my own equilibrium from the force of the wind, and my hair was blown about with such violence that it lashed my face like a whip. The schooner tumbled about fearfully and the sea frequently came over the deck...*[61]

It seems that traditional New Zealand attitudes to service had formed already. Captain Scott called a dark-complexioned American passenger a nigger and the angry man retaliated with 'terms rather highly spiced'. Later that year Rous-Marten took the schooner *Star* to New River (Invercargill). The passengers gave the master a testimonial for the fastest passage from the Otago Heads to Bluff (21 hours), but the entire voyage lasted from 8.00 a.m. Sunday 15 August, when they embarked at Dunedin, until 9.00 a.m. Monday 23 August, when they left the *Star* — eight full days! They had taken three days just to leave Otago Harbour. Along the way they grounded briefly in the Upper Harbour, got buffeted leaving port, and ran into rough seas.

The first steamers to visit New Zealand were naval vessels. The paddle sloop HMS *Driver* arrived in 1846 and was used by Governor Grey to suppress Maori resistance around Wellington. Another paddle sloop, HMS *Inflexible*, spent a couple of months in New Zealand in 1847, but the most important naval visitor was the sloop HMS *Acheron*. Commanded by Captain John Lort

Alexander Turnbull Library F-104998-½

Riverton, or Jacob's River, as it was then known, grew from the whaling station that Captain John Howell managed for Johnny Jones. American whalers had a habit of running contraband there and the Customs waiter appointed in 1858 found that 'all the houses were shut, locked and barred against him'. This early photograph, dated about 1860, shows the bluff lines of a brigantine in the little river port.

Stokes, the ship worked on the first systematic hydrographic survey of New Zealand's coasts between 1848 and 1851, a task that HMS *Pandora* completed in 1855.[62] 'Between them they covered almost the whole of the coastline, surveyed the most important ports and harbours, and sent no fewer than 250 tracings to the Hydrographic Office in England.'[63]

Invaluable though the *Acheron*'s work was, what the settlers really wanted to see were merchant ships. In the Victorian age the smell of success was synonymous with smoky, smelly steam. Colonists whose last sight of Britain had been steam tugs longed for the speed and certainty that steam brought. Unfortunately early steamers were costly and inefficient, prohibitively so for a sparsely populated colony unless public subsidies could be found. Because the provinces were competing fiercely with each other for passengers and prestige the first two decades of experimentation with steam locally generated as much political hot air as coal smoke. Thus, although the *Juno* paid the first visit to New Zealand by a merchant steamer in 1847, steamers did not run regularly until 1854 when the 301-ton steamer *Nelson* arrived at its new home port. The provincial authorities had ambitious plans for coastal and trans-Tasman steam services based from Nelson, but although the *Nelson* completed 11 round voyages and the smaller *Zingari* 10, the service collapsed,

Alexander Turnbull Library A-078-015

H.M.P.S. "Driver" off Barrett's Hotel - Wellington.
1846 with Maori Chiefs on board prisoners after the fight

The old Country built Bg "London"
Ballochs from Sydney in 1846

with the ships returning to Australia in 1855 and 1856 respectively. Auckland made a steadier start in 1854 with the purchase of the 595-ton steamer *William Denny* by the Auckland Steam Navigation Company. Members of the House of Representatives deserted their parliamentary duties to take to the Waitemata to welcome the ship and the band of the 58th Regiment went along to provide the music.[64] The first real national service emerged in 1858–9 when hefty New Zealand government subsidies enabled the Intercolonial Royal Mail Company to connect all provinces to Sydney with the large steamers *Lord Ashley, Lord Worsley, Prince Alfred* and *Airedale*. Steam was here to stay, although it was still too costly to threaten sail in most trades.

Warships were the most common steamers on the New Zealand coast in the 1840s. Matthew Clayton's sketch shows HMS *Driver* lying off Port Nicholson in 1846. Governor Grey used the ship to put down Maori resistance in the Wellington region. The vessel to the left is the migrant ship *London*, a frequent visitor.

❋

CHAPTER 3

White Wings and Steam Kettles

1860-85

Despite our preoccupation with founding myths and the events of 1840, the making of modern New Zealand really occurred in the 1860s and 1870s when two huge waves of immigration broke against our shores. The first was generated by gold fever, part of a mid-19th-century series of rushes around settler Pacific Rim countries: California in 1849, Australia in the early 1850s and New Zealand a decade later. The second demographic tsunami rolled in during the 1870s, generated by recruiting agents for the colonial government's assisted immigration schemes. These two waves enormously increased New Zealand's population. It had taken 20 years for the non-Maori population to rise from 2000 in 1840 to 60,000 in 1860, but that figure would soar to 470,000 by 1881.[1] These two immigration waves swamped and marginalised Maori society and by 1885, in all but a shrinking part of the central North Island and a few other fringes, no one doubted that New Zealand was part of the British Empire. Or that the modern age of cheap and reliable transport and communications had arrived. According to one freight index, costs fell from 185 to 104 between 1870 and 1885.[2] By 1885 most New Zealanders were receiving the British mail in a third the time it had taken in 1860. That year fast steamers plied regularly between its major ports, submarine cables linked us to the world and the first 5000-ton steam ships were poised to halve the voyage time between Britain and New Zealand.

White Wings and Great Circle Sailing

Preceding pages

Victorian New Zealanders liked to relax on and around water, participating in regattas, water carnivals, picnics and excursions. Few people owned purpose-built leisure craft before the 1880s and they usually made use of whaleboats, dinghies or waka, as these people are doing at Kohukohu on the Hokianga.

Henry Wright Collection, Alexander Turnbull Library, G-20439-¹/₁-

Between May 1860, when news of Gabriel Read's discovery of 'gold shining like all the stars in Orion on a dark frosty night' reached Dunedin, and the end of that eventful year, 8000 people had flooded into Otago from Victoria alone. In just two years Dunedin, a struggling, disputatious village of 2000, swelled to a bustling town of 12,000, serving 24,000 people in Central Otago (where fewer than 300 Europeans had lived in 1860). Most came in by sea. The Port of Otago, host to just 69 shipping arrivals in 1860, saw 256 in 1861 and 395 in 1862. In 1863 it handled 983 ships, making it the third-busiest port in the South Pacific. Needless to say, this influx stretched the provincial government's thinly spread harbour department to breaking point. A pilot board met in 1864 and by 1865 the Rattray and Stuart Street jetties had marched out into the bay, but neither Dunedin nor Port Chalmers could take big ships.[3] Pulled between its fiercely pro-Port Chalmers and equally one-eyed pro-Dunedin factions, the Otago authorities embarked on an Upper Harbour dredging programme.

These new port works were needed to support Colonial Treasurer Julius

Vogel's Immigration and Public Works Act of 1870. Gold alone could not create long-term prosperity, he warned: 'A steady influx of settlers was needed, not the tidal rush and ebb of the diggers.'[4] Since young emigrants would not bring in the capital the colony needed, Vogel budgeted for £10 million worth of development. He earmarked £1.5 million of this for immigration in order to make New Zealand more competitive. Geography and costs were loaded against the colony. In 1874 it cost a migrant £15 (five months' earnings for an Oxfordshire agricultural labourer) and took 75–115 uncomfortable days to travel here. The United States, on the other hand, cost British emigrants just £4 and took only 5–10 days. The Canadians threw in free passages and free land. That is why emigration to New Zealand 'was but a small leak in the Atlantic pipeline'.[5] Of the 4.5 million Britons who emigrated between 1861 and 1885, only 17 per cent went to Australasia. Even in the peak years of 1874–75, they represented only about five per cent of British emigration. About 100,000 assisted migrants, 93 per cent from Britain, came here during the 1870s — just over half the net inflow in that decade.

They also took a new route. Early ships followed the old Admiralty route, breaking their journey at Cape Town before sailing east along The Thirties. In 1847, however, John Towson argued that the shortest route between two points on a sphere is a curve and that a line connecting the points and encircling the globe's diameter would be the shortest or 'great circle' route. Few took much notice until the Australian gold discoveries put a premium on speed. In 1852 Captain James Forbes astonished the shipping world by making a round trip to Australia faster than some one-way voyages. Most ships now followed the new route, non-stop all the way, running through the rough, cold, southern seas where drifting pack ice added a freezing frisson to the passage.

Still, speed counted. If you believed the shipping companies, every ship was a 'fast packet' or a 'clipper'. Many were not, of course, but ships with a good table and a reputation for speedy passages lured passengers. Shipping correspondents such as Henry Brett, who later immortalised the migrant ships in *White Wings*, helped to make or break reputations. Their reports of fast passages made headlines. In 1874 the 1053-ton *Loch Awe* set the record for London to Auckland of 76 days, six hours. Speed came at a price, though. The ship took a terrific battering in the Tasman and the married couples and single women were battened down in their accommodation for two days. And it did not always pay to be so quick. The agents were caught unprepared by the *Loch Awe*, which had to wait for the Customs entries and other paperwork to be done.

The clippers of the 1870s were generally larger and better than the migrant vessels of the 1840s. A change in British tonnage laws had enabled naval architects to design more efficient ships and not worry about cheating taxes. Graceful, sharply raked bows and finer hull lines produced the 'clipper' look, and iron hulls, iron shrouds and stays gave more stability and speed. With

"CRUSADER."

D A De Maus Collection, Alexander Turnbull Library G-2016-1/1-

The *Crusader* typified the colonial clippers that brought the Vogel-era migrants out to New Zealand in the 1870s. The 1058-ton ship was not built for the New Zealand trade, but joined the Shaw Savill fleet in 1869, at just four years old. The company kept it until 1898. The *Crusader* was always renowned for its fast passages and even on its last voyage out to Port Chalmers in 1897 made the journey in 95 days. Former passengers formed 'The Clipper Ship Crusader Association' for families of immigrants.

speed came size, 800–1300 tons, compared to the 382-ton *Tory* of 1840 or the 459-ton *Philip Laing* of 1848. Nevertheless, while these Aberdeen or colonial clippers monopolised the migrant trade, older, slower and smaller vessels kept going in the bulk grain and wool trades.

Several shipping lines now worked in the New Zealand trade permanently. Patrick Henderson and Company of Glasgow's Albion Line built a remarkable ship for the New Zealand service in 1857, the Aberdeen clipper *Robert Henderson*. It was a shade under 600 tons but was slim and fast and made a record maiden voyage passage of 79 days land-to-land — not bad at a time when voyage times were still usually over 100 days and frequently 110-130. In the late 1850s the Albion Line joined Shaw Savill and Company, which started with chartered vessels. As imperial troops and gold seekers swelled the traffic during the 1860s, both lines built more ships especially for the trade.

In 1873 they were joined by the New Zealand Shipping Company, or the Shipping Company as it was usually known. Formed in Christchurch in November 1872 with a nominal capital of £250,000, the Shipping Company rode the wave of anti-monopolist feeling generated by the local freight

associations' complaints about high freight rates. The powers behind the Shipping Company were banker J L Coster and Christchurch merchant Charles Wesley Turner. Within months of going to Britain to organise the new company Turner had grabbed the main government contracts. Within a year the new line had sent out nearly 40 ships, had bought four and had the first of a dozen new iron-hulled ships on order. The first, the *Rakaia, Waikato, Waitangi, Waimate* and *Otaki* of 1873–5, were between 1053 and 1161 tons. Shaw Savill's *Oamaru, Timaru* and *Peter Denny* of 1874 were 1364 tons. Typical iron clippers of their day, they were not designed for speed at all costs, but they averaged voyages of between 95 and 100 days.

The Albion Line built the *Invercargill* especially for its New Zealand trade. It was one of the Auckland-class—the *Auckland, Dunedin, Canterbury, Wellington* and *Nelson* were the others—big, 1300-ton iron ships, soundly constructed at Port Glasgow by Robert Duncan, and all except the *Dunedin* served for about 30 years. This Ferrier photograph was taken at Timaru.

'Packed Like So Many Cattle'

What was the experience like for the individual migrant? Fortunately, they have left us their diaries, journals and letters. They do not speak for all who made the journey 'half the world away from home', since many migrants could write little more than their name, but they nevertheless offer a porthole view of the world of the migrant.[6] Most left from London, but there were secondary flows from the Clyde (particularly for Otago) and Plymouth. After reaching the city, they went to the immigration depots, where they waited until shortly before their ship was ready. 'Confusion, distress and bewilderment prevailed at every embarkation,' Charlotte Macdonald recorded. 'There was a great jumble of strange faces, voices, bags and boxes in the unfamiliar surroundings of the main deck where emigrants gathered to watch the constant passing of members of the crew, dock workers, friends, relatives and officials'.[7]

Once the jostle and noise subsided migrants discovered how hierarchical an emigrant ship could be. Passengers were segregated by class, marital status and by gender. First- and second-class cabin passengers occupied the poop (the upper aft deck) and assisted passengers — 80–90 per cent of those aboard — had the lower deck above the cargo. Social mixing varied from ship to ship but Tony Simpson found that 'ships continued to be a microcosm of the class structures those in steerage hoped they had left behind'.[8] First-class passengers lorded it from the drier, more comfortable poop deck and even resented sharing it with fare-paying second-class passengers. On one ship first-class passengers complained about having to share the poop with the second-class, forcing the harried master to divide it in two with a spar.

This was all above the heads of the resentful assisted passengers, huddled in their less salubrious quarters, in the 'tween decks below the main deck and above the lower hold. Being closer to the waterline, they were much more likely to spend days battened down for safety in stormy seas. Their berths, or 'horse stalls', were partitioned by cheap, thin timber, knocked up for the outward voyage and knocked down for the return when wool, grain and kauri gum replaced people. They occupied each side of the 'tween deck and were approximately two metres by two, into which four people were shoe-horned. The migrants were also segregated according to gender and marital status. Married couples, single men and single women each had their own part of the ship: men and boys aged 12 and over in the forward section; single women aft under the poop, as far from the crew and single men as possible. Married couples and young children occupied the centre of the ship. Matrons of varying quality and effectiveness looked after the single women, locking them in their compartment each night.

The 'tween decks were so cramped that the mess tables had to be hoisted up to the deck above when not in use, creating more space especially in the evenings when it was unsafe to venture on deck. Every well-regulated ship put a 'mess captain' in charge of maintaining discipline in his little section. The mess captain drew stores, supervised the preparation of food for the galleys and made sure that nothing in his area would offend the eye of the master during his daily inspection. The emigrants kept their own quarters clean and there were also usually a couple of 'constables', selected from among the male passengers to act as masters-at-arms.

Assisted migrants got an adequate-looking bill of fare but spoilage, vermin or skimping by unscrupulous shipowners or ships' officers could reduce what passengers actually received. The food was fair until the fresh meat and vegetables ran out, which occurred quite early in the voyage. The saloon passengers fared better while the livestock on the deck lasted, but once they were consumed the genteel also faced a diet of salt beef, barrelled pork, tinned mutton, highly smoked bacon, preserved potatoes, carrots and hard biscuits. For desserts they had rice and sago puddings and duffs of questionable quality. Like the seamen, the passengers received a daily dose of lime juice.

With space at such a premium, there was little room for personal belongings, just basic eating utensils, clothing and other necessities. Every three or four weeks there would be a welcome diversion as the hold was opened and boxes were brought up for passengers to replenish their stocks of food, clothing and reading material. This and the occasional shipboard ceremony diluted some of the voyage's discomfort and tedium.

The conditions were unpleasant. As the New Zealand National Maritime Museum's immigrant cabin exhibit shows, it was almost always cramped and dark below decks. Headroom

This engraving from the *Illustrated Australian News* of immigrants landing at Lyttelton captures some of the sense of bustle at the wharfside whenever an immigrant ship discharged its passengers. Along with the port and government officials there would be relatives and friends searching for loved ones, boarding room touts waiting to pounce on 'new chums' and employers seeking workers.

LANDING IMMIGRANTS AT LYTTELTON, N.Z.

THE ILLUSTRATED AUSTRALIAN NEWS.

Alexander Turnbull Library F-81746-½

was 1.8 metres in the older ships and 2.1-2.4 metres in the newer ones. What 21st-century museum visitors miss out on is the smell: spew, sweat and shit mingled with the stench of cargoes past and present. Women on the *Ivanhoe* (1864) inhabited a stinking hold that had not been cleaned out from a previous cargo of sugar and molasses. 'The light was so dim that a lamp had to be kept burning day and night, and the main deck was constantly dirty with drainage from a sheep pen'.[9] 'Vermin, including lice, were commonly present, and rats were endemic to all ships at all periods,'[10] and at least one ship allegedly had 'giant cockroaches whose own cuisine consisted of the toenails of sleeping passengers'.[11] Food standards were at least better than in the 1840s.

Disease was always a risk. Passengers were inspected before embarking, but inevitably some illnesses (and pregnancies) slipped through. The ships carried doctors but not always of much use. After the *England* lost 16 of its 102 immigrants to disease in 1873 the inquiry revealed that the doctor, who 'laboured under a defective memory', had been ill, was epileptic and had signed up for what he saw as his own sea cure.[12] In 1863 the *Brother's Pride* lost 46 people and the *Scimitar* lost 25 children 11 years later. With the likelihood that a family with six children would lose one on the voyage out, migrating really was playing 'New Zealand roulette with their children'.[13]

Then there was the sea itself. The *Dallam Tower* showed that it could punish even a large, well-found ship. It left London on 10 May 1873 for Port Chalmers and made good progress until the night of 14 July when the barometer plunged and the wind and sea rose. By midnight seas were submerging the decks almost continuously and had swept everything moveable off the main deck. This kept up through the early hours as the waves smashed fittings and tore away navigation equipment. The master sent passengers into the forecastle for safety, because 'timber was floating about the saloon in a most dangerous manner'.[14] The gale raged for two days more but somehow the *Dallam Tower* survived, dismasted, leaking and lacking even the most basic chart, sextant or chronometer to navigate by. Only one person was injured, but most lost all but the clothes they stood in. Sixteen passengers transferred to another ship, leaving the rest to sail 2000 miles to Melbourne under jury rig. After repairs the *Dallam Tower* finally reached Otago on 4 March 1874.

While storms, icebergs and collisions with other ships (the *Avalanche*, *St. Leonards* and *Waitara* were lost in the English Channel) brought their terrors, fire stalked everyone's nightmares. These small, closely subdivided ships, lit by naked flame, were deathtraps whenever fire broke out. The better-run ships conducted regular fire drills and ran nocturnal fire patrols, but they had only hand-worked 'fire engines' and buckets should disaster strike. And they carried a fairly explosive mix. In their holds highly flammable substances often shared space with general cargo. The ships' stores of oakum, rope, varnish and paint would also feed any fire that got going.

As colonial ports developed they were able to offer better support for shipping. This photograph shows the Shaw Savill vessel *Hermione* in the Lyttelton graving dock. The ship was broken up at Genoa in 1913 but the graving dock still exists, a registered historic place as well as a vital part of the Lyttelton's maritime infrastructure.

Alexander Turnbull Library
F-14577-½.

One disaster stands out, the burning of the *Cospatrick* in November 1874. This 1220-ton full-rigged ship was far to the west of the Cape of Good Hope, heading for Auckland with a very heavy passenger list, when the dreaded cry 'Fire!' was heard. The crew and passengers did their best but soon the *Cospatrick* was ablaze from stem to stern. Panic ensued as flames consumed some of the boats. Only two boats got away before the main and mizzen masts came crashing down onto the survivors. Then the stern blew out, silencing the shrieks. Soon the survivors would envy the dead. One boat vanished completely and most aboard the other were dead or barely clinging to sanity when they were rescued. Four hundred and seventy of the 473 men, women and children aboard died in a disaster that 'caused a thrill of horror throughout the Empire and particularly in Auckland'.[15]

The vast majority of migrants avoided fire, disease or shipboard accident and arrived in New Zealand healthy and sound. But even after three to five months at sea, their trials were not over. Before anyone could disembark, officials checked the health of the government migrants and the condition of the ship, and heard complaints. If a ship arrived with sickness aboard, it had to raise the yellow flag and go into quarantine, a dismal introduction to the new country given the state of colonial quarantine stations. For the lucky healthy, though, it was time to step ashore, to meet friends or relatives or to make their way to the barracks-like immigration depots, where they waited while officials found them jobs. Little wonder, then, that 'the joy of stepping ashore frequently became a drunken revelry'. Dunedin's chief constable had to intervene when men and women from the *Sevilla* got out of hand.[16] Not surprisingly, the *Otago Daily Times* denounced one shipload as 'certificated scum'.[17]

Building Better Ports and a Safer Coast

Exalted governors and certificated scum had one thing in common: arrival on a dangerous and still poorly lit coastline. On New Year's Eve 1873, 270 Irish, Welsh and French emigrants were celebrating aboard the *Surat*, running up the southern coastline to Port Chalmers, when it struck a rock off Chasland's Mistake.[18] As the ship limped north along the Catlins coast, the pumps failed, drunkenness bred violence and the *Surat* went aground. No one died, but the emigrants lost everything they possessed, relieved of even their luggage by the insurers, who put the wreck, its cargo and passengers' effects up for sale under the rule of 'general average'. Fortunately public pressure won them back their trunks and chests. The *Queen Bee* ran aground on Farewell Spit in 1887, on the last leg of its voyage from London to Nelson in 1877 with one casualty. Even in harbour, though, there were still dangers. In 1863 the *Pride of the Yarra* was ferrying passengers, newly arrived immigrants, from Port Chalmers to Dunedin when it collided with the paddle steamer *Favourite* in thick fog off Blanket Bay. The little steamer sank like a stone, drowning 12 people. On the day of the funeral, Dunedin shops shut early and 2000 people, most of its population, took part in the funeral procession.[19]

As that compelling reference work, *New Zealand Shipwrecks,* shows, the deadliest wrecks in our history took place during this period. The sea exacted its heaviest price in February 1863 when the steam corvette HMS *Orpheus* struck the treacherous Manukau bar on its way in to bolster the forces fighting rebel Maori.[20] On what was really the costliest day of the New Zealand Wars, 189 officers and men drowned within sight of shore, as great rollers pounded the ship, toppling the masts and snatching the crew from the rigging. The second highest toll was exacted at the other end of the country nearly 20 years later. The Union Steam Ship Company's trans-Tasman liner, *Tararua,* smashed onto a reef at Waipapa Point, Southland, on 29 April 1882,[21] drowning 131 passengers and crew, again just a stone's throw away from the shore.

The reports of the Marine Department in the *Appendix to the Journals of the House of Representatives* make depressing reading. Their fold-out Wreck Charts mark the year's casualties in big blacks Xs and they carry long roll-calls of total wrecks, strandings and collisions. H-12 for 1882 runs to five closely set pages of maritime misadventures — 66 casualties, 162 lives, 131 of them from the *Tararua.* In 1883, a year free of major passenger-ship disasters, there were still 85 accidents and 48 deaths. Deaths on the road would not exceed death by drowning until 1928.

New Zealand ports were dangerous, especially in the 1860s when trade grew, but they were still very rudimentary and navigation aids were almost non-existent. The bar harbours of the West Coast ports of both islands were especially dangerous, as the steam corvette HMS *Orpheus* discovered in February 1863 when it was wrecked on the Manukau bar: 189 officers and men drowned.

Gavin McLean Collection

Building River Ports

This plan of Patea harbour improvements shows how marine engineers made river ports safer. Sir John Coode was an eminent British marine consulting engineer who advised many New Zealand harbour boards in the late 1870s. Whether it was Gisborne, Westport, Greymouth or here, Patea, the formula was simple, if expensive: straighten the river, concentrate the flow (and therefore the scour) by closing off diversionary streams and push moles or breakwaters out into deeper water, to create a relatively calm entrance over the bar. Coode felt that Wanganui could

meet Patea's needs, but that was not a message the locals wanted to hear and in true parochial fashion they went ahead with the huge £200,000 project, albeit in stages as money permitted. The photograph, taken in 1904, shows the short eastern breakwater and the guide pier concentrating the river flow. The steamer ashore under the headland in the background is the *Aotea*, which stranded there for the final time that year. Two hundred and fifty tons was about the limit for Patea, but the port was busy until 1959.

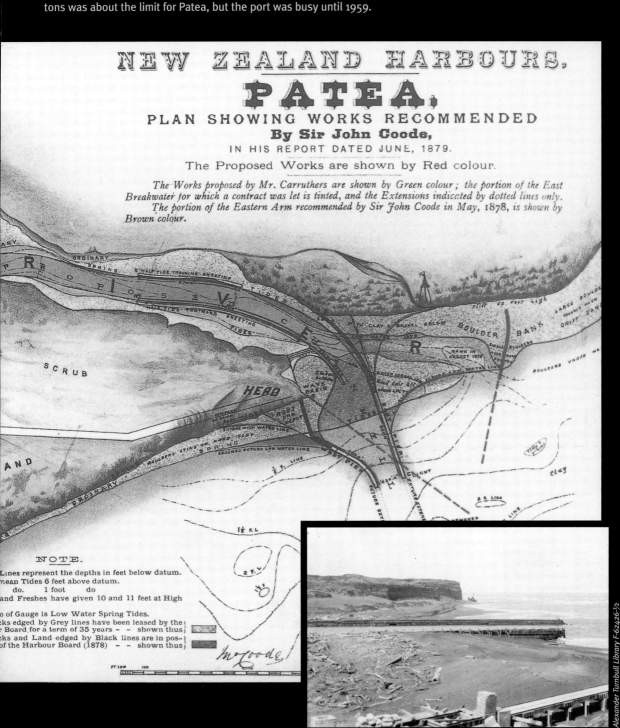

NEW ZEALAND HARBOURS,
PATEA,
PLAN SHOWING WORKS RECOMMENDED
By Sir John Coode,
IN HIS REPORT DATED JUNE, 1879.

The Proposed Works are shown by Red colour.

The Works proposed by Mr. Carruthers are shown by Green colour; the portion of the East Breakwater for which a contract was let is tinted, and the Extensions indicated by dotted lines only. The portion of the Eastern Arm recommended by Sir John Coode in May, 1878, is shown by Brown colour.

NOTE.

Lines represent the depths in feet below datum.
mean Tides 6 feet above datum.
do.   1 foot   do
and Freshes have given 10 and 11 feet at High

o of Gauge is Low Water Spring Tides.
cks edged by Grey lines have been leased by the
r Board for a term of 35 years - - shown thus
cks and Land edged by Black lines are in pos-
of the Harbour Board (1878) - - shown thus

The solutions were two-fold. The most practical solutions came locally through the harbour boards, sanctioned by the Harbour Board Act 1870, that were set up to create safer ports. In time New Zealand would have 60 harbour boards, though many were short-lived and a number were no more than the local road board or county council doubling up as a harbour authority. Of course many ports did not last long. They remained simple anchorages, or else had little more than a signal mast and a thin T-head jetty to dignify their status. They were the sort of places that the Northern Company and Richardson and Company would make their specialty, often loading wool direct from settlers' bullock drays into surfboats and ferrying it out to the little steamer off the coast, its crew anxiously watching for signs of storms. Many places, even ones sorely lacking in any natural advantage, sought port status. 'They were strongly motivated by parochialism and they embarked on development schemes, sometimes out of necessity, but often as a speculation based on the concept that the port would bring the trade,' wrote John O'C Ross in *Pride in Their Ports*, his history of over 100 minor ports. 'Sometimes they were right, but in too many cases they were wrong . . . They over-reached themselves, in some cases to the point of bankruptcy and either fell into the receiver's hands, had to be bailed out by a Government loan, or their port was taken over by the Marine Department.'[22]

Each port had its own characteristics, but they came under three broad categories. In the first group were the major ports, Auckland, Wellington and Lyttelton, which were safe natural anchorages and which required only modest improvement; Otago, with its two-port system within the same harbour, shared these characteristics with those of the next group. Next came the river ports, such as Hokitika, Greymouth, Westport, Wanganui, Patea and Gisborne. These provided a measure of natural safety that could be improved upon if enough money was spent on dredging and building training walls. Finally there were the open roadsteads such as Oamaru, Timaru and New Plymouth. They offered virtually no shelter and could only be made safe by building massive artificial harbours protected by breakwaters and moles.

River ports offered a quick and easy anchorage. New Zealand's mountain-fed rivers are short, shallow and dangerous. Only the Waikato, Wanganui and Clutha were navigable for any real distance and all rivers concealed dangers. Bars — submerged ridges of sand that shifted with every storm — guarded their entrances and many river mouths shifted, cutting fresh entrances after heavy storms. Once safely across the bar, the ship then had to avoid snags, shallows and other hazards. Most of the major river ports are clustered on New Zealand's western seaboard: Greymouth and Westport in the South Island and Wanganui in the North.

Hokitika was the archetypal gold-rush river port, brought to life by the discovery of gold in the vicinity in 1864. It was not much of a place that

December when Captain Leach took the small steamer *Nelson* over the bar and into the snag-infested river. The Canterbury provincial government, desperate for gold revenue, declared Hokitika a port of entry in 1865 and by 1866 a tolerably good wharf (Gibson Quay), a Customs house and goods sheds were doing good business with the ships that thronged there. In the days of sail it was faster to cross the Tasman than it was to sail from the provincial capital, Christchurch, around the coast to Hokitika, so small tenders from the port were soon servicing the ships that anchored off its dangerous entrance in the storm-ravaged Tasman. Between 1865 and 1867 Hokitika had no fewer than 108 strandings — one every 10 days! — and 32 of these resulted in the complete loss of the ships. At one time in 1865 photographers recorded seven ashore at once. Westport, which went bankrupt and was run by the central government for many decades, showed that the river ports never had it easy. They could seldom accommodate large international traders and they required constant maintenance — regular soundings of the bar, dredging and the repair of those vulnerable training walls.

The roadstead ports faced the toughest hurdles and the construction of an expensive breakwater was always a last resort. Napier people never resolved their battle between the inner port (Port Ahuriri) and breakwater factions in the 19th century. Both Oamaru and Timaru looked hard at river port options, the shallow creek in Oamaru's case and Milford Lagoon in Timaru's. Oamaru depended on surfboats from the beach when the town sprang up to serve the new pastoral stations of North Otago in the 1850s. The town boomed in the 1860s but the provincial authorities were reluctant to spend money and built only an exposed jetty in the lee of Cape Wanbrow. The inevitable happened in February 1868 when a huge storm wrecked it, along with the ships *Star of Tasmania*, *Water Nymph* and *Otago*. In fact, Oamaru became something of a shipwreck capital, claiming 22 total wrecks and many more strandings between 1862 and 1875. After beginning and then abandoning a dock in the creek, Oamaru formed a harbour board in 1874 and started work on the 600-metre breakwater. By 1876 it had marched out sufficiently into the Pacific to enable steamers to berth safely against the adjoining Macandrew wharf. Thereafter only one small trading vessel was wrecked at the North Otago port.

Port numbers peaked in the mid 1860s. They fell from 86 in 1867 to 64 in 1881, 21 of them being in the under-developed Auckland province, where the 'mosquito fleet' of small steamers, schooners, ketches, cutters and scows connected the city to its sprawling hinterland. Ports had closed in both islands, but the casualties usually sat in the shadow of the more established ones. All the minor ports trading between Dunedin and Oamaru, for example — Shag Point, Moeraki, Kakanui and Allday Bay — were gone by 1881. The export trade also became more concentrated. Now Dunedin, Wellington, Auckland and Lyttelton were claiming 80 per cent of overseas trade.[23]

Hazardous Hokitika

Like Otago and Thames, Hokitika experienced a gold rush boom. Although the river had an unusually dangerous, unstable entrance that forced ships to enter and leave broadside to the prevailing seas, gold fever enticed masters to cross the bar in 1865. Within weeks the snag-infested river had been gazetted a port. In 1866 the value of its exports exceeded Auckland's. The top photograph shows shipping thickly stretched the length of Gibson Quay. But there was a price to pay. 108 ships stranded there between 1865 and 1867 and the port was sometimes closed completely by shallowing. Like so many other harbours, Hokitika was inspected by Sir John Coode in 1878. He recommended extending the channel out in two 200-metre breakwaters. The harbour board beggared itself building them but cut them short at just over 130 metres. The lower photograph shows an auxiliary ketch leaving port past the Coode breakwaters.

Eventually Timaru built a breakwater to improve the safety of the port. As this photo shows, these structures had to withstand tremendous battering.

BREAKWATER TIMARU N.Z. DURING A HEAVY SEA.   W.F.

William Ferrier Collection, Alexander Turnbull Library G-19954-½

Better progress was also made possible after the abolition of the provincial governments in 1876. The Marine Department that had replaced the earlier Marine Board assumed responsibility for the ports and anchorages not administered by harbour boards. The Department examined seafarers' qualifications, inspected ships, certified boilers and other machinery and inspected fisheries, but its most prominent work was constructing and maintaining lighthouses. The country's first respectable lighthouse had been lit at Pencarrow Head, near the entrance to Wellington Harbour, on 1 January 1859. The early lighthouses were prefabricated of cast iron in Britain and shipped out here, but soon they were being built of local materials to save money. Stone towers were favoured where there was a suitable supply of building materials nearby but others were built locally from timber and cast iron. Run by marine engineer John Blackett, the Department's Lighthouse Service modelled itself on the Scottish service. 'Complete with a strict and authoritarian set of rules, *Instructions to Lightkeepers*', which required employees to be 'sober and industrious, cleanly in their persons and habits, and orderly in their families' and which warned the inhabitants of those phallic structures that 'any flagrant immorality will subject them to immediate dismissal'.[24]

The Marine Department also ran the government steamers. The government had owned earlier vessels, but its steamer service took on its new look in 1876 when the new steamers *Stella* (268 tons) and the *Hinemoa* (542 tons) reached the colony. They and the later ships were maids-of-all-work. They ferried Parliamentarians to and from sittings of Parliament and took governors on summer cruises, but their core work for the Department was more mundane. They carried lighthouse components to new sites, landed stores at existing ones, surveyed the coast, ferried scientific parties to isolated places, searched for missing vessels and transported supplies to the sub-Antarctic islands, castaway depots that the government maintained until 1927.

The New Zealand Wars

By the time that the main Vogel migration waves lapped against New Zealand's shores, the New Zealand Wars were receding into memory. The wars were almost entirely land-based engagements. Maori had no naval capacity and the Royal Navy, the premier fighting arm of the world's only superpower, enabled the imperial, colonial and allied Maori forces to move at will along the coast and to insert forces as required. As early as 1846 Governor Sir George Grey had put into practice Alfred Thayer Mahan's doctrine of the use of seapower by snatching the 'Old Sarpint', Te Rauparaha. Sailors from HMS *Driver* stormed ashore early in the morning, catching Te Rauparaha naked and defenceless. According to one account, 'the old chief struggled desperately until a British sailor grabbed his testicles, so symbolising the low morality and high

Deepening, deepening . . . harbour boards were forever building expensive holes in the seabed to deepen channels for ships that kept getting bigger. This photograph of the paddle steamer *Golden Age* alongside the jetty at Dunedin exemplifies the problem. Small ships meant expensive freight rates.

Wellington Museum, City & Sea

H Winkelmann photograph, Auckland Institute and Museum, neg. 2352

The government steamers made an important contribution to New Zealand history. At the sensible end of the scale, they serviced lighthouses and castaway depots, transported scientific expeditions, carried politicians and governors and searched for missing ships. At the silly end of the scale, governors and colonial politicians fought over using them for seagoing junkets. This is the *Hinemoa* unloading stores by surfboat for the lighthouse at North Head in 1902. The *Hinemoa* had been built in 1876 and served the government for several decades.

effectiveness of Grey's tactics'.[25]

When fighting erupted in Taranaki in the early 1860s, the authorities threw together a scratch fleet of armed auxiliaries. For the Waikato campaign the colonial government built or converted a small flotilla of armed gunboats and barges, New Zealand's first navy. In 1863 it converted the 43-ton paddle steamer *Avon* into an armoured gunboat, complete with 12-pounder gun. From Australia the government ordered its first warships, the 300-ton *Pioneer* (launched as the *Waikato*) and the smaller *Koheroa* and *Rangiriri*. The *Pioneer*, armed at Auckland, mounted two 12-pounders in revolving turrets. Four coastal cutters, the *Ant*, *Midge*, *Chub* and *Flirt* supplemented them; converted to armour-plated barges, fitted with a 12-pounder and a 4.4-inch mortar, they were towed into action behind the gunboats.[26]

The river flotilla played a crucial part in defeating the Kingites. The *Avon* and *Pioneer* took part in the investment and capture of Meremere pa in October 1863 and the capture of Rangiriri two months later. More importantly, from their shipyard base at Ngaruawahia, they defended the supply chain connecting General Cameron's advance to the Great South Road. 'Before *Pioneer*'s advent, the protection of Cameron's logistic chain required no less than 80 per cent of his total forces,' the *Oxford Companion to New Zealand Military History* recorded.[27] The *Pioneer*'s arrival enabled many of these troops to be redeployed to the front.

The last inland expedition came in 1869 when armed constables and Maori auxiliaries built a small flotilla of open boats to confront Hauhau on Lake Waikaremoana. Cutting tracks would have been quicker and cheaper and the troops were recalled before this colonial bath tub navy could be used.

All this time, the colonial gunboats and transports had been operating behind a wider shield. The schooner *Caroline* was fitted with a 32-pounder gun and put on patrol between Manukau and New Plymouth, and the cutter *Midnight*, fitted with a 4-pounder gun, patrolled the Hauraki Gulf. The paddle steamer *Sandfly* mounted two 12-pounders and patrolled the Firth of Thames between 1863 and 1865, bombarding Maori retreating along a beach at Tauranga in April 1864. During the wars, HM ships *Curacoa*, *Esk*, *Fawn* and *Miranda* maintained a presence on the Waitemata and *Eclipse* and *Harrier* did the same on the Manukau. Devonport on Auckland's North Shore developed as the colony's rudimentary naval base.

Colonial Shipbuilding

The government could not have converted steamers for war purposes unless the colony possessed talented shipwrights and engineers. As in pre-colonial times, wooden shipbuilding remained important. Shipwrights were busiest up north, where timber supplies were plentiful. William Brown and Thomas Lane built at Whangaroa, James Barbour built on the Kaipara and the Darrochs built timber craft at Auckland, Mahurangi and then Auckland again. Henry Niccol founded a shipbuilding dynasty in Auckland and Robert Stone built ships in Thames. On Banks Peninsula, numerous small builders turned out fine cutters and ketches.

One distinctive type emerged during the 1870s: the scow.[28] Its origins lie with the flat-bottomed North American sailing craft of that name. Like America, northern New Zealand needed something that could carry heavy loads, take the battering that log cargoes gave and sit on the bottom when the tide went out. In 1873 an American mariner living in New Zealand, George Spencer, ordered the first scow from Omaha shipbuilder Septimus Meiklejohn. Spencer's vessel was based on a Great Lakes scow and, fittingly, was called *Lake Erie* (other early New Zealand scows were called *Lake Superior*, *Lake St. Clair* and *Lake Michigan*). The *Lake Erie* was punt-like, just a wide, shallow box with a sharp end and a blunt end. The cargo sat on the deck, not in the shallow hull. Reporting the launch of the *Lake Erie* in June 1873 the *Southern Cross* said that 'the idea of building a vessel of this description is to enable the owners to run the vessel up the shallow creek, and take in her cargo direct from the mills, instead of having to lie off some distance, as is so frequently the case with cutters and schooners, and so save the lightering off by small punts'.[29] The scows had another advantage — they had low net

William A Price's camera captured the scow *Lady of the Lake* in its intended environment, sitting on the Auckland seabed at low water. Kauri logs lie in the foreground, a timber boom snakes across the middle distance and other scows and small sailing craft bob about in the distance. The *Lady of the Lake* was an early scow, built at Mahurangi in 1876.

tonnages and therefore paid low harbour dues.

The early scows were called 'monster punts' and 'schooner barges' and were treated with some disdain and suspicion but they quickly proved themselves in service. Cheap, tough and very practical, the scow had few vices. Its chief failing came from its need to sit upright when aground. This meant that it lacked a conventional keel, relying instead on a big centre-board (earlier ones had used leeboards) that could be raised and lowered. This gave some stability under sail, but it could not entirely compensate for the loss of grip in the water and so scows tended to drift to leeward when sailing against the wind. They also sported thumping great 'barn door' rudders to help with steering. As with any type, the scow evolved with time and from the 1880s these 'punt-shaped' craft were being built with pointed bows and an easy sheer, taking on an almost respectable appearance. They also crowded the Waitemata. P A Eaddy, the first chronicler of the scows, recorded that 'Niccol turned out scows from his yard like a small builder would turn out rowing boats . . . In quick succession he built the scows *Seagull, Gannet, Tramp, Hawk, Wanderer, Welcome, Haere, Haeremai, Magic, Korora, Zingara, Arrah Na Pogue, Cead Mile Failte*, and many more.'[30]

There were two types. Deck scows, the most numerous, were the original

Alexander Turnbull Library, G-5393-½

design, flat bottomed and flat-decked, built to carry their cargo on deck, like a modern ramped barge. The big deck scows were especially suited to the northern timber trade. They hauled logs aboard with their derricks and parbuckling chains, taking so many that the last were often chained well outside the line of the hull. 'A fully loaded scow resembled a logpile with a bow and sails'.[31] Yet they piled on plenty of canvas and were even raced for many years in the Auckland Anniversary Day Regattas. Some crews were so enthusiastic about racing that they entered the race even if they had not completely cleared their deck of cargo.

The *Rangi* was one of the most famous scows. George Niccol built the big deck scow in 1905. This photograph shows the *Rangi* at Whangaparapara at Great Barrier Island, discharging logs for the local sawmill.

Less common than the deck scow was the hold scow. Hold scows ranged in size from the tiny 17.2-metre *Pakihi* to the 36.4-metre, three-masted *Whangaroa*. There were fewer hold scows, but they made up for their lack of numbers by their longevity. The *Echo* and *The Portland* carried cargo across Cook Strait as late as 1965 and 1972 respectively and still survive — just — in 2001.

About 130 scows were built. They proved tough, adaptable little ships and several survived multiple sinkings or strandings. The first ones kept close to Auckland, but they proved themselves on longer coastal trips and even crossed the Tasman with timber. Living conditions were tough. In big ships, such as the three-masted trans-Tasman traders *Whangaroa* and *Zingara*, the crew was seven including the master. In most, though, it was just three to five men.

Many more brigs, schooners, ketches and cutters were built than scows. More steamers were also built. After the initial failure of the *Governor Wynyard* New Zealand shipbuilders returned to building steamers, launching 34 between 1853 and 1869, 22 of them in Auckland. Steamers were built throughout the country, sometimes from components manufactured in Britain but more commonly locally. While Auckland yards did build in iron and steel, they specialised in timber construction, drawing on the rich resources of their hinterland. Timber was less plentiful in Otago but Dunedin shipbuilders could draw on their city's position as the principal manufacturing centre of the colony to build in iron and steel. During the 1870s James Kincaid & Charles McQueen and Robert

Dunedin was the commercial and industrial heartland of late Victorian New Zealand and its shipbuilders dominated New Zealand's modest iron and steel shipbuilding industry. The dredge *Progress* was built for the Oamaru Harbour Board by Kinnear and Imrie and assembled at Port Chalmers by J Davidson. Here we see it about to be launched from the Port Chalmers dockhead on 9 February 1883. Dredges such as this kept ports competitive and freights low. The 350-ton craft served at Oamaru until 1916 when it was converted to a sailing coaster and then a steamer. The very old ship sank in 1931 off the entrance to Wellington Harbour with the loss of four lives.

Hocken Library

Sparrow and his several partners forged a solid reputation for their skills at building iron and steel ships. In 1873 Kincaid & McQueen showed that a steamer could be built from materials made entirely in the city when it delivered the 45-ton *Fairy* to Napier shipowners John Campbell and George Richardson. Although the ship proved a success, its launching was anything but. The builders intended to run the hull on a carriage down to the beach but all of Kincaid's horses and all of Kincaid's men could not get ship and sea together that day. The carriage wheels sank into the soft road metal and then a tight street corner halted progress. As darkness fell Dunedinites gazed at the odd sight of a steamer stuck in a city intersection and it took another day of sweaty exertion before the *Fairy* got to the water.[32] Dunedin shipbuilders seem to have had a problem with getting to the water's edge, which reclamation was pushing further from their workshops. In April 1876 Sparrow and Henderson were sliding their new steamer *Iron Age* towards the Stuart Street jetty when the soft ground gave way, stranding the steamer firmly across the busy Dunedin–Port Chalmers railway line — a rare, albeit temporary, victory for ship over train.

But Dunedin yards persevered and during the 1870s they turned out ships such as the *Jane Douglas, Iron Age, Jane Williams, Invercargill, Iona, Kakanui, Mountaineer, Tui, Reynolds* and *Vulcan*. These southern shipyards also built boilers for factories and for decades were constructing large gold- and tin-mining dredges for New Zealand and overseas customers (201 in 1903 alone).[33] Gold mining led to New Zealand's strangest shipbuilding contract. In 1873, inspired by the latest speculative idea, the New Zealand Submarine Gold Mining Co. ordered a small gold-mining submarine from Sparrow & Company.[34] It was 10.7 metres long and built of 95-mm iron plate. The *Platypus*, as it was named, was designed to submerge to the riverbed, where the current would provide power to the main shaft, from which a belt transmitted the drive to a counter-shaft operating the air-pumps. It was tested off Pelichet Bay in Dunedin Harbour on 30 January 1874, when four company representatives and an *Otago Daily Times* reporter spent 45 minutes sealed in. Unfortunately the grand public demonstration a little later went off less successfully and the eight men spent rather longer — over four hours — on the seabed than planned. This dampened investor enthusiasm for the venture and the *Platypus*, knocked down at a cheap price, sat on the Rattray Street wharf for many years before being cut up and carted away.

At all the major ports hundreds of people worked away at repairing ships. Again, Otago led the way. In 1868 a syndicate launched the wooden floating dock *Alpha*, which could accommodate 45-metre-long ships. Four years later the impressive stone-lined Port Chalmers graving dock opened at Port Chalmers; the much larger Otago Dock supplemented it in 1909, giving Port Chalmers unrivalled repair capacities. In 1897 the Union Steam Ship

S.S. POHERUA

D A De Maus Collection, Alexander Turnbull Library G-3383-1/1-

Port Chalmers was also the location for the colony's biggest repair works. The Union Company began servicing its fleet there in 1876 and later that century the company built a large marine repair works complex, which survived until the 1970s. This late Victorian photograph shows the company's cargo carrier *Poherua* (1175 tons, 1890) alongside the sheerlegs.

Company would build substantial carpentry and engineering shops to service its steamers there. Other major ports also built docks. Lyttelton's opened in 1883 when the Shipping Company's flag-bedecked clipper *Hurunui* entered, after which invited guests celebrated with food, wine and a staggering 30 speeches.[35] Auckland opened Calliope Dock in 1888 and at Wellington, John George Rees built the Wellington Patent Slip in 1873. Like the ports they inhabited, these docks were powerful symbols of parochial pride. Lyttelton's lost money for years and Otago critics derided theirs as 'an expensive piece of marine furniture', but it built the 1909 one to keep ahead.

Steam Kettles and Engines of Progress

Before the 1870s New Zealand shipping lines were generally small. Their titles might have been grand, but most were single-ship ventures, owned by an individual or a group of friends who split the shares in the traditional 64ths. One of the few early exceptions was Henderson and Macfarlane's Circular Saw Line. This Auckland venture owned or chartered numerous small steamers and sailing craft and ran in the coastal and Islands trades for many decades from the mid 1840s.[36] By the 1860s several inter-provincial mail services were being provided by the Inter-Colonial Royal Mail, McMeckan Blackwood and the New Zealand Steam Navigation Company. Sailing craft were still common, but as Simon Ville notes, 'It was in the 1870s that steamers came to predominate: by the end of the decade they were responsible for more than half of coasting vessels and as much as 80 per cent of tonnage'.[37]

The first of the large joint stock companies was the New Zealand Steam Navigation Company Ltd. It was formed in Wellington in 1862 with a capital of £50,000. The NZSNCo. slurped up provincial subsidies like a frenzied vampire, but it did provide the first reasonably comprehensive coastal service. By 1864 six steamers — the *Wellington, Wonga Wonga, Ladybird, Rangatira, Queen* and *Stormbird* — were running around the coast while the company was running to ruin. Shareholders could not decide whether to wind up or go on and by the late 1860s the NZSNCo. 'was dispirited, introspective and defeated, despite supposedly having the cream of Wellington's business community on one side or the other of the argument'.[38] In 1871 it was finally wound up, only to be replaced by a new company called the New Zealand Steam Shipping Company Ltd, which inherited some of

The *Wellington* (seen here at Picton) was built in 1863 for the New Zealand Steam Navigation Company. Its bowsprit, slender lines and masts fitted for carrying auxiliary sail typified early steamships, although it must be said that the *Wellington* was advanced for its day and went on to serve most major shipping companies, the New Zealand Steam Shipping Company, the Union Company and Northern. It was hulked in 1909.

Gavin McLean Collection

Compound and triple-expansion engines finally made steamers competitive. This photograph shows the big trans-Tasman passenger/cargo steamer *Wakatipu* in the Port Chalmers dry dock shortly after arriving in the colony in 1876. It could make 13 knots but usually did 11 in service. Built for a syndicate friendly to the Union Steam Ship Company, the 1797-ton *Wakatipu* joined the Southern Octopus's fleet in 1878. It was twice the size of most migrant ships.

the fleet, and most of the muddled ways of its predecessor.

The NZSSCo. would soon succumb to competition from the south. Dunedin had also had its share of steamship company crashes. Johnny Jones, E B Cargill and other leading merchants had formed the Otago Steam Ship Company in 1863 to contest the trans-Tasman trade. Unfortunately only half the shares had been placed before Jones rashly ordered the steamers *Scotia* (872 tons) and *Albion* (668 tons). Even more rashly, he sent the ships to sea underinsured. When the *Scotia* ran ashore at Stirling Point on just its second round trip, the company had to sell two small feeder vessels and two lighters cheaply merely to stay afloat. The company that had planned to run six big steamers across the Tasman went into voluntary liquidation in 1867.

The Union Steam Ship Company of New Zealand began in 1875 in Dunedin, which was then at the peak of its commercial pre-eminence. Its presiding genius, James Mills, had been born at Wellington in 1847, two years before the family moved to the new Otago settlement. The bright young man attracted the attention of Johnny Jones and before long 'Little Jimmy' was running another Jones-led shipping line, the Harbour Steam Company. He was also a trustee for Jones, which was fortunate, because Jones died suddenly in 1869. Under the old system of loose partnerships, where shares were owned

in 64ths, sudden death or emigration could threaten ventures such as Harbour Steam, since unlike land-based partnerships, 64ths could be transferred without the consent of all members. Mills decided not to let this happen and delayed the sale of the fleet until he and his friends could build up their stake in the business. While ship owning could be very profitable, Mills knew that the harbour traffic would not survive rail competition. He wanted to run big modern steamers between the islands.[39]

After one failed attempt, Mills established his company in 1875. Like most colonials, he succeeded through a combination of talent, drive and access to British capital. Mills took letters of introduction back with him to Britain but his greatest coup was his chance meeting with Dumbarton shipbuilder and investor Peter Denny. Denny invested in shipping lines as a means of bringing in new business and he liked both Mills and his plans. He offered to build two new ships on favourable terms and to bring in other investors. Mills was elated. Denny was an envied builder of fine, fast, short-sea steamers. For nearly 30 years the Dumbarton yard would construct almost every new Union

The Union Company made its biggest splash with the graceful, yacht-like, 15-knot *Rotomahana*. This 1727-tonner was the world's first oceangoing steamer to be built of mild steel and the first with bilge keels. It could carry 332 passengers and served on the Tasman, Cook and Bass Strait runs from 1879 until the 1920s. But all colonial-era passenger ships also had to carry cargo and this photograph (circa 1910) at Nelson brings home the reality of life in New Zealand. Even the *Rotomahana* had to carry sheep!

Alexander Turnbull Library 93071/1

Company ship and the Scottish town would be home to the Union Company's marine superintending engineers and marine superintendents.

Although Mills was initially concerned about expansion diluting his personal power, he was now in a very strong position. Denny and his friends supplied the technology and much of the capital from the United Kingdom. In Dunedin, Mills's fellow directors, who included members of the prestigious Cargill and Ritchie families, supplied further capital, local knowledge and contacts with shippers. This powerful combination of talent and capital quickly sidelined its rivals. In 1876, just months after Mills got back to Dunedin, Denny's takeover of the troubled New Zealand Steam Shipping Company added the steamers *Phoebe*, *Taranaki*, *Wellington* and *Ladybird* to Union's five ships.[40] Denny also kept the British lines out of local waters. They still ran sailing ships to New Zealand but the Albion Line was planning coastal feeder services to bring cargo to its ships. In 1876 Albion's 438-ton steamer *Taiaroa* entered the Timaru–Port Chalmers trade against Union's chartered steamer *Wanganui*. Mills was determined to end the experiment before the *Taiaroa* could prove its worth and Denny got Albion to sell Union the ship and promise to leave the coastal trade to the Dunedin business.

The Union Company also had its eyes on the vital trade between New Zealand and the Australian colonies. Denny delivered the big passenger-cargo vessel *Wakatipu* to a friendly syndicate in 1876 (Union acquired it in 1878), and in 1877 the *Rotorua* made the company's first intercolonial voyage. In 1878 Union took over the principal trans-Tasman shipping line, McMeckan Blackwood & Company of Melbourne. Between 1879 and 1882 Dennys built seven new passenger-cargo liners for this route, all between 1700 and 2000 tons: the *Rotomahana*, *Te Anau*, *Manapouri*, *Wairarapa*, *Hauroto*, *Tarawera* and *Waihora*. Although the *Te Anau* was a more profitable ship, the *Rotomahana* stood out. It was the world's first ship built of mild steel and the first with bilge keels. At 1727 tons, this Tasman Sea steamer dwarfed the Shipping Company's latest British-trade sailing ship, the *Wanganui* (1136 tons, 1877). With its bowsprit, clipper bow, that raked funnel and masts that made it look like a millionaire's steam yacht, the rakish, 15-knot 'Greyhound of the Pacific' was a powerful mobile advertising billboard for the new company.

The Union Company made its money by offering its customers safe, high-quality services. The first new ships built by Denny for the Union Company in 1875 had been the *Taupo* and the *Hawea*. Many modern New Zealand factory trawlers are much bigger than their 720 tons gross, but in 1875 they were seen as coastal giants. They were almost as big as the smaller sailing ships that the Shipping Company, Shaw Savill and the Albion Line were using to bring migrants all the way out from Britain. More important than size were their new compound steam engines. These were a development from the old single-cylinder reciprocating engine in which the steam, after leaving the first

Alexander Turnbull Library G-2348-1/1

cylinder, was passed through a second low-pressure cylinder of larger diameter before being drawn off to a condenser to be changed back to boiler feed power. This second use of the steam produced higher engine efficiency and enabled steamers to compete economically with sail for the first time. That is why people flocked aboard them during their triumphal first sailings and the colony's business leaders toasted the company's fortunes in the steamers' luxuriously panelled saloons.

As a rule, the coasters that the Union Company ordered from Denny were big and comfortable rather than flyers. The notable exception was the high-speed coastal mini-liner *Takapuna* of 1883, built for an express service between Port Chalmers and Onehunga. The 930-ton ship caused ructions with Denny, who first said the specifications were impractical and then sulked when Mills built it elsewhere. The *Takapuna* chewed up coal in costly quantities but cut travelling time between Wellington and Auckland (Onehunga) to 23 hours, a big improvement on the

The *Takapuna* was a less successful Union Company steamer. It was designed for an express mail service from Onehunga to Wellington and Lyttelton, and had to meet tight length and draft restrictions for the Manukau Harbour. Regular builder Peter Denny felt that too much was being expected of the ship and refused the job. The 930-ton *Takapuna* proved a costly ship to operate but it nevertheless had a long career with the company. Here it is working cargo at Queen's Wharf, Wellington, dwarfed by the New Zealand Shipping Company's 'Home boat' *Papanui* of 1898.

three wearying days that ships on the Wellington-Auckland East Coast route
were taking.

Saving Time and Making Tracks

Even ships slower than the *Takapuna* slashed travelling times. The first steamers
may have had their terrors and wayward ways but they brought speed and some
certainty to travel for the first time. In 1859 the fastest way to get from
Dunedin to Auckland was to take a series of small steamers via Lyttelton,
Wellington, Nelson and New Plymouth and then land at Onehunga. Even
with a six-day interlude at Nelson, waiting for a connecting steamer, the 15-
day journey time was a tremendous advance on the uncertainties of sail.
Twenty years later our traveller could cut that by two thirds by taking the train
to Christchurch and then boarding better, faster steamers. In 1898 using the
Dunedin-Christchurch and the Wellington-New Plymouth trains and the

The Union Company issued its *Pocket Guide*
monthly. The little booklet also included a guide
to Government Railways. The map in the centre
traced the steamer routes and marked the
reassuring lighthouses.

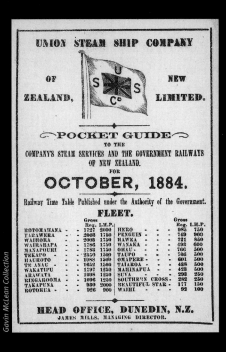

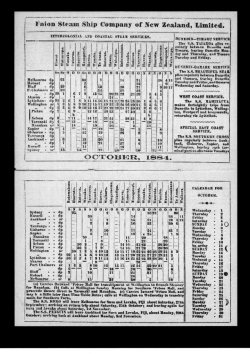

Gavin McLean Collection

Onehunga-New Plymouth steamer shaved another day off our Dunedinite's travelling time.[41]

Notice the trains. Conventional wisdom has them poised to shunt coastal shipping into an historical siding. Certainly, they were the talk of the day. The South Island main trunk railway was finished in 1878 and rails were advancing throughout the colony, aided by Vogel's money and central government enthusiasm for these new engines of progress. As the tracks advanced, they took business from some ships, harbour lighters and short-distance passenger-cargo steamers. Rail competition made the modern 412-ton *Waitaki* uneconomic on the Oamaru-Dunedin run within three years. It was replaced by smaller, older craft, which struggled on until 1890. But it is worth noting that these old steamers held out for another decade and that the *Waitaki* found work elsewhere on the coast. Since most of New Zealand was less developed than the prosperous Otago-Canterbury seaboard, it is more helpful to see the railways' role as an auxiliary to coastal shipping, opening up the back country and feeding its produce down to the ports. From there coasters either distributed it to other parts of the colony or took it to the export ports.

Rollo Arnold thought that the railways had been over-estimated. Government ownership and public accounting requirements gave them a profile higher than the privately owned coasters, whose results were 'murky, ambiguous and complete'.[42] In 1885, the terminal year for this chapter, Arnold calculated ton-mileage to estimate the total amount of work being done by these ships. He warned that his figures had to be qualified, since official statistics excluded the very small ports and the anchorages served by the mosquito fleet. Nevertheless, depending on the carrying co-efficient assumed, he produced ton-mileages in the range of 455,000,000 and 925,000,000 or 'seven times and 14 times the year's ton-mileage on the railways'.[43] Little wonder that the Union Company's monthly *Pocket Guides* to its services also included timetables for the railways.

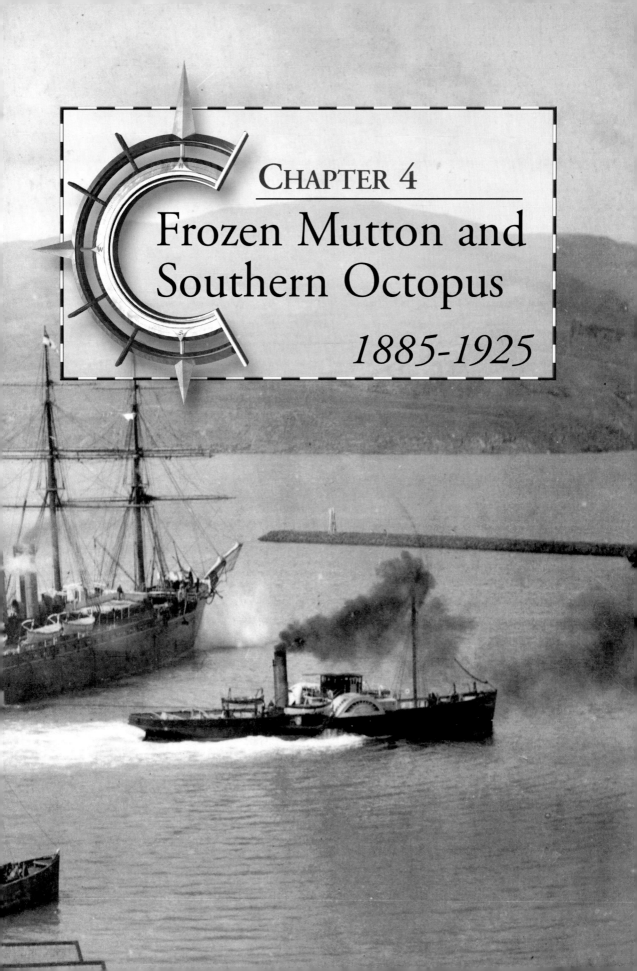

Chapter 4

Frozen Mutton and Southern Octopus

1885-1925

In just two decades the marriage of iron and steel hulls to efficient steam engines transformed the shipping industry and along with it the lives of ordinary New Zealanders. During the Late Victorian period world trade expanded vigorously. It was a time of business as well as political imperialism and the heyday of the Atlantic economy. In the last quarter of the 19th century world trade roughly doubled in volume and increased by a third in value, while the international merchant fleet nearly doubled to 30 million tons net between 1870 and 1900.[1] New Zealand ports reflected this upsurge in activity. Two hundred and thirty-eight overseas ships totalling 65,504 tons net had entered the colony's ports in 1853. Seventeen years later the figures were 756 ships and 273,151 tons. By 1900 only 616 ships were calling but they totalled 854,632 tons. By 1920, towards the end of the period covered by this chapter, 744 overseas ships were calling annually and they were 2,062,370 tons in total.[2]

For the average New Zealander transport got faster, cheaper and more reliable. Simply replacing wooden hulls with iron is estimated to have improved the sailing ship's carrying capacity 14–28.6 per cent.[3] Steel-hulled steamers brought even greater improvements. As we have seen, the single-cylinder steam engine was barely viable even on short, subsidised routes. The compound engine, perfected from the late 1860s, halved fuel consumption and made more room for cargo. Coal consumption fell another 30 per cent when boiler pressures were raised in the early 1880s to accommodate a third cylinder. Triple expansion engines and an expanded colonial export base finally made steam shipping economic on the long haul between New Zealand and Britain. As James Watson notes, passengers' preference for steam meant that 'carrying live people could act as a profitable sideline to the carriage of dead sheep. Above all, the fact that steamers quickly grew to several times the capacity of large sailers brought great economies of scale . . . In 1932 the freight rate per pound of meat to Britain was under half the 2¼d charged on the *Dunedin*'s cargo.'[4]

Frozen Meat and Home Liners

Until the early 1880s New Zealand's major export, apart from gold, timber and grain, was wool. Since gold took up very little space, and grain exports had been falling, the trade was unbalanced, seasonal and costly. Ships that had brought passengers and general cargo down from Britain often returned 'Home' lightly laden outside the wool season. Everyone regretted the waste of meat. Visitors to the colony often wrote home with amazement at New Zealanders' diet of meat three times a day, but the colonists were too few in number to roast, fry and grill their way through all those woolly millions. Refrigeration pioneer William

Preceding pages

The 1884 Shaw Savill liner *Arawa* typifies the first steamers built specially for the New Zealand-United Kingdom trade. Although the *Arawa* and *Tainui*'s triple-expansion engines were more efficient than their competitors', all these 5000-ton ships carried plenty of auxiliary sail. They made 14 knots on trials and normally cruised at 12.5. The rig was not the only hangover from sail; despite being fitted with refrigeration equipment, they had four sheep pens and four fowl coops! The *Tainui* carried 95 first-class passengers amidships, 52 second-class in the poop and 670 steerage-class in the 'tween decks. This shows the ship leaving Lyttelton in 1891, escorted by the paddle tug *Lyttelton*.

Alexander Turnbull Library F-12547-¼

Soltau Davidson recalled that: 'I had seen the flocks in New Zealand increase from the want of an outlet until the old sheep were unsaleable, and I had vivid recollections of having to erect yards at the edges of cliffs, into which thousands of these old sheep were driven, so that they might be knocked on the head and thrown over the precipice as a waste product.'[5]

The solution, as we know, lay in freezing meat and exporting it to where consumers and carcasses were more evenly matched. Successful French meat shipments from South America encouraged Andrew McIlwraith to fit the *Strathleven* with a Bell-Coleman refrigerating plant in 1879 and send it to Australia to load a trial shipment of butter, beef, lamb and mutton. This caught the attention of Davidson, the young general manager of the New Zealand and Australian Land Company, a Scottish-owned trans-Tasman pastoral empire with 16 runs in New Zealand. The Land Company wanted its pound of flesh from its sheep along with their wool. Just weeks after the *Strathleven* docked, Davidson took James Galbraith, a director of the Albion Line, to see the Bell-Coleman Company. Since New Zealand had neither freezing works nor steamer services to Britain, they had to improvise, fitting out a sailing ship and freezing the carcasses on board. Nevertheless, they decided to give it a try.

The Land Company built a killing shed at Totara Estate, just outside Oamaru, while the Albion Line fitted a Bell-Coleman plant to one of its big 'Auckland'-class iron ships. The *Dunedin* retained much of its general cargo and passenger space, insulating only the forehold and the 'tween deck abaft the fore hatch. Above deck the main clue was an ungainly funnel between the fore and main masts for the machinery.[6] At Totara, Davidson and Thomas Brydone supervised the slaughtering and shipment. Oamaru's harbour works were incomplete, so they railed the carcasses to Port Chalmers for freezing aboard the *Dunedin*, a costly and time-consuming process. At first things went badly. A broken crankshaft led to the first carcasses of frozen lamb being consumed by New Zealanders instead of Britons. Loading resumed after Kincaid & McQueen made a new shaft and on 15 February 1882 the *Dunedin* left Port Chalmers carrying 4311 carcasses of mutton, 598 of lamb, 22 pigs, 2226 sheep tongues, 246 kegs of butter and two passengers. Sixty passengers were meant to have gone but the crankshaft incident had scared off most. The *Dunedin* landed the cargo in perfect condition, to the delight of the Land Company and the other shippers; the Albion Line charged 2¼d per pound and the mutton averaged 6¼d on the London market.[7]

Both the Shipping Company and the Shaw Savill & Albion Company (formed that year through a merger) converted sailing ships to refrigerated cargo carriers. By late 1882 the *Dunedin* had been joined by another Albion clipper, the *Marlborough* and the Shipping Company's *Mataura*. This work kept the immigrant carriers of the 1870s going for another decade or more but the real interest was now in steam ships. In 1879 the Shipping Company and

D A De Maus Collection, Alexander Turnbull Library G-12669-½

The *Dunedin* created a milestone in New Zealand's economic history when it left Port Chalmers with the first shipment of frozen meat in 1882. There were a few problems along the way—sparks from the funnel tended to set fire to the sails in these early conversions—but the cargo arrived safely and New Zealand now had a new source of wealth. This photograph shows the *Dunedin* in the Port Chalmers dock in the Albion Company's black hull colour. The ship went missing in 1890 after leaving Oamaru for London.

Shaw Savill & Company had chartered the *Stad Haarlem* to test steam on the migrant trade. The ship brought out its 600 migrants successfully in just 57 days, but lost money. The chartered steamer *Marsala* took frozen meat from Dunedin in September 1882 but the first steamer built for the New Zealand frozen meat trade was the *Elderslie*, ordered after North Otago runholder John Reid teamed up with Turnbull, Martin and Company to trade directly between Oamaru and London. When the 2761-ton *Elderslie* berthed at Oamaru on 24 August 1884 to load a record export cargo of 23,305 carcasses, a delighted local press dubbed Reid 'the Napoleon of the meat freezing industry'.[8]

Over the next few decades refrigeration reshaped the New Zealand economy, adding meat and (less rapidly) dairy products to wool as sustainable staple exports. Freezing works became New Zealand's first large-scale industrial plants and 'a new economy and society was created in New Zealand', the *New Zealand Historical Atlas* noted. 'One of sheep bred for meat as much as for wool, of owner-occupier farms rather than stations with large numbers of hands, of freezing works and their associated communities, and of ports, some of the activities of which were dominated by this industry.'[9] By 1902 the frozen meat trade accounted for 20 per cent of all exports. Elsewhere, particularly in the North Island and in Southland, it was joined by dairy products — the butter and cheese that went almost exclusively to Britain.

The history of ports around the world has been the struggle between naval architects designing ever-bigger ships and harbour engineers struggling to provide the depth of water in which to float these creations. Annihilation threatened any port that could not keep up. Refrigeration tested harbour boards, as ports used to handling 800–1300-ton sailing ships geared up for ships of 4000–5000 tons or even larger. Some could not do it. Wanganui, Gisborne, Napier, Tolaga Bay and Tokomaru Bay all relied on lightering well into the 20th century. But the major ports plunged deep into debt to deepen channels and build bigger wharves. The Otago Harbour Board, still fighting the old Port Chalmers/Dunedin battle, improved the entrance with a training mole and deepened the bar. Timaru and Oamaru pushed their artificial breakwater ports out into stormy seas. Oamaru ordered a prefabricated dredge from England and deepened the port, now taking shape behind the nearly finished breakwater. The new export wharf,

In contrast to the major ports, the shallow river ports had to rely on lighters to take cargo out to the 'Home boats' lying in the roadstead. Here the *Shamrock* is returning from the Indra Line freighter which is lying off the port. Lightering was slow, costly and dangerous and was phased out as ports either closed or built better facilities; Napier retired its fleet in the early 1940s and Gisborne was the last major port to use lighters, retiring them in the 1960s.

Oamaru about 1875.

Oamaru Harbour

The frozen meat trade started in North Otago and the Port of Oamaru spent recklessly to meet the challenge of handling the big new steamers. It had to, for nature had not intended Oamaru to be a port. Cape Wanbrow offered some protection from the southerlies, but the coast was generally exposed, as the top photograph of the landing service, taken in the mid 1870s, shows). Passengers, parcels, pianos . . . all made their scary way through the surf in open boats, the Victorian equivalent of whitewater rafting.

Oamaru experienced many shipwrecks in the 1860s and early 1870s until the harbour board built the breakwater port (top right). The breakwater, built between 1872 and 1884, protected Macandrew wharf, the stone Cross and Normanby wharves and the new export wharf, Sumpter, against which a large overseas freighter is seen in the late Victorian era. The Burton Bros photograph (lower right) looks across the now sheltered harbour from Macandrew wharf to the pioneering refrigerated steamer *Elderslie* alongside Sumpter Wharf.

3282. OAMARU HARBOUR,
BURTON BROS. DUNEDIN

5178. PICTON.
PHOT'D 20.9.04. Muir Moodie, DUNEDIN.

Sumpter, was ready in time for the *Elderslie*, *Dunedin* and *Mataura* in 1884 and with 6.7 metres of water alongside at low tide gave Oamaru a lead over most rivals. Local boosters crowed. It was an engineering triumph. Financially, though, the port's finances were rockier than the seabed dredged away so expensively. Even with record export cargoes and profits from its endowments, the Oamaru Harbour Board had to sell surplus cement to balance its budget. When the board defaulted on half the interest owed on its 1879 London loan seven years later, 'The name of Oamaru [became] an unpleasant one in the ears of London money lenders and the *Financial Times* spoke of the "recklessness or worse" of colonial borrowers.'[10]

From the mid 1880s the regular lines phased in their first purpose-built steamers to replace temporarily chartered tonnage. The Shipping Company ordered five high-class craft from J Elder & Company. The *Tongariro*, *Aorangi* and *Ruapehu* (4163 tons) and the *Kaikoura* and *Rimutaka* (4474 tons), all delivered in 1883–84, were almost as big as Atlantic liners. Their clipper bows, figureheads and barque rig, 'gave them much of the "grace and glory" of the sailing ships whose death knell they sounded when they entered the New Zealand trade'.[11] No passengers shed any tears for the old windbags. They loved the new steamers, four times the size of the sailers and much faster, safer and more comfortable. One of Shaw Savill's first steamers, the *Arawa*, for example, took 38 days to get to New Zealand and 32 to return to Britain. Not only could these steamers carry more people and passengers than sailing ships, they could make three round trips a year instead of the sailer's one. With speed came certainty. Travellers could book their passage to or from New Zealand and know almost to the day when they would arrive. Shaw Savill's first pair, the *Arawa* and *Tainui*, were even bigger, 5000 tons. Like the Shipping Company quintet, they carried some sail, but their triple-expansion engines were more economical than their rival's compounds, which ate into its profits with every shovelful of coal.

These were in fact the last of their type. The first generation 'Home boats' needed government contracts and mail subsidies. The next Shipping Company passenger ship, the *Ruahine* of 1891, still carried sail on its two masts, but the straight-up-and-down bow and funnel, and the quadruple-expansion engines spoke of sobriety and efficiency. By the turn of the century the Shipping Company was building two types of ship. The passenger-cargo liners *Rimutaka*, *Ruapehu*, *Tongariro* and *Turakina* of 1900–02 were of about 8000 tons, and slower than the 1884 quintet, but were far more economical carriers. In starkly hierarchical fashion the *Rimutaka* carried 40 first-class passengers on

A shortage of shore freezing space gave the *Edwin Fox* a new lease of life. The ship has an interesting background. The *Edwin Fox* was built in 1853 at Sulkeah, Bengal Province, for the Honourable East India Company and later also served as a Crimean War transport, a convict ship to Australia and a migrant ship to New Zealand. In 1885 Shaw Savill & Albion converted it into a freezing storage hulk. The *Edwin Fox* served at Port Chalmers, Lyttelton, Gisborne and Bluff before arriving at Picton in 1897. There it has remained ever since, first as a landing stage and coal hulk, then as an abandoned derelict. Fortunately, local preservationists recognised the old ship's significance and the *Edwin Fox*'s old hull has been refloated and placed in a permanent dock, where it is open to the public while conservation proceeds as funds permit.

Alexander Turnbull Library C-25268-½.

The full majesty of Britain's naval and economic might ride at anchor in Wellington in this splendid photograph from the late 1880s. HMS *Nelson* served on the Australasian Station for most of the 1880s. The 7473-ton ship was an armoured cruiser, mounted with four 10-inch and eight 9-inch guns and could steam at 14 knots: about the same as the fastest liners of the day. The Shaw Savill & Albion liner *Tainui* was a sister to the *Arawa*.

the bridge deck, 50 second- and 80 third-class passengers on the upper deck and 170 emigrants in temporary dormitories that could be fitted up in the holds on the outward voyage. The *Rakaia, Mataura, Waimate, Wakanui* and *Whakatane* of 1895–1900, were slightly smaller, at 5600–5800 tons, and were primarily cargo carriers, but they, too, carried 26 first-class passengers above decks and could squeeze emigrants into dormitories in the 'tween decks when required. In 1901–03, the 12,230-ton heavyweights *Athenic, Corinthic* and *Ionic* entered a new Shaw Savill-White Star joint service.

The big steamers brought a new sense of security to ocean travel. People still got seasick, but the big ships shook off the storms better and their well-lit, spacious public spaces offered more comfort to the afflicted and to those recovering their appetites. That jolly booster, 'Mrs Robert Wilson', who published *My Journal in New Zealand* in London in 1894, succumbed to a touch of mal de mer but recovered quickly to consider that travelling on the *Rimutaka* was 'quite the most delightful form of yachting possible'. The ship's elegance appealed, the captain was solicitous and the awning under the poop deck sheltered dancing in the evenings and music and games by day. She was something of a delicate flower — she hated the locals calling the Napier landing place 'the Spit' when 'the Maori Ahuriri is much more euphonic' — but nothing could prepare her for landing at a choppy roadstead:

The sea was so rough that it was useless to put the gangway down to the tender; so, instead, we had to be lowered in a very ignominious way. A large, square piece of sailcloth was spread on the deck and we sat down upon it, when the four corners were gathered together by ropes fastened into a ring, kept

*at work near the hold, hooked, and then swung into mid-air, with no more
ceremony than if we had been frozen mutton, its usual freight. There was a
feeling of utter insecurity for a breathless moment, when the extraordinary
thing begun turning round and round like a teetotum; however at length we
reached the tender's deck in safety.*[12]

The new steamers were also much safer. Few 'Home boats' came to grief in New
Zealand waters now. The *Elginshire* ran ashore in fog south of Timaru in 1892,
and there was a small spate of wrecks just before the First World
War. In 1912 the *Star of Canada* was blown ashore at Gisborne
while lightering in the roadstead, the *Devon* was wrecked when
entering Wellington Harbour in filthy weather in 1913 and the
Tyrone piled up near Taiaroa Head in thick fog the same year. But
mechanical mishaps did dog the early ships, especially single-shaft
steamers. The Shipping Company's *Waikato* made international
history on 5 June 1899 when it broke a shaft south of the Cape of
Good Hope on the way out to New Zealand. 'That big steamer,
dying by a sudden stroke,' Joseph Conrad wrote, 'drifted, an
unwieldy corpse, away from the track of other ships'.[13] The crew
raided the cargo when their stores ran low and put oil on the galley
fire every night to send distress signals up its funnel, but with no
passing traffic to see it, the big freighter had to wallow there until
15 September when the steamer *Asloun* took it in tow. The two
ships reached Fremantle on 9 October, after the *Waikato* had
drifted an amazing 4500 miles back and forth.

Shipwrecks became much less
common from the 1880s on, especially
for overseas steamers. Lighthouses,
better port facilities and the power that
steam engines provided made it rare
for a 'Home boat' to get into serious
trouble. Nevertheless, it occasionally
happened. One unlucky ship was the
Scottish Shire Line steamer *Elginshire*.
It was sailing from Oamaru to Timaru to
complete loading for London on the
morning of 9 March 1892 in thick fog
when it ran onto Normanby Point, just
south of the South Canterbury port.
The 4579-ton, five-month-old
Elginshire became a total loss.

Two Rimutakas: a Contrast in Style

D A De Maus Collection, Alexander Turnbull Library G-3399-1/1-

A contrast in styles. The *Rimutaka* (top) was one of the New Zealand Shipping Company's first generation of 'Mountain'-class mail liners. The 4474-ton ship could carry 77 first-class passengers, 58 second-class and 230 emigrants and made 14 knots. Its bowsprit and heavy rig suggested something of the sailing ships of the day, although the engines were its primary power source. They were also its downfall. The compound engines ate up coal on the long run between Britain and the colony and, even with mail subsidy payments, the ships lost money. The second *Rimutaka*, built in 1900 by Dennys of Dumbarton, replaced the first after just 16 years. It was 50 per cent larger, at 7765 tons, carried 40 first-class passengers, 50 second-class, 80 third-class and 170 emigrants, and had much greater cargo capacity. The second *Rimutaka* was also fitted with light rig, but this had been removed by 1905-06. The ship's economical triple-expansion engines gave a speed of 13.8 knots on trials.

The new ships came too late to save the Shipping Company's shareholders. Those 'coal eaters' of 1884 had cost the line dearly and an anonymously published broadsheet, *Other People's Money*, was crucifying it before the year was out.[14] By 1886 it was heavily in debt and the fleet was mortgaged to its bankers and builders. That year London shareholders voted to transfer control to a British committee headed by shipbuilder and shipowner Sir William Pearce, to whom the *Aorangi*, *Ruapehu* and *Rimutaka* were mortgaged. After Pearce's death control passed to Edwin Dawes, who in turn later transferred majority shareholding to a partnership headed by his son William, and Allan Hughes, of Birt, Potter & Hughes. For appearance's sake, the new masters kept on a New Zealand 'local board of advice', top-heavy with pastoralists and other colonial bigwigs. The Shipping Company also had a large New Zealand staff and management, but from now on the crucial decisions would be taken in London, where the interests of the meat trade and shipping intersected ever more closely. In 1906 Hughes, who controlled powerful meat-processing interests in Australia, broke into the New Zealand-United Kingdom trade with his Federal-Houlder-Shire service; Federal and Houlder had been running to South Africa for a few years. In 1912 he took control of the Shipping Company. Publicly, the deal was described as a Shipping Company takeover of Federal, but as Charles Holdsworth, managing-director of the Union Company, told chairman Sir James Mills, it was really a case of 'the tail wagging the dog'.[15]

The Union Company also entered this trade that year, one that it had coveted for a very long time. Before 1912 the company had developed few long-distance overseas routes apart from the mail services. The 5704-ton *Aparima* of 1902 ran on the Indian service and the *Waitemata* (5432 tons) of 1908 served on several routes, but most growth had gone into the 'Pacific Slope' service, the West Coast of North America run. The *Wairuna* of 1905, (3947 tons) and the *Waihemo* (4283 tons), were bigger than most company freighters. Union got its hoped-for break in 1912 when Hughes, reshuffling his empire, offered it the Houlder 'Irish County' service of four ships, the *Limerick*, *Roscommon*, *Tyrone* and *Westmeath*, and conference loading rights to West of England ports. Union welcomed the opportunity to get a foot in the door.

The only other New Zealand company left in the trade was something of a curiosity. For a start — except for a few old sailing ships scratched together during the First World War — it never owned any ships. It also had some very peculiar articles of association — only registered sheep-owners could own shares. Geo H Scales, as it was known, had emerged in 1897 amid protests by the farmer-led Freight Reduction Committee. Angry at being charged higher freight rates than Australian farmers, the FRC hired a Dunedin company to run charter ships against the Liners (an earlier term for the Conference Lines). When that company foundered, a Wellington auctioneer, Geo H Scales — the so-called 'Knight of the Hammer' — made a go of the business. Scales never

The harbour boards also had to provide better towage services for the new deep-sea steamers. Wellington relied on private operators until the 1970s but most other major ports built at least one large harbour tug. The *Lyttelton*, originally named the *Canterbury*, was built at Port Glasgow in 1907 and is a screw tug, unlike the paddle tug *Lyttelton*, seen assisting the *Arawa* on pages 92–93. It had twice the power of the earlier ship. It is 292 tons gross, 38.10 metres long and now lovingly cared for by local preservationists, and enables 21st-century New Zealanders to enjoy the sight, sound and smells of a classic British steam tug.

carried more than a fraction of the New Zealand wool clip but it forced down freight rates.

In 1897–98 the Liners were pre-occupied with the task of dividing up the meat and dairy trades. They did not welcome Scales, but as their local adviser, Dunedin businessman J M Ritchie, counselled: 'The sailer rates ought to have been reduced this year all over New Zealand in order to avert a growing belief that the shipping companies are joining to take too much out of shippers'.[16] Scales kept running and by 1904 had signed an agreement with the Liners. Their truce lasted until 1908 when Scales switched to steamers. Although the Liners trusted Scales, they feared that the owners of his chartered steamers might enter the New Zealand trade permanently. The two sides traded threats, then sketched out a deal in Wellington. However, when Scales went to London in 1912 to confirm that arrangement, Allan Hughes decided to play hardball. 'There's your agreement!' Scales shouted, as he pushed back his chair and swept out of the office, Hughes's threats to crush him ringing in his ears.[17] Hughes could not, however, and Scales signed up the Clan Line to supply his steamers. That year his farmer supporters formally registered Geo H Scales Ltd, New Zealand's quirky little toehold in its main export trade.

The Southern Octopus Stretches its Tentacles

The Union Company continued to grow. Soon to be dubbed 'The Southern Octopus' by its critics, the company had ended the 1870s in a position of strength. It dominated the coastal and trans-Tasman services and before the century was out it would do the same with the Tasmanian services (acquiring the Tasmanian Steam Navigation Company's eight large steamers in 1891 and buying some smaller Bass Strait traders later in the decade) and the Pacific Islands trades.

It had bought the Auckland Steam Ship Company's *Southern Cross* and rights to the subsidised Fiji service in 1881. Next year it acquired McEwan and Company's steamer *Suva* and the Melbourne-Fiji run. In 1896 the company bought Donald and Edenborough's Auckland-to-Rarotonga and Tahiti service and the steamer *Richmond*. It had also been pioneering its own services and in 1890–91, it built three ships especially for its Pacific Islands services, the *Taviuni*, *Ovalau* and *Upolu*. These and other ships gave the company a commanding position in the Pacific Islands trades, running scheduled passenger-cargo services as well as cruises that appealed to winter-weary New Zealanders. The growth of the company's business was measured by the size of the Islands steamers that it now ordered: the *Navua* (2930 tons, 1904), *Atua* (3444 tons, 1906) and *Tofua* (4345 tons, 1908), were just a shade smaller than the trans-Tasman liners of their day.

Gavin McLean Collection

When Dunedin architect David Ross designed this splendid head-office building for the Union Steam Ship Company in the 1880s, he chose the fashionable Italian style. The lower part of the building was Port Chalmers stone, the upper portions brick cemented over. Attention to detail extended from the minarets on the roof to Ashbury's mechanical heating process in the basement. The company swapped Water Street premises with the National Mortgage Agency Company when it moved to Wellington after the First World War. Although shorn of much of its rooftop finery, the old building survives in Water Street and has recently been upgraded for new owners.

The Union Company also entered the trans-Pacific mail services. Mail services were extremely prestigious. Companies cherished the title 'Royal Mail Steamer', often received government subsidies and their mail liners received priority at ports. So, the Union Company moved quickly in 1885 when the Pacific Mail Steamship Company dropped out of the subsidised service to San Francisco. Union ran its new trans-Tasman liner *Mararoa* (2466 tons) for a year before dropping out, only to return in 1890 with the specially designed *Monowai*. A larger ship, the 3915-ton *Moana*, followed in 1897. The company had been running in uneasy alliance with the American Oceanic Steam Ship Company but had to pull out in 1900 when the American annexation of Hawaii made it impossible to carry cargo on the San Francisco to Hawaii leg of the route. It would resume a different San Francisco service 10 years later.

By then the subsidised imperial mail service to Vancouver, part of the 'All Red Route', was the company's premier service. The Union Company entered it in 1901 when it bought into the troubled Canadian Australian Royal Mail Line service run by James Huddart and the Shipping Company. It acquired Huddart's old *Warrimoo* — known as the 'Weary Mary' — and by 1910 had the whole line. The Canadian-Australasian Royal Mail Line, as it became known, soon had Union's biggest ships. The 8075-ton *Makura*, which could accommodate 450 passengers in three classes, came out in 1908 and in 1913 it commissioned its masterpiece, the 13,415-ton liner *Niagara*. The *Niagara* could carry over 700 passengers and was the first passenger ship to be certificated by the British Board of Trade for oil burning. Significantly, the *Niagara* was larger than any Shipping Company or Shaw Savill liner running to Britain.

Union Liners Around the Coasts

But the company earned its bread and butter in the trans-Tasman, Tasmanian and New Zealand coastal trades. On the coast it expanded its network by buying rivals and by building new ships. The coal business became extremely important to the Union Company in the mid 1880s as it bought up the country's collier fleets. The first to fall was Captain W R Williams's Black Diamond Line (steamers *Mawhera*, *Koranui*, *Manawatu*, *Maitai* and *Grafton*), which Union bought in 1885. Two years later it took over the financially troubled Westport Coal Company's colliers *Kawatiri*, *Orowaiti* and *Wareatea*. In 1888 the Brunner Coal Company's *Brunner* and J Kilgour's *Oreti* joined the Union fleet.

In a sense the ships were merely the tip of Mills's iceberg. Williams's fleet had come with a struggling coalmine (the Koranui), and a branch railway line. That short track was worth its weight in gold, because every tonne of the Westport Coal Company's huge output had to cross it to get to the government

Gavin McLean Collection

Wellington Museum, City & Sea

James Mills, Shipping Baron

James Mills is New Zealand's most important businessman. Unusually for his cohort, he was born locally, in 1847. The smaller photograph shows him as a young director of the Union Company. Take a look at the larger photograph. It was probably taken about the time that he represented New Zealand at an imperial shipping conference. In 1906 he became the first New Zealand-born person to be knighted; three years later he was made a KCMG. When he stepped down as managing director in 1913 (he kept the chairmanship until his death in 1936), the board gave him a golden handshake of £10,000: more than a skilled worker could earn in 30 years. There he sits, confidently staring into the future while the New Zealand Prime Minister, Sir Joseph Ward — no hayseed himself — stands behind the shipping baron.

railway that led down to the Westport wharves. Mills stepped up production at Koranui and put pressure on the WCC by levying a charge on coal wagons crossing Union's track. As he predicted, the WCC quickly came to terms. The two companies were both based in Dunedin's Water Street, shared directors and soon settled the fuel and transport businesses amicably. In 1889 Westport agreed to sell Union its entire production, giving Union its shipping business and the power to set the rate for the colony's fuel supply. By then Mills had also bullied Martin Kennedy, the leading force in the Grey Valley mining industry, into submission, giving Mills 'a practical monopoly of the coal trade of New Zealand'.[18] There were few independents. The Shipping Company's Blackball Coal Company ran three colliers from 1908–13, but under strict agreements with the Union Company. After 1907, when the Australian shipowners and colliers drew up a deal, the company was able to extend that control over even imported fuel.

The pages of fading copies of the company's monthly *Pocket Guides* show that its coastal passenger-cargo vessels now linked every major port in New Zealand and eastern Australia. Whether you were a local inhabitant or a visitor to the colony, you now took a Red Funnel Line ship. Travel guides extolled their virtues and one, written by the composer of the 'New Zealand Anthem', Thomas Bracken, was published by the company. Even outsiders acknowledged the company's omnipotence. According to 'Wanderer', who published his *Antipodean Notes* in London in 1888, most Union Company vessels sailed at night and spent their days in port, 'whence the New Zealand saying that the Union steamers ship cargo every day, and go rock-hunting at night. For the coasts of the colony are very rough and dangerous'. He went on to say:

> On the larger steamers of the Union Company the accommodation and food are good, but the smaller vessels leave much to be desired, while no one who has not gone through a prolonged colonial training should take passage in the local vessels, which are mostly engaged in the coal trade. The steamers are small, and heavily laden; the food is coarse and ill-prepared, and the firemen sit in the saloon to eat it, without washing themselves first. They carry but few passengers and are not organized for the purpose.[19]

Obviously it paid to select your ship carefully. Sometimes, though, this was not possible, as storms delayed ships or companies adjusted their schedules. American writer Mark Twain, who sailed from Lyttelton aboard the *Flora*, thought that steamer was 'about the equivalent of a cattle scow'. Twain's book, *More Tramps Abroad*, criticised the Union Company for practices he recognised from America. 'They give no notice of their projected depredation,' he lamented, 'you innocently buy tickets for the advertised passenger boat, and

then you get down to Lyttelton at midnight, you find that they have substituted the scow. They have plenty of good boats but no competition — and that is the trouble.' That night Twain and 200 unhappy others settled down aboard a ship licensed to carry 125. 'All the cabins were full, all the cattle-stalls in the main stable were full, every inch of floor and table and in the swill-room was packed with sleeping men and remained so until the place was required for breakfast, the chairs and benches on the hurricane deck were occupied, and still there were people who had to walk about all night!' Twain found a berth, but in a calico-partitioned space 'as dark as the soul of the Union Company, and [that] smelt like dog kennel'.[20]

In fairness, he described his next Union ship, the *Mahinapua*, as 'a wee little bridal-parlour of a boat . . . clean and comfortable; good service; good beds, good table and no crowding'. The fancy menus, the lengthy descriptions of the first-class saloons of new ships straight from the builders' yards should not blind us to the fact that many people travelled second- or third-class. Often they did this aboard small, elderly ships. The company could be very cautious, as the early history of one of its premier routes, the famous Wellington-Lyttelton ferry service, showed. At first people travelled between these ports aboard ships that ran on longer routes. From 1895 the

The *Taviuni*, one of the Union Company's Pacific Islands steamers, spent over a year ashore at a most unlikely port, Westport, in 1908-09. The *Taviuni* went ashore at the notoriously dangerous port on 23 April 1908 and was refloated in 1909 after a herculean salvage job. The 1465-ton ship had been built in 1890 and served until it was laid up at Sydney in 1921 and partly dismantled three years later.

F N Jones Collection, Alexander Turnbull Library, G-12118-½

elderly *Penguin* was running exclusively between the two ports. The service became daily in 1900 and ran all year from 1905. Then in 1907 Denny delivered the first purpose-built ferry, the *Maori*. A slightly larger *Wahine* followed in 1913. These ships were big (about 4000 tons) and fast (over 20 knots), making them and their successors strategic assets during both world wars. *Wahine* served off Gallipoli and later was a minelayer. The newspaper *Truth* grumbled about the 'U Shan't Sleep Co' and fares were always too high for some, but the country took to the Lyttelton ferry service, or 'the steamer express', as the company pompously styled it.

Away from the Lyttelton run, few new passenger steamers were built, just the 1200-ton *Rotoiti* and *Mapourika* of 1898 and the 1600-ton *Arahura* of 1905, all built to serve the isolated West Coast and the New Plymouth-Onehunga runs. People now preferred to travel by rail and the completion of the North Island Main Trunk line in 1908 further eroded long-distance passenger traffic.

During the early 1900s the company replaced its 2000-tonners of the early 1880s. For its trans-Tasman service, it built a batch of 3000–4500-tonners, the

This jubilant scene of bandsmen returning from a contest gives an indication of the social role played by wharves in early 20th-century New Zealand. The ship is the Union Company's steamer *Arahura* of 1905. The 1596-ton ship was an improved version of two other shallow-draft passenger/cargo steamers, the *Mapourika* and *Rotoiti*. It could carry 155 first-class and 66 second-class passengers on the overnight service between Wellington, Nelson, Westport and Greymouth. The *Arahura* was Union's last such coastal passenger ship. From now on it would build only ferries for the Picton and Lyttelton runs. In 1921 the company withdrew from the historic West Coast passenger trade and transferred the *Arahura* to its associate company, the Anchor Company, which put the ship on its Wellington-Nelson ferry service.

Waikare (1897), *Mokoia* (1898), *Moeraki* (1902) and *Manuka* (1903) before opting for the more ambitious steam turbine-powered *Maheno* of 1905. The 5282-ton, 16-knot ship had a long career but the company paid a price for innovation because the *Maheno's* turbines chewed up coal. In 1914, in one of the most ambitious repair jobs yet undertaken in New Zealand, Union's Port Chalmers Marine Repair Works replaced the original engines with geared turbines. Two more trans-Tasman liners, the 6437-ton *Marama* of 1907 and the 7527-ton *Maunganui* of 1911, reverted to less ambitious triple- and quadruple-expansion steam engines respectively.

Coastal Minnows

The Union Company acquired many new cargo vessels in the early 1900s to replace the small ships bought in the 1880s and the early 1890s. It was as happy to buy off the stocks as to design its own ships. Most were in the 1000–2000-ton range and after 1900 the Union Company built very few small ships. It had no need to, for in the first decade of the new century the 'Southern Octopus' swept up its remaining coastal competitors. In 1899 the company had taken a quarter-share in Levin & Company's coaster *Himitangi*, but it generally preferred to stay away from the small ships and the risky ports they served. This began to change around 1905 when, as the result of the spread of intensive farming and a decade of general prosperity, many regional ports flourished. Mills and his managers could ignore scows and clapped-out little steamers but not the arrival in 1904–05 of the first of a new breed of coaster. Small crews, big carrying capacity and economical engines let these modern 500-ton British or Dutch-built coasters range far and wide. Even their names — George Niccol's *Squall* (369 tons) or the Canterbury Steam Shipping Company's *Storm* (405 tons) — suggested dark clouds coming unless the company acted decisively.

That is precisely what it did. In 1905 Mills decided to take secret control of these new regional carriers. Union would curb their expansionist tendencies while offering the public the illusion of competition — 'as a means of satisfying a certain class of shipper who always like to have two strings to their bow', as he put it. This left the day-to-day running in the hands of the minnows, deluding local shippers into thinking that they had a choice and gave the Union Company control of more ships than its published fleet lists showed.

In 1906 the Union Company bought half the shares of the Canterbury Steam Shipping Company, by then partnering the *Storm* with the 413-ton *Breeze*.[21] A tight agreement specified where Canterbury could trade to and the rates that it had to charge customers. Later that year Union bought Niccol's *Squall*, and put the ship in its Gisborne trade. Two smaller concerns passed into

Alexander Turnbull Library G-21864-1/1-

The Union Company decided to invest in smaller coastal firms after the new Canterbury Steam Shipping Company imported modern coasters like the 405-ton *Storm*. Two brothers, A H Turnbull from Christchurch and D C Turnbull from Timaru, had formed the company in 1904 with Captain Hugh Monro. The company's ships took their names from meteorological conditions.

Union Company control in 1907, the Wairau Steam Ship Company and the Invercargill Shipping Company. A year later it bought part of the Anchor Shipping and Foundry Company of Nelson. Anchor ran a network of services centred on the West Coast–Nelson coal trade and Cook Strait passenger-cargo services.

Although most Union Company buy-ins had been made amicably, some targeted companies put up a fight. Napier's Richardson & Company was one that did. Richardsons dated from 1899, although the firm traced its roots back to a private partnership formed in 1859.[22] The Union Company had no interest in its little 'rock-hoppers', the feeder ships that it ran to the small anchorages around the East Coast, but it objected to Richardsons running the 413-ton *Ripple* (acquired from Canterbury in 1910) against it in the Wellington-Napier-Gisborne trade. The *Ripple* trounced both the big Red Funnel steamers, which had to lighter in the roadstead, and the smaller *Squall*, which, while able to use the inner harbour like the *Ripple*, was slower and less manoeuvrable. The Richardson directors held out until 1912 when Union bought 25 per cent of its shares.

Another reluctant seller was the Maoriland Steamship Company, formed in 1906 by sailing ship owner Ferdinand Holm and two embittered former Union Company masters, Gerald Hall and Charles Macarthur.[23] At first Maoriland promised to stick to low-value timber and grain cargoes, but Holm annoyed Union by putting the 1148-ton steamer *Ennerdale* on the Tasman and the 267-ton *Torgauten* (renamed *Holmdale* in 1908) on the coastal trade. Holm gave a verbal agreement to play by Union's rules but by 1907 Maoriland's losses were forcing it to compete too vigorously for Dunedin's liking. Macarthur needed to cash up his shares and was willing to do business, but many Maoriland shareholders had taken shares in order to secure port agencies and other business and they frustrated the deal for several months. In 1908 Holm stormed out rather than settle with the Union Company, leaving the way open for it to buy half the Maoriland shares. In 1915 it bought the rest and absorbed its three ships into the main fleet.

Only two businesses worth mentioning remained independent. One was

what would become registered as the Holm Shipping Company in 1926, but which traced its roots back into the 19th century. Its founder, Pehr Ferdinand Holm, was one of the coastal trade's enduring characters and over time the Holm family would become a minor Wellington shipping dynasty, with son Sydney and grandson John Holm chafing at the restrictions imposed by Union Company.[24] Ferdinand's other sons also went to sea, Mariner Holm as a master mariner and Ferdinand and John Herman as marine engineers. Ferdinand senior always preferred sail, but he and Sydney laid the company's real foundations in 1911 when they bought the 12-year-old coaster *John*. For the next 60 years the green-funneled Holm ships would be a Wellington institution, controlled from 1935 by the Union Company but managed by stroppy, independent-minded Holms.[25]

The 'Foundry' part of the Anchor Shipping & Foundry Company built and serviced ships at Nelson, including those of its own fleet. Here we see the *Koi* about to be launched sideways. The ship had been assembled from components built by John Shearer & Co., Glasgow. The 136-ton ship was lengthened in 1910 and served Anchor until 1930, when the Peranos bought it for use as a coal hulk at their whaling station.
Alexander Turnbull Library G-2186-1/1-

The other independent was the Northern Steamship Company, which dated from 1881 when Captain Alexander McGregor persuaded several Auckland ship owners to consolidate their efforts. The Northern Steamship Company (its own documents frequently also spelled its name 'Steam Ship') served the northern North Island, basically from Wanganui north on the West Coast and from East Cape north on the East. Generally it operated services that were beneath the Union Company. By the mid 1890s the Northern Company had grown to 20 vessels. Like Richardsons, Northern was a regional institution, sending its small ships into every creek, beach, estuary or bar harbour in the

Tyree Collection, Alexander Turnbull Library G-1721-10x8-

Robert Logan built the small screw steamer *Tasman* in 1903 for an Auckland owner. Like most small ships of its time, it passed through several fleets and trades, such as the Golden Bay service, where it briefly served under the Anchor Company and other flags. Here the ship is seen at the port of Collingwood. Collingwood had been declared a Port of Entry in 1858 and had a turbulent political history until it finally closed after the Second World War.

North where a paying cargo could be found. Its timetables were adjusted to suit the tides as well as the settlers, for whom it hauled building supplies, fencing materials and groceries and loaded their wool, gum, animals and timber. 'Passengers were woken, given ship's tea and biscuits and dropped off at jetties or helped overboard into dinghies. In the roadless and rail-less North the whistles and tall black and white funnels of the Northern Company's fleet meant that civilisation was at hand.'[26]

The Northern Company had many vessels but few were big. In 1914 only three of its steamers topped 500 tons gross, the *Manaia* (1159 tons), *Ngapuhi* (703 tons), and the *Clansman* (635 tons). The *Manaia* was the Union Company's *Rotorua* of 1898, bought in 1912 and run under strict agreement with the

Gavin McLean Collection

'Southern Octopus' on the fading Onehunga–New Plymouth route. Indeed, Northern's independence was qualified and restricted by pooling, rates agreements and the companies' joint ownership of the United Repairing Company in Auckland.

The late Victorian era and the early 1900s saw the peak of ferry traffic on the major harbours. Auckland's wooden, double-ended ferries were particularly distinctive. Many were built from the 1880s onwards, with the *Albatross* of 1904 setting a new style. *The Peregrine* of 1912 was 245 tons and could carry 1,364 passengers and 4 crew. Like so many of the old steam ferries, *The Peregrine* was withdrawn in 1959, victim of the new harbour bridge.

The Seafarers' Life

What of the men who manned these ships? As the question suggests, it was a masculine world. The bigger passenger ships carried a few stewardesses, but the vast majority of this floating workforce was male. It is easy to forget what a significant employer seafaring was. There were about 3500 officers and seamen in 1860. Census data, which excluded owner/operators, engineers and other specialist employment categories, showed a stable 2700–3100 between 1901 and 1921, when the seamen's union alone had 4462 paid-up members.[27] With thousands of other seafarers ashore at any time from visiting overseas ships or trying their hands at shore jobs, the country must have been saturated with what Belich calls 'crew culture'. For all but a few, seafaring gave only intermittent employment. Crews were paid off at the end of voyages or whenever ships were sold or wrecked. This kept them moving about constantly while remaining part of a distinctive subculture. 'Raw recruits were quickly indoctrinated, quickly encouraged or pressured into conformity with prevailing mores. Crews were *prefabricated* communities into which new members could easily slot.'[28]

Harding-Denton Collection, Alexander Turnbull Library G-17012-¼

New Zealand's short, fast-flowing, mountain-fed streams are poorly suited to navigation. Only three rivers sustained long-term steam shipping services — the Clutha, the Wanganui and the Waikato. The most heavily trafficked was the Wanganui, which was promoted in the late 19th century as 'The Rhine of New Zealand'. Perhaps the most magnificent of all river steamers was the *Manuwai*, built for Alexander Hatrick in 1894 by Yarrow & Co. The 117-ton stern-wheeler was sold for service on the Waikato in 1922 and was laid up in 1939, the same year that the last Clutha River steamer was withdrawn from service.

Those communities varied, of course, depending on ship type, size and ownership. The large steam ship brought new hierarchies, new jobs and larger complements. A steam ship such as the Union Company's trans-Tasman liner *Mokoia* of 1898, with its 24 officers and engineers, 36 stokers and seamen and 39 cooks and stewards, was an extraordinarily hierarchical place. Reporting the new ship, the *Evening Post* explained that:

> *The officers have their quarters in a special house forward from the bridge, and the cooks and stewards are accommodated in the forecastle; while the seamen live right aft. The engineers' rooms are along the port alleyway of the main saloon deck, and the various galleys and messrooms are situated in the same vicinity. The captain's cabin is a luxurious apartment under the bridge, and it marks the beginning of the promenade deck...*[29]

There were two departments aboard a freighter: deck and engineering, (catering formed a third department in passenger ships), and even the officers tended to divide into these two camps. At the bottom of the heap — literally — were the stokehold trimmers, who shovelled coal from the dark, cramped bunkers through the hatch onto the stokehold floor, where the firemen, or stokers, heaved it into the furnace. 'For two four-hour spells each day firemen stoked the boilers, scorched by the heat and choked by coal dust and gases,' Neill Atkinson notes. 'Ventilation was often inadequate, and the work was usually performed on a rolling, moving surface.'[30] Strained muscles, burns and scalds went with the territory in these rolling steel dungeons. Stokehold hands earned more than deck hands but their working conditions were so appalling that they and the firemen usually gave the most trouble aboard ship. 'The firemen were a tough bunch in those days,' a Union Company Westport employee recalled of even the late 1940s, 'and verbal altercations in the office between these gentlemen and the office staff were regular features of the office routine'.[31] The sound of ships' whistles punctured the night air as masters tried to get crews back from the wharfside pubs in order to catch the tide.

On deck, 'boys', usually aged 15–18, served as apprentices for one or two years before becoming ordinary seamen. After four years as ordinary seamen, they became able-bodied seamen, or ABs. In the bigger Union Company coasters they seldom worked cargo — watersiders did this — but at the smallest ports, roadsteads and beaches, the men did everything. In the Richardson boats off the East Coast, the seamen loaded wool bales and other bulky items into surfboats from farmers' drays backed into the surf. The surfboats carried an average of 2.5 tonnes of cargo, or 16–25 bales of wool, but in practice transported everything from cattle to grand pianos. The men worked waist-deep in water. 'When work ceased at the end of the day, wet clothes were hung over the boiler-room fiddley to dry out'.[32] Accidents and drownings were common. Up north the scows loaded on calmer beaches but shingle pushing (pushing wheelbarrows up a narrow plank), was no less backbreaking.

Then there were the officers. Their ranks varied according to the size and business of the ship. Traditionally, ships' masters had had a semi-entrepreneurial role in addition to their management functions. As large companies such as the Union Company developed, however, they imposed their own ways of doing things on even their most senior seagoing employees. The Union Company had its own *Instructions to Masters*, and was particularly tough on officers and men who drank. In the early days Mills had required all masters to report to him personally whenever their ships passed through Otago

S C Smith Collection, Alexander Turnbull Library G-20019-1/1-

Coal was an important cargo at almost every port during the Age of Steam and one of the dirtiest. Sydney Smith took this photograph at Wellington about 1910. Note the large baskets.

Harbour but by the 1890s the company had a full-time inspector working with branch managers and masters to sniff out tipplers and other miscreants. 'Alcoholism troubled it more than socialism until well into the 1900s.'[33] The engineers were also officers, and were disproportionately Scottish in ethnic make-up. An MP said while welcoming the new *Maheno* in 1905, 'He supposed there was the usual number of Scotchmen in the engine room, and if one called out "Mac!" it would be hard to say how many would answer.'[34]

But the process of modernisation also proceeded unevenly and was more evident in the South Island, where the Union Company's big steel steamers ruled the roost. In 1910 the average size of a ship on the Dunedin register was 1625 tons, many times the Auckland average of 121 tons. Average crew sizes were 45 in Dunedin, 32 in Wellington and 13 in Auckland. As a consequence, the Federated Seamen's Union's militancy, weaker than many unions at a time when industrial militancy was sweeping the world, tended to fade the further north you went.[35]

Although masters, deck officers and (especially) engineers had transferable skills, most seafarers were regarded as unskilled labourers. 'Together with most unskilled labourers, seamen faced low wages and intermittent employment, their work was dangerous and accidents were frequent, they often put up with poor conditions and cramped accommodation, and they worked in isolation from other classes'.[36] Deck hands caught fingers in winches or ropes, were hurt handling cargo or fell during rough seas. Living conditions were poor. The crew usually slept in the forecastle, which could leak in bad weather. In small craft the quarters doubled as the mess. Firemen and trimmers would collapse exhausted and covered in coal dust. Furthermore, unlike other workers, seafarers could not just walk off the job, even when in port. They signed legally binding and enforceable articles of employment. In one year, 1911–12, 77 seamen were convicted under the Shipping and Seamen Act 1908, mostly for failing to return to ships after drinking sprees. As Atkinson observes, 'A common working-class perception of the workplace as a prison seems particularly relevant to the experience of seamen'.[37]

It is therefore not surprising that ships and wharves formed the main battleground for New Zealand's most historic confrontations between capital and labour. One of the more novel occurred in 1887 when the Northern Company reneged on an agreement with the seamen. Since Auckland shipowners always found it easier to recruit replacement labour for their small boats, the Federated Seamen's Union chartered the Australian steamers *Stormbird* and *Bellinger* and ran them against the Northern Company. They lost money, but so did Northern, and support from Australian unions kept the battle going until the Union Company stepped in. Ignoring both the Steamship Owners Association of Australia (of which Union was the largest member) and the Northern Company, James Mills cut a deal with the seamen.[38]

Alexander Turnbull Library F-72153-

That lasted only until the Maritime Strike brought shipping to a halt on both sides of the Tasman in 1890. The Union Company did not like trade unions, but it took a generally tolerant attitude until 1889 when a local officers' union appeared and talked about forming a trans-Tasman association and enrolling the ships' masters. At this point the Red Funnel Line saw red. Although the company's centralised bureaucracy had taken away some of the masters' autonomy, the directors still saw them as their representatives. Both J A Millar, the strike leader, and the company found themselves drawn into the strike by others, for the unions' biggest complaints were about the smaller lines' old tubs, and the Australian shipowners, all smaller than Union, were more militant. Timing was on the employers' side in spring 1890 and they won the two-month struggle, albeit at considerable cost.

Ships stretch the full length of the Wellington roadstead during the 1913 waterfront strike. Although the employers won, they paid a high price in disruption to their shipping schedules.

The companies sought revenge. The Union Company blacklisted and victimised former unionists, set up a 'yellow dog' officers' union and created a Mutual Benefit Society, nicknamed the 'the Deaf and Dumb Society' by employees. Eventually, however, the unions recovered and the courts forced the companies to recognise them. In the 1910s a chronic shortage of labour obliged Union Company senior management to restrain its branch managers. It had its problems with its seafarers, particularly the crews of the larger passenger ships, but the FSU had stayed aloof from the second major industrial dispute in New Zealand history, the 1913 waterfront strike, until the very last stage, when it climbed aboard a sinking ship. In 1913, unlike

F N Jones Collection, Alexander Turnbull Library G-14741

The unions were crushed in 1913 by the government and farmers, the shipping companies and new unionists took over the waterfront. Frederick Jones photographed 'new union men' discharging the coaster *John*. The *John*, a 339-ton steamer, had come to New Zealand after Ferdinand Holm bought it. Ferdinand always preferred sail to steam, but his son Sydney made the 'Irish gunboat' (so-called because of its green funnel) the nucleus of the Holm Shipping Company.

1890, the government took sides. William Massey's farmer government leaped in, gumboots and all, to crush the unions with the help of Royal Navy sailors and rural strikebreakers, 'Massey's Cossacks'.

The First World War

When war broke out the presence of the cruisers from the German East Asiatic Squadron caused much concern. Politicians were reluctant to dispatch the New Zealand Expeditionary Force without adequate naval escort, which had to be cobbled together from British, Australian, French and Japanese warships. In the event, the German cruisers went hunting elsewhere and only one German ship entered New Zealand waters during the war. In 1917, off the Kermadecs, the converted merchant raider *Wolf* captured the Union Company freighter *Wairuna* and the American schooner *Winslow*. Mines that it had laid earlier would later claim the freighter *Port Kembla* off Cape Farewell and the trans-Tasman liner *Wimmera* off Cape Maria van Diemen. Twenty-six passengers and crew went down with the *Wimmera*.

Most casualties occurred far away in Europe where U-boats sank the Union Company ships *Aotearoa* (a larger *Niagara*, requisitioned before completion by the Admiralty), *Aparima*, *Limerick*, *Roscommon*, *Waikawa*, *Waihemo* and *Waitemata*. The worst tragedy was the loss of the *Aparima*. On 19 November 1917 the company's cadet ship was steaming around the south-east coast of Britain when a submarine torpedo blew off its stern, sinking the ship in eight minutes. Half the crew of 114 died, 24 of them New Zealanders, but the youngest had a remarkable escape. Thomas Bevan was asleep when compressed air from the explosion blew him up through a ventilator and onto a floating liferaft.[39]

With so many of the biggest and best ships requisitioned or diverted, shipping lines literally scavenged 'Rotten Row' for laid up hulls. The Port Chalmers firm R C Miller bought the Oamaru Harbour Board's ancient dredge *Progress* and expensively rebuilt it twice, first as a schooner and then as a steamer. In 1917 Daniel Reese of Christchurch towed the hulk *Opihi* (1117 tons, 1886), to Lyttelton for conversion to a coastal steamer. Geo H Scales also raided Rotten Row. It needed new business after the liners took advantage of wartime circumstances to elbow it from the wool trade. Scales decided to go into the coal trade and bought three dilapidated old sailing ships for hulking. However, when the experts advised that it would cost as much to re-rig the ships as to hulk them, Scales refitted the barques *Rona* and *Louisa Craig* (renamed *Raupo*) and the barquentine *Ysabel* and ran them to North America and the Pacific Islands. Like most other shipping lines, it made extraordinary wartime profits.

The war brought profound changes to the New Zealand shipping industry. Ships such as the Wellington–Lyttelton ferry *Wahine* were requisitioned for Royal Navy service and the diversion of trans-Tasman liners to trooping and hospital ship duties led to the temporary cancellation of the historic Dunedin–Melbourne service. War marked a loss of local control of the merchant fleet. Within weeks of hostilities breaking out, 18 of the Union Company's biggest ships were re-registered in London for insurance purposes. Control of the company itself soon followed.

As we have seen, the New Zealand Shipping Company had come under British control in 1886. British shipowners had been consolidating their holdings in the face of threats from other nations and because of the death and aging of founders. Just before war broke out Allan Hughes had opened talks with the Union Company to work more closely together. In 1916, however, Hughes sold the New Zealand Shipping Company and Federal to P&O, which was expanding aggressively. Just a year later Sir James Mills opened talks with the big British company. There was no pressing need. The Union Company was the biggest commercial organisation in New Zealand, had vast hidden reserves and was profiting almost indecently from the war. But Mills, who was 70 and had been living in England for a decade, saw it as a way of protecting Union as a separate entity within the ambit of a larger combine that could compete with foreign firms. P&O's chairman, Lord Inchcape, also reported, correctly, that 'at the back of the mind of Sir James Mills is also a desire to hide away the profits which have been made . . . from the public of that country'.[40] 'Obtaining full value by public flotation involved revealing information that could induce merchants to request lower rates and encourage governments to investigate conferences closely, all of which would undermine the value of the firms' intangible assets,' Gordon Boyce believes. 'A private sale

Kinnear Collection, Alexander Turnbull Library, G-6205-1/1-

A highlight of the pre-war era had been the 1908 visit of the United States Navy's 'Great White Fleet', seen smoking and shining in the Waitemata roadstead.

enabled owners to secure the full price by transferring these assets intact.'[41] Despite considerable outcry (P&O would never be popular in New Zealand), the sale went through (British investors already held more shares than New Zealanders). Four years later the Union Company moved its head office from Dunedin to Wellington, acknowledging that the days of southern power were over.

Post-War Reconstruction

Opposite

The Union Company freighter *Aparima* was one of the costliest casualties of the war. The big freighter had been built in 1905 and had also been doubling as the company's cadet training ship when it was sent to the bottom by a submarine torpedo. This photograph shows the *Aparima* in happier days, in Auckland's Calliope Dock.

Kinnear Collection, Alexander Turnbull Library, G-6205-1/1-

After the war the shipping companies enjoyed a brief burst of prosperity as they took over ex-German shipping, bought war emergency ships and ordered new ships of their own. For its post-war fleet, the Shipping Company and Federal turned out no-nonsense freighters of the *Kent* type. Of between 8500 and 9800 grt, these 13–15-knot ships, with their straight bows, long bridge decks, stumpy masts and vertical funnels, looked exactly like what they were: simple floating refrigerators. G D G Jensen, who shipped aboard one of the *Otaki*-class of 1920, acknowledged that some ships are so beautiful you fall in love with them. The *Otaki*, on the other hand, 'was so ugly she made you feel sick. Everything about her was strictly utilitarian, with no concessions to comfort or convenience. She was a bare steel box. The crew's fo'c's'le was a triangular space right up in the bows, furnished with wooden bunks, a long table and two backless benches.'[42] The company had sprayed the unlined bulkheads with a cork compound to prevent condensation. The only ventilation was provided by the doorway at the top of the access ladder, and that opening had to be closed at sea except in fine weather.

Jensen had been hired because the Shipping Company 'manned its vessels mainly with Ordinary rather than Able Seamen, who had to be paid a few shillings a month more', but the Conference Lines went far beyond petty

The Union Company's huge fleet gave New Zealand a strategic asset that it willingly placed at the disposal of the imperial authorities. Many New Zealand ships were requisitioned for war service that took them far from their normal trade routes. None was more valuable than the Lyttelton–Wellington ferry *Wahine*, built in 1913 to partner the *Maori* of 1907. With their powerful steam turbines and their bow rudders, they were both very fast, manoeuvrable ships, making the *Wahine* an ideal minelayer. Here it is seen in wartime camouflage and weaponry.

Opposite

In 1909 New Zealand gave a capital ship to the Royal Navy. HMS *New Zealand* was an 'Indefatigable'-class battlecruiser, a larger and even less capable version of the original 'Invincible' battlecruiser design. The ship was mounted with 8–12-inch guns and had a maximum speed of 26 knots, five more than contemporary battleships. The ship visited New Zealand twice, in 1913 and 1919, and drew enormous crowds, as this Lyttelton photograph shows.

The Press (Christchurch) Collection, Alexander Turnbull Library G-2294-1/1-

John Dickie Collection, Alexander Turnbull Library G-16582-

penny-pinching in order to maximise those profits. They had been doing their best to restrict competition for many years. As early as 1873 Shaw Savill, the Albion Line and the Shipping Company had agreed on uniform freight rates. The 'Davis' pool, which regulated freight rates and sailings, began three years later in Australia.[43] They never quite pulled it off during Victorian/Edwardian times. The seasonal peaks that attracted outsiders to load wool or grain always frustrated their efforts but they strengthened 'Davis' in the mid 1890s and by 1897 the companies had divided the refrigerated trade between them. They made more progress just before the First World War. The war prevented them from tying things up but they achieved greater cohesion in another way when P&O absorbed the Shipping Company, Federal and the Union Company in 1916–17. In 1916 the Commonwealth and Dominion Line — better known as the Port Line, whose constituent parts had strong meat industry associations — was admitted to the trade.

In 1922 the liners completed their prewar talks and signed what became known as the Benmacow Agreement (named after H C Benson of Commonwealth & Dominion, J MacMillan of Shaw Savill and C J Cowan of the Shipping Company). Benmacow 'established the conference which controlled the carriage of New Zealand produce until the advent of container ships'.[44] Non-British lines eyed the trade hungrily at times but the only new entrant before the French and Dutch lines that fought their way in during the early 1960s would be another British concern, the Blue Star Line. An offshoot of the Vestey meat industry dynasty, Blue Star barged in in 1933 after the Ottawa trade agreements threatened its South American trades.

The Conference Lines maintained the illusion of choice through their networks of branch offices and port agencies. Shippers might develop loyalties to one line or

another but the companies' managers observed the strictest secret agreements about freight rates, loading frequencies and even the ports that could be used.

The Conference Lines made New Zealanders unwelcome in their main export trade. In 1921 the Poverty Bay Farmers' Meat Company bought a large freighter, the *Admiral Codrington*, insulated it and ran it against the Conference Lines. The Lines fought back and the unsuitable *Admiral Codrington* made just three voyages before it was withdrawn. The Lines also tried to keep Geo H Scales out. They had used wartime shipping shortages to oust it from the trade but Scales fought its way back in, by using sail, of all things. In the 1920–21 season, the company chartered the *Pampa* and the *Rewa*, at 2999 tons, owned by George Scales's separate company, Geo H. Scales Pacific, the largest sailing ship on the British register.

During these years the country also finally sorted out its naval policy. For decades the dominions had been torn both ways on the issue of contributing to the Royal Navy or establishing their own local forces. Australia went its own way, but New Zealand held back. In 1909 that old political magician Sir Joseph Ward gave Britain a battlecruiser to shore up its lead over Germany. We were still paying it off decades later, long after it had been scrapped under the naval limitation provisions of the Washington Naval Conference. HMS *New Zealand* made two very popular flag-waving tours of the dominion in 1913 and 1919. Not even the Naval Defence Act 1913 provided for the automatic transfer of any local ships to Admiralty control in war. We did, indeed, transfer our old training cruiser HMS *Philomel* to Admiralty control. The *Philomel* served as a convoy escort and in the Middle East theatres until the worn-out old ship had to be sent back to New Zealand to become a stationary depot ship. With its boilers dead, the old cruiser nevertheless provided the nucleus for the New Zealand Division of the Royal Navy, the brainchild of Admiral of the Fleet (and later Governor-General) Lord Jellicoe.

As its name suggests, the Division was a halfway house, using ships borrowed from the Royal Navy. Jellicoe recommended three light cruisers, six submarines and a depot ship, with six destroyers and other craft to follow, but the government tested the waters with a single cruiser, cancelling the patrol boats and submarines that it applied for. The coal-burning light cruiser HMS *Chatham* arrived in 1921 and served until 1924 when it was replaced by the first of the modern oil-burning cruisers, HMS *Dunedin*; HMS *Diomede* followed in 1926. Throughout most of its two decades, the New Zealand Division would comprise a pair of cruisers, the old oiler *Nucula*, the Castle-class minesweeper *Wakakura* and a pair of imperial sloops attached to it for administrative purposes.[45]

For a decade from the mid 1920s the D-class light cruisers HMS *Diomede* (left) and HMS *Dunedin* (right) were the mainstay of the New Zealand Division of the Royal Navy. The eight Ds were completed too late to see war service. The 4900-ton ships mounted six six-inch guns in single shields, smaller weapons, and torpedo tubes and could make 29 knots. *Diomede* could always be distinguished by the unique enclosed forward six-inch mount.

New Zealand Free Lance Collection, Alexander Turnbull Library G-100601-½-

Chapter 5
Home Boats and Slow Greens
1925-62

Between the 1880s and the 1940s, they say, New Zealand was 'recolonised'. As one historian put it, the country 'became London's town supply district; London became New Zealand's cultural capital; refrigerated meat ships bridged the gap as if inter-island ferries of a single entity . . . The favourite child traded prolonged adolescence for special access to Mother's ear, purse, and markets, and for higher living standards'.[1] Others call it 'Britannic nationalism'.[2] Whatever term we choose to apply, it is clear that for all but the very end of the period covered in this chapter, British ships, British trade, British migrants and British wars dominated New Zealand's maritime world. You could read 'London', 'Southampton' or 'Glasgow' on the stern of a ship here as readily as 'Dunedin' or 'Wellington'. Our ships flew the same 'red duster' as Britain's, our Navy League branches presented Union Jacks to schools and the British Sailors' Society ran dry-as-dust sailors' rests at our major ports. Even as late as 1960, we prolonged adolescents waited expectantly for a British-flag Conference Line ship to ferry out the next shipment of Matchbox toys or *Beano* comics.

The flag, they also say, follows trade. Take a look at the figures, which were certainly not good news for the Union Company, now locked into the Pacific region by P&O:

DESTINATION OF NEW ZEALAND TRADE 1920-60				
% exports/ (imports)	% exports/ (imports)	% exports/ (imports)	% exports/ (imports)	% exports/ (imports)
UK	Australia	Japan	USA	Others
75/(49)	5/(17)	../(2)	15/(18)	5/(14)
81/(47)	3/(8)	../(2)	5/(18)	11/(26)
90/(47)	1/(16)	../(..)	3/(12)	6/(23)
66/(61)	2/(12)	1/(3)	10/(7)	21/(20)
53/(44)	4/(18)	3/(3)	13/(10)	27/(25)

(Year column: 1920, 1930, 1940, 1950, 1960)

Conferences and Collusion

Throughout the middle of the 20th century the Conference Lines pulled our strings quietly from behind the scenes. Their methods varied. They slipped opinion-makers sweeteners in the form of free or discounted fares. They bullied when they really had to. Most effectively, perhaps, they relentlessly traded on our loyalty: loyalty to Empire, loyalty to flag and loyalty to our 'shared' history with the ships they encouraged European New Zealanders to think of their ancestral 'waka'. The Conference Lines made sentiment a bankable commodity. As late as 1971 when even politicians as pro-British as Robert Muldoon were condemning the Lines for gouging New Zealand producers and consumers by shamefully pulling out of containerising the New Zealand trade, even though ports already were building the facilities, the editor of a maritime journal warned his countrymen not to knock the Lines. 'Through all the vicissitudes of peace and war for over a century these companies have served New Zealand and served it well,' he advised. 'The tradition of service and reliability, the expert knowledge of our very special requirements, are theirs. Let us cease this criticism of our old friends. Let us help them to maintain our trade routes to the old world as they have done for so long'.[3]

Unfortunately, anyone who has seen the film *Deliverance* will know what our 'old friends' had been doing to us while they held our trade captive. Gordon Boyce, who sees the conference as a British alternative to American and German amalgamation into vertically integrated empires, notes that they 'sought to align the supply of tonnage with demand in order to maintain rates that supported the cost of regular service using high-class vessels'.[4] Liners keep schedules regardless of whether ships are full and the conferences undoubtedly benefited shippers by guaranteeing frequency of service and quality tonnage, important considerations for New Zealand, whose seasonal exports required guaranteed access to expensive refrigerated tonnage.

But that cannot disguise the fact that shipping conferences are 'primarily agreements organised by shipping lines to restrict or eliminate competition . . . they generally control prices, i.e., freight rates and passenger fares' and aim above all 'to minimise losses or to maximise profits'.[5] Or, to put it another way, 'you pays your money, you gets no choice'. The Lines tied shippers to them with deferred rebates. Under this system merchants who used only conference vessels for a specified period received a rebate a further six months in the future. 'Conferences deflected competition away from pricing to service rivalry.'[6]

The Conference Lines sometimes fought dirty, as the government discovered while renegotiating the three-year freight contract due to expire in September 1939. The lines demanded 15 per cent more, even though they were doing so well that Lord Essendon, Shaw Savill's chairman, warned his henchmen that he did not want to do anything that might lead to the Lines' books being inspected. 'I do not much care for the sake of verifying of having

As this Shaw Savill booklet cover shows, the Conference Lines liked to suggest that European New Zealanders had their own 'canoe traditions'.

J R Wall Collection, Alexander Turnbull Library G-10182-1/1-

In 1914 four family firms merged to form the Commonwealth and Dominion Line. In practice that cumbersome name soon gave way to the Port Line in everyday usage and from 1936 officially. The Port Line introduced several firsts to the New Zealand-United Kingdom trade; the *Port Dunedin* was the first motor vessel and in 1933 the *Port Fairy* carried the first shipment of New Zealand chilled meat to Britain. The *Port Caroline*, photographed alongside New Plymouth's Moturoa Wharf about 1930, did not make any headlines. The 8236-ton steamer was completed in 1919 and served uneventfully until 1950, one of the last coal-burners in the Conference Lines' fleets.

an independent umpire in London who might ask for all kinds of particulars,' he confided. He just hoped that their New Zealand manager 'did not literally tell them we have the whip hand and can name our own terms from 1st September 1939'.[7] He did not, but Minister of Finance Walter Nash felt that lash when he travelled to Britain to renegotiate the conversion of a loan. Before leaving he had annoyed the Lines by asking for better terms. But the Lines had no intention of acquiescing. They resented Labour's import restrictions (which they feared would reduce trade) and its waterfront reforms, so Essendon went to see the Governor of the Bank of England, with whom Nash would soon have to plead his case. Essendon suggested that 'as a consideration for the loan that is required, it might be possible to negotiate some amelioration of the import restrictions, which in turn, would make it easier for the Shipping Companies to agree some amelioration of their freight proposals'.[8] The bank did that and when it was through with him, passed him on to 'our old friends', the Conference Lines, who unilaterally imposed a 10 per cent freight increase. Nash gnashed his teeth, but could do nothing.

Little analysis has been done of the profitability of the New

Zealand–United Kingdom trade but the financial returns of the local firm, Geo H Scales Ltd, may shed some light. It was an unusual venture, a charterer rather than an owner, and it exported only wool. Nevertheless, although Scales had its disputes with the Conference Lines, it had reached a private understanding with them in 1905 and in 1924 it signed a more comprehensive agreement that 'stuck Scales to the Conference like an insect to flypaper'.[9] Scales had the occasional bad year when charter rates soared, but the company, running under the Conference umbrella and charging its rates, usually made good money. Between 1926 and 1934, for example, its net profits averaged 68.6 per cent of gross income. Between 1958 and 1962, when the company's revenue included more investment and agency work, the figure was 45.5 per cent.[10] Nice work if you could get it.

The Conference Lines also concealed what today would be described as significant transfer pricing, the cross-subsidisation of consumers from one country by those of another. Unknown to all but a few Union Company senior executives, P&O milked the company. The 'Southern Octopus' had used New Zealand's weak company legislation to artificially deflate profits and build up hefty secret reserves by depreciating assets at a very high rate. It did this so well that P&O later considered that it had got £11.6 million worth of assets for just £2.9 million in cash and shares.[11] The Union Company's reserves swelled even more as this rare cash cow in a now troubled P&O group salted away millions of pounds.

Those bulging reserves proved too tempting for P&O, which between 1921 and 1936 siphoned off over £8 million from Union to prop up its teetering empire. Conventional histories have stressed the autonomy allowed Union and other P&O subsidiaries, but Lord Inchcape, P&O's chairman, lent heavily on the company to make these transfers. He ignored Sir James Mills and even managing-director Sir Charles Holdsworth and corresponded directly with general manager David Aiken. In 1931 he sold half of Union's Canadian-Australasian Line (*Niagara* and *Aorangi*) to CPR without consulting it and then demanded most of the proceeds of the sale.[12] In 1934 Inchcape's successor sailed out to New Zealand to ensure that Union paid a colossal secret dividend of £4.5 million (enough to pay for six *Awateas*) to P&O just to keep it afloat. P&O kept this clandestine pillaging secret from Union Company preference shareholders, customers and the New Zealand government, all of whom might have preferred higher benefits or cheaper freights. 'Had these transfers been disclosed at the time, it is likely that Union would have come under pressure within New Zealand to reduce its rates,' Christopher Napier considers. The impact on the New Zealand economy was significant. 'Resources that could have been invested within that economy were repatriated to Britain, where they were in one way or another ploughed into P&O's less profitable fleet or dissipated in dividends'.[13]

From Coal to Oil — New Ships

New Zealanders paid higher fares and freights than they might otherwise but they did at least get better ships. Geoffrey Blainey found that between 1920 and 1960 bigger ships, oil fuel, cheaper Suez Canal charges and more frequent use of the Panama Canal cut costs even if 'some of these gains were possibly lost by bedlam on the Australian waterfront and the cartel or conference of foreign shipowners which regulated most of Australia's overseas traffic'.[14] Because we shared so many lines and ships, it would be fair to assume that the same applied to New Zealand. We shall return to the waterfront bedlam later in this chapter, but it is now worth looking at the new oil-fuelled motor vessels.

The diesel-powered motor vessel was cleaner and easier to operate and cut labour costs, especially stokehold crew — the men who usually gave the most trouble on a steamer. Productive cargo-carrying space increased since oil, unlike coal, could be stored in unproductive parts of the ship. British shipowners have been criticised for being slower than their Continental and Scandinavian competitors to embrace the new technology. New Zealand lines, with ready access to plentiful supplies of West Coast and Australian steaming coal, had little incentive to switch, especially as they had to create a new distribution system for the new fuel. And there were also doubts about the efficiency of the early plants. Not until 1930 did *Brassey's Naval and Shipping Annual* consider the two-stroke diesel as reliable as steam machinery.[15]

Nevertheless, the Union Company adopted a cautiously innovative approach, building sample motor vessels, converting some steamers to oil-burning — a half-way house — and continuing to build oil- and coal-fired steamers for trades where they still had an advantage. Using information gathered from throughout the company and within its P&O parent group, and wanting to take advantage of the oil available on the American coast, the company ordered two significant motor vessels, the freighter *Hauraki* and the liner *Aorangi*. Both were big. The 7113-ton *Hauraki*, a trans-Pacific freighter, had four of the few North British Diesel engines ever built, which 'proved not very reliable in service'. Nevertheless, the ship served for 20 years before being captured by the Japanese in the Indian Ocean in 1942.[16]

Two years later Fairfield Shipbuilding and Engineering completed the trans-Pacific liner *Aorangi*. It was the largest (17,491 tons) and fastest (18 knots) motor passenger vessel in the world. This time the company used more reliable Sulzer diesels. Like most early motor ships the *Aorangi* was 'a bit of a workhouse down below' and, compared to later ships, its engine room was a 'chamber of horrors'.[17] Oil was cleaner than coal, but as former engineer G A Ricketts, recalls, such terms are relative. 'I shall never forget the sloshy mess we had to endure on the plates when walking between each inner and outer main

Gavin McLean Collection

engine,' he wrote. 'There was always a generous coating of oil to skid on but the spillage onto the plates of hot salt water from the piston-cooling tundishes, especially in the tropics and at full speed, made watch-keeping in that area very hazardous'.[18] Air locks in the drainpipes and their inability to cope with the quantity of hot drain water frequently spurted hot salt water all over the surrounding area. The men's feet were always wet and their boots seldom lasted more than one or two round trips to Vancouver and back.

The Depression dried up cargoes and many ships spent several years laid up at 'Rotten Row' at Port Chalmers or Wellington. Nevertheless, the Union Company built a respectable number of ships between the wars. On the coast its engines-aft colliers *Kaponga, Kartigi, Kiwitea, Kaimiro* and *Karepo* and the East Coast South Island-Auckland 'main trunk' freighters *Waipiata* and *Waimarino* set a new family style. Three of its four notable passenger ships of the period were oil-burning turbine electric steam vessels. Two ferries, the 1989-ton Wellington-Picton ferry *Tamahine* (1925) and the 6152-ton Wellington-Lyttelton ferry *Rangatira* (1931) served for over 30 years and developed devoted followings. But overshadowing them all was the trans-Tasman liner *Awatea* of 1936, built to head off competition from the American Matson

The Union Company built oil-burning steamers and motor vessels for its trans-Pacific services to take advantage of cheap American oil supplies. The Vancouver Royal Mail liner *Aorangi* of 1924 was briefly the largest (17,491 tons) and the fastest (18.5 knots on trials) motor liner in the world. Seven years later P&O's unscrupulous chairman, Lord Inchcape, piratically sold a half share in the *Aorangi* and the *Niagara* to CPR and pocketed most of the proceeds in order to keep his rickety empire afloat. Nevertheless, the Union Company managed the ship until its sale for scrap in 1953.

Alexander Turnbull Library C-25269-½

They slipped ships at the Patent Slip in Wellington's Evans Bay until the end of the conventional shipping era. The steamer pictured high and dry here is the Union Company's collier *Kartigi*, one of a series of engines-aft colliers and freighters built for the company in the mid–late 1920s. The 2347-ton *Kartigi* replaced traditional wooden hatches with patented steel hatch covers, had plenty of cargo handling gear and was fitted with additional ballast tanks to provide stability during voyages in ballast.

Line. It was smaller than the *Aorangi* — 13,482 tons — but at 23 knots, was the fourth fastest liner in the world. The elegantly shaped liner broke new records — 55 hours and 28 minutes Auckland to Sydney and 55 hours Sydney to Wellington — and carried its 377 first-class and 151 second-class passengers in art deco style.[19] The ship and its popular master, Arthur Davey, represented the pinnacle of the company's achievement and at Wellington on its first visit, Governor-General Lord Galway attended a formal welcome luncheon.

But cargo carriers remained the cornerstone of its business. In 1935 the company commissioned its first new motor coaster, the 1044-ton *Karu*. Another popular ship was the 4166-ton Pacific Islands cargo-passenger ship *Matua* of 1936. Other motor vessels followed, in a decade that saw the company order many one-off types, but it is worth remembering that as late as 1938–39 the Union Company was still launching new coal-fired steamers, the trans-Tasman freighters *Korowai*, *Kurow* and *Komata*. In 1943 it took delivery of its last purpose-built steamer, the *Kaimanawa*.

The company's subsidiaries and associates also built motor vessels in the 1930s. Three stand out, the Canterbury Company's *Gale* and *Breeze* and

Richardson & Company's *Kopara*. The Canterbury pair attracted more attention than any of their generation. In 1932, when chairman Hugh Monro went to Britain to order a new ship, motor vessels were still mostly passenger ships or large freighters. The Union Company permitted him to experiment, though, and he ordered the new *Breeze* from Scott & Sons, of Bowling. The three-island-type *Breeze*, a fine-lined motor coaster of 622 tons, 53.4 metres long, could carry 800 tonnes of cargo. Its five-cylinder British Polar Atlas diesel gave a service speed of 10 knots (11.5 knots on trials). The hatches were long and all the masts and derricks were of steel. The *Gale* followed in 1935. Richardson's *Kopara* was a strikingly handsome three-islander, built by the Union Company's favourite yard, Henry Robb Ltd, in 1938. The 679-ton ship had a high service speed of 12 knots. All three ships would prove their usefulness in war, *Breeze* and *Gale* as armed anti-submarine minesweepers and the *Kopara* as a freighter. Other lines also bought new steel-hulled motor vessels. Scottish shipyards delivered the 927-ton *Puriri* to the Anchor Company in 1938 and the 158-ton *Ranginui* to the Northern Company in 1936.

All but the last were too big for New Zealand's shipyards. From the 1930s on they turned out few trading vessels. Almost their last gasp came from the traditional Auckland shipbuilder George Niccol. He built several small

Like the earlier *Rotomahana*, the *Awatea* was another 'poster ship' for the Union Company. This profile shows the new greyhound at its best.

The coaster *Foxton* was one of the last general cargo vessels built in New Zealand. Like most of its generation, it was a product of Auckland shipbuilder George Niccol, who sold it prior to completion to the Canterbury Steam Shipping Company. For 10 years the 224-ton *Foxton* ran between Lyttelton, Kaiapoi and Foxton, although the last port was then dying and strandings were frequent. In 1939 Canterbury sold it to the South Taranaki Shipping Company. For the next 20 years the *Foxton* ran between Wellington and another little river port, Patea, until that, too, closed.

Alexander Turnbull Library F-135541-½

wooden-hulled motor vessels on speculation in the early 1930s. These were the 224-ton *Foxton*, which he sold to the Canterbury Company before completion in 1929, the 268-ton ship that became the Anchor Company's *Taupata*, the 236-ton *Waka* (1930) and the 208-ton *Atua* (1932). Niccol ran the last two on his own account until 1934 when he sold them to the Northern Company, which renamed them *Clansman* and *Waiotahi*. From now on few cargo vessels would be built locally. One of the last was the 137-ton powered lighter *Kaiwaka*, built by W G Love and Son Ltd, Auckland, for the New Zealand Refrigerating Company to take frozen meat out to the 'Home' boats loading off the Wanganui roadstead.

Although the coal trade remained significant, it had peaked by the time the last pre-war motor vessels entered service. The Otira rail tunnel (1923) had eliminated the carriage of coal by sea from West Coast ports to many South Island ones. But the new fuel also required ships to carry it. Until then it had been carried around the coast as 'case oil', usually in five-gallon tins, packed in wooden cases, first as part cargoes in general cargo ships and then, as trade increased, as full cargoes in special 'case-oil' ships.[20] Most big ports got their supplies direct from overseas tankers but in 1927 Shell built the 1260-ton tanker *Paua* to distribute oil around the coast from the Miramar depot. In 1950 the 3060-ton *Tanea* replaced it.

The 'Home' boats were slightly slower to switch to diesels. In 1925, however, the Commonwealth & Dominion Line — the Port Line — placed the first motor vessel on the Britain–New Zealand run. The 7527-ton *Port Dunedin* set

Wilkinson Collection, Alexander Turnbull Library

several records: the first motorship built for the trade, the first refrigerated motorship and the first twin-screw ship fitted with Doxford engines.[21] The other lines followed C&D. Shaw Savill built its four *Zealandics* from 1928 and the New Zealand Shipping Company its three *Otaios* from 1930. The signing of the Ottawa agreements in the early 1930s gave the lines the incentive to build larger and faster ships. Arguably the best of these 'Empire Food Ships' were Blue Star's *Imperial Star* class of 1935. With their fine lines, single masts and cavernous holds, the 12,400-ton, 17-knot *Imperial, New Zealand, Australia*, and *Empire Star*s set the pattern for Blue Star reefers for over a decade.

But the new passenger liners captured the most attention. In 1929, after a protracted building period, the New Zealand Shipping Company introduced the three *Rangitiki*-class liners. The *Rangitiki* had a few teething problems — the funnels and some kingposts had to be cut down to improve stability — but the *Rangitiki, Rangitata* and *Rangitane* quickly became icons, so much so that it is easy to forget that they were primarily cargo carriers. Above decks the ships catered for 100 first-, 85 second- and 410 third-class passengers but their enormous holds packed away 13,200 DWT of refrigerated and general cargo.[22] Nevertheless, they were some of the most potent symbols of Britain's links with the dominion in the 1930s.

Shaw Savill went one better with its *Dominion Monarch* of 1939. The ship was 10,000 tons more than the *Rangitikis* — 27,155 tons — and would remain the

In names as well as in appearance, the *Imperial Star* symbolises the 'Empire Food Ships' built in the 1930s to take advantage of the Ottawa trade agreements that brought in Empire preference tariffs. In fact the *Imperial Star* was launched at Harland & Wolff's Belfast yard from New Zealand by Governor-General Lord Bledisloe, who pressed a button to send the signal across the world by radio. The big 12,427-ton *Imperial Star* was fast for its day, 17–knots. It sank in 1941 in a submarine attack.

Steffano Webb Collection, Alexander Turnbull Library F-9191-1/1

The Shipping Company's *Rangitiki*, *Rangitata* and *Rangitane* of 1929 made a big impression with their sturdy lines, imposing superstructures and those distinctive twin funnels.

The *Dominion Monarch* was the largest passenger liner ever built for the New Zealand service.

largest ship in the Conference Lines' fleets throughout its long career. Indeed, the 207.8-metre-long *Dominion Monarch* set new port records; 32 years later the Lyttelton Harbour Board history reported that 'the special posts fixed for her lines on the far side of Gladstone Pier east still remain as evidence of the requirements imposed by her great size'.[23] Unfortunately, by the time the *Dominion Monarch* reached dominion ports in late 1939 the movements of overseas shipping were no longer being reported. For the second time in a generation, war had broken out.

Heron Collection, Alexander Turnbull Library, F-9429-1/4

The Second World War

The war came to our shores very abruptly in 1940–41 when German auxiliary cruisers — fast cargo vessels heavily disguised and fitted with six 5.9-inch guns, torpedoes, mines and other weapons — struck deep into our sealanes. The *Orion* sowed contact mines in the Hauraki Gulf in 1940 and next year the *Adjutant* laid more in the approaches to Wellington and Lyttelton. The later ones did no damage, but early on the morning of 19 June 1941 the *Orion* claimed the Vancouver mail liner *Niagara*. Aussie the ship's cat was the only casualty, but the loss of part of the cargo, 590 bars of Bank of England gold bullion, payment for desperately needed American arms, set an epic salvage job in motion.[24] On 15 May 1941 another *Orion* mine sank one of the hastily converted minesweeping trawlers, HMS *Puriri*. Five men, including the commanding officer, went down with the *Puriri*.

More disturbing were the gun actions that took place off the coast. After making a swing up through the Pacific, the *Orion* returned and on 20 August 1940 intercepted the Shipping Company freighter *Turakina* in heavy seas off the West Coast of the North Island. The *Turakina* was slow and carried just a single old 4.7-inch gun. It was no match for the *Orion*, but Captain J B Laird decided to fight it out and to radio a warning. The battle was hopelessly one-sided. Within 20 minutes the *Orion* had reduced the *Turakina* to a blazing wreck and killed or wounded half the crew, but even then, Laird refused to give up. He raced through the flames to the gun crew to urge the gunners to 'have another shot at the — !' In late November the persistent *Orion* returned with another raider, the *Komet*, and a supply ship. Off the East Coast they intercepted the Chatham Islands supply ship *Holmwood*. The old ship surrendered to save the lives of its passengers and crew. Two days later the raiders claimed the largest ship ever sunk by ships of their type, the *Rangitane*. It had been sailing unescorted, because its speed normally protected it from attack. The *Rangitane* sent off a distress message and then halted, under fire from the Germans. Eleven passengers and crew died.

New Zealand had entered the war with minimal naval forces. Since the mid 1930s we had manned the modern 'Leander'-class light cruisers, the *Achilles* and *Leander*. They displaced about 7000 tons, mounted eight six-inch guns and could steam at about 32 knots. Also in our waters were two modern imperial sloops, the *Wellington* and *Leith*; like the survey ship *Endeavour*, they departed for their war stations in September 1939. The only other naval 'asset' was the old armed minesweeping trawler *Wakakura*.

The navy expanded rapidly to fill the gaps left by the departure of the imperial vessels, requisitioning many small coasters, trawlers and pleasure craft for use as patrol boats, mine warfare vessels and auxiliaries. Many were too old

S C Smith Collection, Alexander Turnbull Library G-45191

New Zealand's most famous warship was the Royal Navy cruiser *Achilles*, which served the dominion from 1936 until 1946. This prewar view shows the ship in Wellington. The 'Leander'-class cruisers were about 7000 tons standard, mounted eight six-inch guns in twin turrets forwards and aft, four single four-inch dual purpose guns, torpedoes and carried an amphibian.

and too slow to be of much value and the most combat-worthy was undoubtedly the Union Company liner *Monowai*, which became an armed merchant cruiser and later served the British as a troop transport. Three multi-purpose 'Bird'-class corvette-style ships, the *Moa*, *Kiwi* and *Tui*, provided valuable reinforcements in 1941. New construction included the locally built 'Fairmile'-class launches, the 'Castle'-class minesweeping trawlers, over 20 harbour defence motor launches and in 1944 two modified 'Flower'-class corvettes, the *Arabis* and *Arbutus*.

New Zealand warships fought in several engagements. In the best known, the *Achilles* fought alongside two British cruisers against the German armoured ship *Admiral Graf Spee* off Uruguay in the first major naval engagement of the war. *Achilles* and *Leander* both sustained heavy damage in the Pacific in 1943. *Achilles* was still under repair in the United Kingdom when the war ended. In 1943 New Zealand took over the 'Fiji'-class cruiser HMNZS *Gambia*. The 8000-ton ship, mounting 12 six-inch guns, is the largest warship ever to fly the New Zealand ensign. Two New Zealand warships were sunk. Japanese bombers sank the corvette *Moa* at Tulagi on

7 April 1943, killing five men and injuring 15 others, and the auxiliary minesweeper HMNZS *South Sea* sank in Wellington Harbour in December after hitting an inter-island ferry. All three 'Birds' fought close encounters with Japanese submarines several times their size.

We also built ships for our own navy and for allies. There were two basic types. The larger were the 'Castle'-class minesweeping trawlers. An old First World War design, they displaced about 550 tons, mounted a 12-pounder gun, machine-guns and depth charges, and could make about 10 knots at full power. The first three, built in Auckland, used engines salvaged from condemned ships from Auckland's 'Rotten Row' and were of composite wood/steel construction to make the best use of available skills. The rest were steel-hulled. The Wellington Patent Slip Company built the *Awatere* and two Auckland yards built the *Rimu*, *Tawhai* and *Hinau*, but most came from a Port Chalmers partnership led by Stevenson & Cook Engineering. In all, 15 were handed over to the navy and others were completed for mercantile use or cancelled. The 12 'Fairmile' large anti-submarine launches were 34 metres long and could make 18.5 knots. The British shipped out the engines and some components, but Auckland shipyards, Associated Boatbuilders, Baileys, Shipbuilders and Vos, built everything else.[25]

The outbreak of war brought change to shipping schedules. New Zealand ships were requisitioned or diverted, export loading was concentrated on the major ports and ships seldom seen here in peacetime called to load troops. This photograph of Kings Wharf, Wellington, shows two huge liners impressed as troopships, the *Empress of Japan* (left) and the *Mauretania* (right). Both ships were bigger than others seen here in peacetime. The Canadian Pacific liner *Empress of Japan* was of 26,032 tons. The 35,738-ton Cunarder *Mauretania* was brand-new, having been completed in May 1939.

W H Raine Collection, Alexander Turnbull Library G-21750-1/1-

One of the most successful ventures of the war was the large shipyard at St Marys Bay, run co-operatively by a consortium of shipbuilders, United Ship and Boatbuilders, which constructed ships for New Zealand and its allies. Here a number of small 13.7-metre wooden tugs destined for the US armed forces are poised to take to the water on 21 August 1943. The boat nearest the camera, the *Kaihau*, was launched along with the *Kawa*, *Kiwa*, *Karokai*, *Kupe*, *Kanapu*, *Koroki* and *Kahu*.

John Pascoe Collection, Alexander Turnbull Library F-597-½

New Zealand yards were fully stretched when the Americans asked for small craft for the Pacific, but Commissioner of Defence Construction James Fletcher ensured that two hastily constructed shipyards were working in Auckland. At St Marys Bay a consortium of Baileys, Lowes, Vos Shipbuilders, Roy Lidgard and Associated Boatbuilders (itself a consortium) and United Ship and Boatbuilders, built 62 13.7-metre tugs, 10 powered lighters and five small cargo vessels.[26] Just along the harbour at Mechanics Bay, Steel Ships built 25 steel tugs. Port Chalmers also built two powered lighters. Official statistics showed that the ships built for the Royal New Zealand Navy (as the New Zealand Division of the Royal Navy had become in 1941) cost £1,270,000 and the ones for the Americans earned the country £2,213,000 under reverse lend-lease. The official war history considered this 'good value in money and in organisation, labour skill and timber'.[27]

Rangi Liners and 10 Pound Poms

Although aviation had made tremendous strides during the Second World War, no one knew whether it would be commercially viable as a mass form of transport. Long-distance seaplanes from Imperial Airways and Pan American had captured public attention in the late 1930s and military aviation had progressed by leaps and bounds during the war, but many still doubted whether it could entice any but the wealthy or people for whom time was precious. It was against this background of vague concern that most shipping lines laid their plans for rebuilding their passenger fleets. Many of the liners serving New Zealand had survived the war but took time to be released from postwar trooping and repatriation duties and be converted back to peacetime standards. The *Monowai* and *Aorangi*, for example, did not return to their trans-Tasman and Vancouver runs until 1949.

Shaw Savill & Albion led the Conference Lines' rebuilding programme with the four *Corinthic*-class passenger cargo liners of 1944–48. These 15,000-ton ships carried 85 passengers in first-class berths and an enormous amount of cargo. Next came the Shipping Company's *Rangitoto* and *Rangitane* in 1949. Once again a generation of *Rangis* caught public attention. When the *Rangitoto* arrived at Wellington on its maiden voyage it 'was the centre of attraction on the waterfront and . . . was visited by many

Shaw Savill & Albion's *Corinthic*-class were the first passenger-cargo ships built after the war for the New Zealand trade. The *Corinthic* was one of the first pair. Completed in 1947, the 15,862-ton ship carried 85 first-class passengers, but was principally a cargo vessel and indeed from 1965 ran as purely a freighter. The second pair, *Gothic* and *Ceramic*, had larger, streamlined funnels and the *Gothic* is best remembered as the white-hulled chartered Royal Yacht during the 1953–54 Royal Tour to New Zealand.

Alexander Turnbull Library 3313-½-

Museum of Wellington, City & Sea

The old and the new. The Shaw Savill & Albion liners *Dominion Monarch* (left) and *Southern Cross* (right) show contrasting styles at Wellington Harbour. The older ship, the *Dominion Monarch*, was a big cargo carrier as well as a passenger ship, and had numerous hatches and derricks. The *Southern Cross*'s sweeping, near-unbroken superstructure showed that it was a pure passenger ship.

hundreds of people'.[28] They were bigger than the surviving pre-war *Rangitikis* — 21,809-tons, and 185.6-metres long, and they replaced the three classes of tickets with a more egalitarian single tourist-class concept — but they and the smaller *Ruahine* of 1951 remained traditional combination passenger and cargo liners.

In 1955, however, Shaw Savill & Albion introduced the revolutionary 20,204-ton *Southern Cross*. Even without the dubious innovation of a puke-green superstructure, the *Southern Cross* would have turned heads. The ship's long, streamlined superstructure ended at the stern with a small funnel, and the decks, freed of hatches and cargo-handling gear, could be used for pampering passengers. The *Southern Cross* also made 20 knots, three knots more than the *Rangis*. But what really set the *Southern Cross* apart was that it was a pure passenger carrier. Its only cargoes were the passengers' luggage and mails. This gave more space for the 1160 passengers, but, more importantly, cut time in port handling cargo. Shaw Savill estimated that the *Southern Cross* could make one round trip a year more than its older ships. In 1959, when Shaw Savill said that the minimum round-the-world fare cost its passengers just twopence halfpenny a mile, the line ordered a larger *Southern Cross*, the 24,733-ton *Northern Star* to replace the *Dominion Monarch*.[29] P&O's huge *Canberra* of 1961 also followed the trend.

They set the standards. Refurbished vessels and the new liners attracted a diverse clientele. Politicians and businessmen continued to book favoured suites aboard the prestigious *Rangis* and new governors-general were always advised to travel by the Shipping Company. At the other end of the travelling market came the '10 pound Poms', the British assisted migrants. This scheme, which would bring out 77,000 British men, women and children between 1947 and 1975, was the biggest wave of assisted immigration since the days of Vogel. Its motivation was part humanitarian, part pragmatic. 'Huge numbers of job vacancies, a desire by the Labour government to avoid the possibility of the kind of postwar slump that had happened in the early 1920s, public concern about a declining rate of natural population increase,' Megan Hutching notes, 'and the continuing development of secondary industry were all factors in the decision to introduce an assisted immigration scheme for British workers in 1947'.[30]

Many '10 pound Poms' came out in regular Conference Lines ships. The *Rangitata* brought out the first draft in August 1947, but shortages of shipping space and high demand forced the government to enter the passenger liner business. In 1948 it chartered the former hospital ship *Atlantis*. Three years later it chartered two more ships, the symbolically named *Captain Cook* and the *Captain Hobson*, new *Endeavours* to convey middle-class shopfitters from Birmingham to the New World. None, it must be said, was in the first flush of youth. The *Atlantis* dated from 1913 and could carry 900 emigrants. The 13,876-ton *Captain Cook*, dating from 1925, survived a fire in Wellington in 1957 and soldiered on until 1960. The last ship, the 1920-vintage *Captain Hobson*, was smaller and slower than the others. Migrants remembered them with mixed feelings. The food aboard the *Captain Hobson* always seemed to taste of oil. A male passenger on the *Captain Cook* recalled being separated from his wife. 'Six husbands in Cabin B80-something and six wives in cabin B106 made for a careful exercise in diplomacy.'[31]

Not all migrants were Brits. Two hundred years after Tasman had fled from New Zealand in disgust, a wave of Dutch migrants, the largest non-British group, took to sea in ships such as the *Sibajak*, *Groote Beer*, *Waterman*, *Zuiderkruis*, *Willem Ruys* and *Volendam*. One enterprising couple, Ben

Evening Post Collection, Alexander Turnbull Library F-58472-?

The main wave of migrants came out in the 1950s, many of them aboard specially chartered immigrant ships. During the war and immediately afterwards, however, many also used ordinary passenger ships. This photograph shows British children arriving in Wellington Harbour aboard the *Rangitata*.

Recreation

Organised excursions and workplace picnics often took place at the beach. Days Bay was a popular day trip destination for Wellingtonians, who travelled across the harbour in the steam ferries *Cobar* and *Duchess*, seen here at the wharf. This photograph from the 1920s shows youngsters making the most of the shallows.

Many of the postwar migrants were drawn to the country by its climate and occupational opportunities. Early racing boats were working craft, run for pleasure on special anniversary days and carnivals but from the 1880s specialist pleasure craft began to appear. One of the earliest designs, the mullet boat, was designed to be used for fishing as well as racing. This is one of the more splendid Logan Bros. products, the *Celox*, caught about the time of the First World War by J H Kinnear's camera on the Waitemata, with a distinctive harbour ferry in the background.

D A De Maus Collection, Alexander Turnbull Library G-3384-1/1-

Grummels and Elizabeth Maas, bought their own voyaging waka, an 18-metre Bermuda-rigged ketch, and sailed it out to New Zealand.[32] Where the Dutch ships led, other Europeans would follow. After the war the British lines let the Scandinavian lines, Wilh. Wilhelmsen, East Asiatic and Transatlantic, send freighters to New Zealand. In the early 1960s Sitmar Line (Italian) and Chandris Line (Greek) began running to New Zealand.

Streamlined, stylish and sparkling in fresh paintwork, the *Port Auckland* (seen here at Port Chalmers) was the standard-bearer for the new streamlining era. The 11,945-ton ship had a long life under the Port Line flag, from 1949 to 1976, when it was sold for conversion to a livestock carrier.

The Conference Lines launched dozens of new cargo liners between the late 1940s and the early 1960s as they discarded pre-war and war emergency vessels. The Shipping Company and Federal ships were conservative looking, but the eight big *Haparangi* class ships of the late 1940s each gave about a quarter century of profitable service. The Port Line got more adventurous in its styling. Underneath, its *Port Brisbane* and *Port Auckland* (1949) were basically similar to the *Port Napier* of 1947, but with their curved bridge fronts and tapering funnels swept back into the surrounding superstructures they set off the era of streamlining. Shaw Savill steered a mid course between these companies. Its *Doric, Persic, Cedric* and *Ionic* class ships evolved gradually and gracefully throughout the decade from the pre-war 'W's to the elegantly streamlined *Ionic, Illyric, Icenic* and *Iberic* of 1959–1961. These ships were mainly 17–18 knotters and conventional, although by the early 1960s deck cranes were replacing traditional samson posts and derricks in some ships. Deck cranes offered faster cargo-handling and Blue Star's *Fremantle Star* of 1960 had nine. Other ships mixed derricks and cranes.

Indian Summer on the Coastal Trade

The New Zealand coastal trade enjoyed its last, long Indian summer during the late 1940s and the 1950s. The country was still shaking off wartime restrictions, making up food parcels for Britain and making do with shipping worn out by wartime use, but times were good and most people felt optimistic. Sheltered by protective tariffs, the manufacturing hubs at Auckland and Wellington were creating plenty of work for any old tub that could float. The last scows, now motorised, were refitted one last time and even veterans' groups started shipping lines using refugees from Rotten Row.[33] Our only war booty became the coaster *Kamo* but war-built British, Canadian and American ships plugged the gaps while European shipyards built new ships. For 20 years the little British-built coasters *Kanna* and *Katui* would shuttle between South Island East Coast ports and the North; in Wellington two 'Empire' tugs *Tapuhi* and *Taioma* would fuss about the harbour until the early 1970s. Six Canadian-built standard ships rejuvenated the company's trans-Pacific freight business and the American-built *Wairata* and *Wairimu* entered its South East Asian trade.

The lines went shopping for shipping on an unprecedented scale. One item, 'Union Steam Ship Company Expansion', stands out from the first issue of the New Zealand Ship and Marine Society's journal in 1949. That year the Union Company's order book was bulging: from Henry Robb, Leith, six *Kaitangata*-class twin screw colliers of 3030 DWT; the motorship *Kamona*, 2000 DWT, and the trans-Tasman

The sturdy *Kaitangata* was the first of six sturdy shallow-draft coasters built for the trade out of Greymouth and Westport in the late 1940s and early 1950s. They served until 1968-71 when all but the *Kaitawa* (which sank off Cape Maria van Diemen in 1966) were sold to Far Eastern owners. This shows the ship leaving Greymouth for Gisborne in February 1952.

L A Inkster, Gavin McLean Collection

Gavin McLean Collection

The *Koraki* was one of the last of the 5300-DWT trans-Tasman 'slow greens', built like so many in Scotland, where it is seen running trials in 1957. Solid, traditional-looking ships, they carried a variety of cargoes between Australia and New Zealand. In 1973 the *Koraki* became the last trans-Tasman freighter to call at Oamaru; two years later the Union Company sold the ship.

motor vessel, *Kurutai*, 5170 DWT; Alexander Stephen & Sons was building *Kawaroa*, a sister to *Kurutai*. Australian builders were working on two colliers and one cargo motor vessel of 3033 DWT and W Denny & Bros was about to build the Islands passenger/cargo ship *Tofua*.[34] Thirteen ships in all! Between 1946 and 1959 the Union Company built 38 new ships and bought another 15.

The company built new ships for all its runs but the most numerous were the trans-Tasman freighters, the mainstays of its core business. They were about 5300 DWT and came in two batches of seven, the *Komata* class (1947–53) and the *Kawerau* class (1955–58). The stiff, conservative lines of the 'AC's, the *Komatas*, showed their pre-war design ancestry, although the ships had innovations such as enclosed winch houses, MacGregor steel hatch covers, hot water radiators and hot freshwater showers for the crew. The 'AE's, the *Kawerau* ships, were slightly modified *Komata*, with soft-nosed stems, rounder bridges, shorter, fuller funnels and four masts and a set of derrick posts instead of the *Komatas*' two masts and three sets of derrick posts. They were plain things, but the builders tweaked them subtly so that by the time the *Katea* and *Waikare* entered service in 1958, all but the cadets had their own cabins, complete with bunk, built-in settee and wardrobe. They never won any prizes for speed. Their six-cylinder diesels gave them 12 knots and earned them the nickname 'slow greens', even if they were not green at first. For decades the Union Company had been painting its coastal and trans-Tasman freighters in drab but practical colours of black hulls and orange-buff superstructures. From 1960, though, with coal carriage declining, it painted its workhorses in the same green hull and white superstructure style as the rest of its fleet.

The company also built a few new passenger vessels. In 1946 it built a new Lyttelton ferry, the 6911-ton *Hinemoa*, a single-funnel development of the *Rangatira*. In 1953 it added a larger ship, the 8303-ton *Maori*. Two years earlier the company had built the 5299-ton *Tofua* for the Pacific Islands trade, but

Aircraft competition killed the Anchor Shipping & Foundry Company's historic ferry service between Nelson and Wellington. In 1950 the company bought its largest ship, the 20-year old Hawaiian *Hualalai*, and renamed it *Ngaio*. The sun was already setting on the happy scene shown here, however, and in 1953 the *Ngaio* was laid up in Wellington Harbour.

Archives New Zealand: National Publicity studios Photographic Collection [Alexander Turnbull Library] F-20499-1/2-

that was all. Already aircraft were chipping away at the passenger market, starting with internal and trans-Tasman traffic. The Anchor Company bought a big Hawaiian ferry for its Wellington-Nelson service in 1949, but the *Ngaio* had to be withdrawn in 1953, beaten by NAC's DC-3s. In 1960–61 the historic trans-Tasman passenger service finally came to an end, when the Union Company and Huddart Parker withdrew their *Monowai* and *Wanganella* respectively. It was now cheaper and easier to fly to Australia.

The Union Company's subsidiaries also built new ships for the coastal trade. Richardson & Company built the *Pateke*, *Parera* and *Pukeko* between 1954 and 1961; the Canterbury Company added the *Calm*, *Squall* and *Storm* between 1950 and 1961; the Holm Shipping Company built the *Holmwood*, *Holmglen*, *Holmburn* and *Holmdale* between 1953 and 1961 and also bought two second-hand ships. The Anchor Company built two stiff-looking, cut-down 'slow greens', the *Mamaku* and the *Puriri*, bought a couple of second-hand ships and turned to Dutch builders in 1957–58 for the 850-ton coasters *Titoki* and *Totara*. These new British and Dutch-built coasters were streamlined little works of art. The *Pateke* of 1954 could carry 1100 DWT and had a maximum speed of 13 knots, although in service most coasters averaged 11–12 knots. Things were tighter aboard these smaller craft, so read between the lines of a contemporary comment that crew accommodation, 'though not spacious, is adequate'. Officers had individual small cabins, equipped with hot and cold water; the crew shared less elaborate twin-berth cabins, although they were expected to be delighted by having a refrigerator in their mess-room.[35] Like all but two of this last generation, the *Pateke* was

M Berthold Collection, Alexander Turnbull Library F-24818-½-

an engines-aft vessel. The exceptions came, typically, from the Holm Shipping Company, where the strong-willed Sydney and John Holm still held 10 per cent of the shares and wanted 50 per cent of the say. John in particular still felt that he could lecture the Union Company. Its managing director scratched 'Holm & Co. have never paid a Div.[idend] since we have had an interest in the Coy.' across the bottom of a Holm broadside, but agreed to the three-island *Holmwood*, Holm's first built-from-scratch vessel, and to the *Holmdale*.

The only major independent, the Northern Steam Ship Company, also splashed out. Much loved by Aucklanders, this old firm had entered the war with a ragbag fleet of wheezy old steamers and new 150–300-ton motor vessels. These slips of ships worked well enough in the traditional short-haul trades but, like James Mills 70 years earlier, Northern knew that this business was moving to land transport. It had to escape its regional ghetto to survive, so Northern began buying bigger ships for longer-distance trading. The first, appropriately named *Goldfinder* (later *Apanui*), was not much to look at, but it set the pattern for later coasters, which, like the 594-ton *Hotonui* purchased in 1950, were all engines-aft vessels. For nearly a decade from the mid 50s, fine, new 800–1200-ton coasters streamed out of Dutch and later Hong Kong shipyards for the Northern Company: *Awanui, Moanui, Poranui, Maunganui, Tawanui, Tainui*, their names ring down the years like a Maori chant.

With the demise of the *Ngaio*, the Anchor Company became purely a cargo carrier. The *Towai* typified the smaller ships in its postwar fleet. The 565-ton *Towai* had been laid down as a Royal Navy aircraft transport and had been completed on the stocks as a merchant vessel in 1949. It was five years old when Anchor acquired it. For the next 15 years the *Towai* carried cargo to Wellington from Nelson, Motueka and Mapua. This shows the little ship at Wellington in 1969, the year in which it was sold.

Archives New Zealand: National Publicity Studios Photographic Collection [Alexander Turnbull Library] 33093-¼-

The *Monowai* was the Union Company's last trans-Tasman passenger ship. The company had bought it second-hand in 1930 to replace the *Tahiti*. The *Monowai* was refitted at great expense and re-entered the Tasman service in 1949. Already, though, aircraft were taking much of the business. In 1960 the company withdrew the ship, closing an 83-year involvement with the business of carrying passengers between the two nations.

The Melbourne firm Huddart Parker ran the *Wanganella* as the *Monowai*'s consort on the postwar trans-Tasman passenger service. With its stumpy funnels, the *Wanganella* typified the Belfast-built motor liners of the early 1930s. It is better remembered not for its lines, but for running aground on Barrett's Reef, near the entrance to Wellington harbour in 1947 and as a floating hostel for workers on the Manapouri hydro scheme from 1963–70. This photograph shows the *Wanganella* after getting off the reef on 6 February. It had been pinned there since 19 January and only fine weather — 'Wanganella weather', as elderly capital residents still say — prevented the ship from becoming a total loss.

New Zealand Free Lance Collection, Alexander Turnbull Library G-100278-½-

The Big Blue and Other Black Clouds

Yet there were hints that all was not well. Silting from up-river land clearance had been silently choking small ports for years, ports such as Hokitika, once the 'wreck capital of New Zealand'. Elsewhere, shallow-bar harbours could cope with the silt — just — but not with the rapidly improving road and rail transport systems. Whakatane had battled to keep its port going but the wreck in 1956 of the coaster *Clansman* effectively killed it.[36] Patea's long history of shipping dairy produce to Wellington for export ended when the dairy companies merged and concentrated exports at New Plymouth. The South Taranaki Shipping Company ceased trading in 1959 and sold the *Foxton* and *Inaha*.[37]

By then most of Auckland's Devonport ferries had also gone, killed off by the new harbour bridge. As delighted Auckland motorists drove across the bridge to colonise the sparsely populated North Shore, the Devonport Steam Ferry Company sold its fleet to the North Shore Transport Company and went out of business. The vehicular ferries were sold or dismantled and commuter favourites *Albatross*, *Pupuke*, *The Peregrine* and *Ngoiro* also drew their fires. The *Ngoiro* became a floating restaurant, but most mouldered away for years in a bleak corner of St Marys Bay while North Shore Transport maintained a vestigial service. The day of the harbour ferry, it seemed, had passed.

So had the conventional coaster. Throughout the 1950s and the 1960s all the coastal lines complained about the cost of doing business. They said that seafarers were pricing themselves out of business. Disputes always got prominent media attention. In fact, though, things were more complex than they seemed. Bear with a few figures. Statistics prepared by the Canterbury Company for two *Storms* 50 years apart are revealing. They showed that many costs had actually fallen in real terms: Crew costs (including overtime) were remarkably stable – 18.66 per cent of freights in 1966, down from 21.67 per cent 50 years earlier. Fuel had fallen from 10.16 per cent in 1916 to 3.15 per cent in 1966. Agents' commission had gone down from 7.98 per cent to 5.92 per cent and port charges from 3.86 to 2.38 per cent. Insurance had also fallen from 3.84 per cent to 2.3 per cent. The cost blowouts came from handling the cargo.[38] In 1916 this had absorbed 19.05 per cent of freights; in 1966, in painful contrast, labour at ordinary and overtime rates, 'contract surplus' and tally clerks swallowed up 44.99 per cent of earnings.

The problems were complex, especially for the coastal lines, which usually got lower priority for berths and waterside labour. In 1951 the Northern Company had warned that liquidation loomed unless work practices changed. Complaining that strikes and port congestion took up 24.7 per cent of ships' working time, company chairman E H Rhodes cited 'one of the company's vessels, capable of making two round inter-island voyages a month, which took 27 days to complete one round voyage and was steaming only four days'.[39] Five years later he was complaining that the company's inter-island traders lost on average 26.52 days a year; 22.78 through lack of labour, 1.74 because of berth unavailability, one through shed congestion and one because of shortages of rail wagons.[40] The costliest bottlenecks were the two major ports, Auckland and Wellington. By 1964 Richardsons was paying $3.04 per tonne to handle cargo at Auckland; in contrast, it cost just $1.35 a tonne to work at Oamaru.[41] Delays at Wellington kept John Holm apoplectic.

The 1951 waterfront lockout—'the big blue'—still casts its shadow over New Zealand history. Robert Chapman suggested that smashing the unions 'was eventually to transfer the role of being the normal party of government from Labour to National'.[42] Most commentators have also focused on the political fight between the government and the unions. Recently, though, Anna Green has put the shipowners back into the picture, highlighting their stevedoring operations. Stevedores organise and supervise the loading and discharge of ships and it was an extremely profitable business. In 1937 Shaw Savill said that 'stevedoring paid the SS and A Co. so handsomely that they would not lightly abandon it'.[43] Geo H Scales Pacific did very well out of stevedoring in the postwar years.[44] Yet despite the profitability of stevedoring, the lines paid its supervisors badly and went to counter-productive lengths to cut costs. According to Green, 'In pursuit of maximum profits, the shipping companies engaged in a policy of minimum investment on the waterfront. Anxious to secure a fast

As more of the land-based workforce moved towards permanent employment, the 40-hour week and home ownership, the clash between its values and that of the still largely casualised maritime workforce became more apparent. Both watersiders and seafarers increasingly resented their casualised status, which kept them vulnerable to petty victimisation and graft, made their income erratic and deprived them of many of the sick-leave provisions enjoyed by the rest of the workforce and management. This interwar photograph shows watersiders 'waiting for the pick up'.

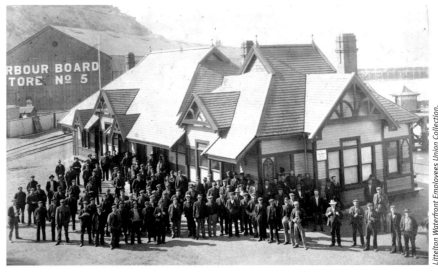

Littelton Waterfront Employees Union Collection, Alexander Turnbull Library F-8214I-1/2–

Archives New Zealand: National Publicity Studios Photographic
Collection [Alexander Turnbull Library F-33093-1/2-(A4014)]

These men are loading an unnamed coaster at Auckland in 1945. The coastal shipping companies complained that they got second choice of berths, labour and priorities.

turnaround in port while employing the cheapest possible labour, they came into constant conflict with the waterside workers, culminating in the extremely damaging dispute of 1951'.[45]

New Zealand waterfront management was appalling. Until 1937 stevedores selected labour by the 'auction block system'; men gathered at the wharf for the morning and afternoon 'calls'. It was open to petty graft, and the workers detested the casualisation at a time when the rest of the country was moving to permanent employment. In the late 1930s new labour bureaux spread work more evenly among union members and removed the foreman's power of victimisation.[46] In 1940 the government created the Waterfront Control Commission (later the Waterfront Industry Committee). The Commission brought in a new system of co-operative contracting which loaded and discharged vessels at an agreed price. The profit from each job was paid back to the workers and their unions as an efficiency bonus. Hypocritically, the Conference Lines, who did everything in their power to stamp out competition in their industry, screamed about the WIC monopoly.

Strikes and go-slows became more common after the war as pressure piled up and the men found themselves working ever-longer hours, 'punch drunk with work' as union leader Jock Barnes put it.[47] Between 1945 and 1950 the main issues were over dirt rates (22 per cent), WIC order negotiations (21 per cent) and danger rates (18 per cent).[48] In 1948, in the highly publicised *Mountpark* dispute, a judge had to order the Union Company to alter the unsafe hatches on its charter ship. Next came strikes over handling lamp-black, a cargo so dirty that even National Party leader Sidney Holland admitted it was a terrible cargo to handle. There was politics on both sides, but the underlying issues arose from poor management, antiquated gear and dangerous practices and, above all, wearyingly long hours that forced men to offer resistance through practices such as go-slows and spelling.

John Pascoe Collection, Alexander Turnbull Library F-1870-?.

On the wharf, where this man is loading frozen beef into a sling for the *Rangitiki* at Wellington in 1945, it was merely hard work. In the freezer compartment, where the men worked without any mechanical aids or protective gear, cramp was common from the cold and the physical exertion. After being dumped in nets into the hold, mutton carcases might have to be stacked three metres high — as high as a fit man could throw.

The employers had their divisions — the coastal lines were more amenable to negotiation than the Conference Lines — but the labour movement was thoroughly riven between the small, militant Trades Union Congress and the conservative Federation of Labour. In February 1951, when the watersiders were locked out after imposing an overtime ban in support of a wage claim, they lacked public support, a clearly articulated grievance, and much of a strategy. Among the seagoing unions, the officers and the engineers welcomed the opportunity to get back control of crew selection and talked more militantly than either the Union Company or the government. The Merchant Service Guild, the officers' union, may have had to walk away 'with a worthless scrap of paper rather than the 30 pieces of silver it had hoped for',[49] but the officers and the engineers helped keep things moving — just.

'The government proclaimed draconian emergency regulations that prevented donations to strikers and their families, censored publications and banned meetings, even those involving opposition politicians'.[50] For 151 dramatic days ships lay idle, or worked under military and non-union labour — employers called it 'free labour', unionists 'scabs' — but the unions lost ground, gagged by the National government's extraordinarily repressive measures and by the use of service personnel.[51] By late March 1951 3200 service personnel were working on the wharves or elsewhere in the distribution system. Naval personnel manned coasters and ratings from HMNZS *Taupo* and *Lachlan* moved coal on the West Coast. Servicemen handled 809,390 tonnes of cargo during the emergency and performed well, despite a growing feeling that 'the armed forces were being used as a political instrument'.[52] On 11 July the national executive of the deregistered union told its men to return to work. The dispute had involved 20,000 workers at its peak and cost the country £40 million.[53] New port unions emerged, but the watersiders gradually rebuilt their union structure. The Seamen's Union emerged more or less intact from the dispute and the officers and engineers soon realised that they had gained nothing from siding with the government. The 1951 lockout solved nothing. Nor could it, given that even 'our old friends', the Conference Lines, quietly acknowledged that they had been the cause of much of the trouble. From the safe distance of London's Leadenhall Street boardrooms, Shaw Savill's managing director, Basil Sanderson, worried about the health of his scabs. 'Past tactics of spelling and knocking off work upon every conceivable pretect [sic] was [the] inevitable consequence [of the] attempt to make men work unconscionably long hours,' he telegrammed.[54]

Indeed, in the late 1930s Shaw Savill and Port Line local managers had warned their more aggressive London principals that the wharves could not handle all the work that longer shifts might generate.[55] Some improvements were being made at the country's ports. At Napier they finally resolved the long dispute between the inner harbour and the breakwater port factions in favour of the latter. A modern new port emerged at Mount Maunganui to handle forestry, dairy and other exports. Several established harbour boards thought innovatively. At Bluff the Southland Harbour Board planned an ambitious 45–hectare 'island harbour', creating eight modern berths, each with its own cargo shed. By 1963 the first of the new mechanical all-weather meat loaders was ready for use.[56] In the 1960s the Lyttelton Harbour Board built its technologically innovative but initially surge-prone eastern extension project, Cashin Quay.[57] But, as long as cargo had to be worked in the traditional, laborious and time-consuming way, and managed so badly, these ad hoc improvements counted for little while the main ports' layout and management left so much to be desired.

But still the work built up. Overseas shipping arrivals surged from 597 ships of 2,688,223 tons in 1950 to 818 ships of 3,800,255 tons in 1960. Coastal arrivals and departures also increased during the same time. Something new was needed if the country was to cope with its burgeoning trade flows and the rising expectations of its workforce. Unknown to most, its squat lines had been glimpsed briefly in the shape of a war-surplus American tank-landing ship. The *Rawhiti III* had been bought in 1948 by Waikato River shipowner Caesar Roose. He has the distinction of running the first seagoing roll-on, roll-off ship on the New Zealand coast. Run was perhaps the wrong word, for although the *Rawhiti III*'s bow doors freed it from conventional wharf facilities and labour practices, 'red tape kept her unregistered for a year'.[58] Roose eventually gave up and sailed his ship away. It would be another decade before anyone would break the mould with a successful roll-on, roll-off.

✺

Fascism is Here !

Protest !   Demand !   Act !

The POLICE under Holland's Instructions have occupied

LABOUR'S OWN HALL

This Concerns YOU ! ! !

No Freedom of Speech
        No Freedom of Assembly

Every N.Z. Worker MUST ACT NOW !

JOIN WATERSIDERS — SEAMEN
        MINERS, & OTHERS

Defend Peace - Living Standards - Liberty

Swell the Thousands at

**TRADES HALL, HOBSON ST.,
Wednesday Morning, 11th April**
Commencing 8 a.m.

Issued by Combined Trade Union Committee

Courtesy of the NZ Waterfront Workers Union, Auckland Branch

In 1951 the government suppressed free-speech rights to combat locked-out workers and their supporters. The language of this union-produced poster captures the intensity of the feelings of the day.

CHAPTER 6

The Second Revolution

1962-90

In just three decades, a two-pronged revolution — technological and political — turned the New Zealand maritime scene upside down. It had been a long time coming. The last major revolution had been in the mid 1880s when triple-expansion engines finally made steam competitive on the long route between New Zealand and Britain. Later changes had been more evolutionary than revolutionary. Even the 'Home boats' had grown little in 60 years. In 1907 Shaw, Savill & Albion's new *Arawa* was 9372 tons gross and made 14 knots. The New Zealand Shipping Company's *Tongariro* of 1967 was a little bigger (10,795 tons), a third faster at 20 knots, sported fancy new Hallen derricks and burned oil instead of coal, but an Edwardian seafarer would have recognised it readily enough. But would he have known what to make of the cellular container ship *Resolution Bay* when it emerged from a German shipyard just a decade later? Probably not. For a start, Overseas Containers Ltd's new ship was four times bigger (43,995 tons) and had no derricks, cranes or even masts worth mentioning. Despite its elephantine size and slab sides, the *Resolution Bay* made 23 knots: *Awatea* speed. It also performed differently. Instead of calling at any of the numerous New Zealand ports sending cargo 'Home' in 1907, it could call at just four and even there it had to use designated cellular container terminals. The *Resolution Bay* carried an even greater variety of goods than ever but our seafarer would not have known from looking, because everything was hidden inside those multi-coloured boxes. Nor would he have known that this ship would spend most of its working time at sea rather than alongside a wharf. Finally, he would have had no inkling of just how drastically those very boxes had transformed the entire inland distribution system. This really was revolution!

Preceding pages

The 19,145-ton *Columbus New Zealand* shows the uncluttered topsides of a modern container ship. Although the ship initially had its own gantry crane, once suitable port facilities were developed, ships relied entirely on shore-based gantry cranes.

Columbus Line New Zealand

In 1962 Railways Sailed the Ocean Blue

In 1962 one of the most important ships in New Zealand history arrived on the coast, an ungainly looking ship with a big door in its stern, the rail ferry *Aramoana*. Here was revolution shaped like a seagoing municipal bus! Before the *Aramoana* and its all-enveloping door showed up, inter-island commerce had entered from many points. As long as cargo had to be loaded in and out of ships' holds from railway wagons and trucks, it made as much sense for bagged flour to be loaded at, say, Oamaru, and taken to Napier for discharge as it did to rail it to Picton or Lyttelton to undergo the same laborious process. That all changed in 1962. The roll-on, roll-off (RO-RO) rail ferries let an Oamaru miller load a wagon at the mill and send that wagon straight through to Napier, reducing pilfering and damage, and saving time and money.

Above all, time. The handling of cargo in a conventional coaster was a time-consuming business. Taking into account delays caused by bad weather, shortage of labour, shortage of berths and occasional industrial trouble, it used to be considered that to load or discharge 300 tons was all that could be expected in an average day in port. Now Railways staff could load 30 rail wagons in an hour or two through the stern link span.[1] Virtually overnight, the *Aramoana* became the 'Pathway over the Sea', turning Cook Strait into a virtual extension of the main trunk railway and State Highway 1.

The *Aramoana* was 4160 tons gross and could carry 1050 tons DWT and 1150 passengers. Thirty-four rail wagons or a mix of wagons, trucks and buses could fit onto the spacious three-lane rail deck. A side span took 31 cars up to the upper vehicle garage.[2] Six English Electric diesels gave a service speed of 17 knots (19 knots maximum), cutting the crossing to three hours 20 minutes in all but the foulest of weather.[3] With twin screws, twin rudders, bow rudder and a bow thruster at his disposal, the master could turn the ship virtually in its own length.

There were, it must be said, a few teething problems. At Wellington someone had got the berth dimensions wrong and the ship was sent cruising around the harbour, ostensibly to test compasses, while workers hurriedly blasted away with gelignite and stared menacingly at over-inquisitive photographers. Things went no more smoothly at Picton, where the *Aramoana* hit the wharf while ferrying the Minister of Railways and 300 other VIPs.[4] To add insult to injury it backed into the berth flying its ensign upside down — the international signal of distress![5] Once the wrinkles were ironed out of the ship and the service, the *Aramoana*'s bookings defied the critics. The Railways needed 85,000 passengers, 20,000 cars and 100,000 tonnes of freight in its first year but got 207,000 passengers, 46,000 cars and about 181,000 tonnes of freight.[6] Other ferries followed: the *Aranui* (1966) and the cargo ferries *Arahanga* (1969) and *Aratika* (1972) converted to carry passengers. They ruled the route until the big 7583-ton, 19-knot *Arahura* replaced the *Aramoana* and *Aranui* in 1984.

With every crossing public enterprise undermined private un-enterprise. Those raised link spans were like giant steel fingers waved in the Union Company's face. Union had made the costliest decision in its history by announcing that it would withdraw the old Wellington–Picton ferry *Tamahine* in 1958. Within weeks the National Roads Board was investigating a vehicular service across Cook Strait. While the Cook Strait Transport Committee deliberated, the government subsidised Union to keep the '*Tam*' going until 1961. The committee's report recommended a 'modern drive-on drive-off car ferry . . . equipped with rails to carry rail wagons'.[7] Even at this eleventh hour the government would have preferred the Union Company run the service but it again refused.

The ferries soon became national institutions even though the headlines they generated were not always good. The book *Strikebound* wallows in the

Arrival of the 'Cook Strait Bridge'

The old method of loading vehicles aboard a ferry was time-consuming and nerve-wracking for vehicle owners. Here a car is being swung aboard the Union Company's Wellington-Lyttelton ferry *Rangatira*.

The stern door of the *Aramoana* offered speedier and safer ways of loading vehicles and rail wagons. The ship, flag-bedecked on its arrival, manoeuvres just off its berth.

negative aspects: demarcation disputes, bar scams, peep shows in the crews' quarters and even a steward spreading butter with his fingers because he was too lazy to find a knife.[8] Passengers took their chances with unappealing food items such as 'savoury mince', pies and curling sandwiches, 'handed over rather than served'.[9] Industrial relations between management (the Union Company until 1971, then Railways) and the unions were not always good, and unhappy travellers endured disputes that always seemed to coincide with school holidays and other peak periods. In fact, there was less strife than people thought. Over 97 per cent of cancellations came from weather and mechanical problems. From 1986 to 1991 only 557 of the 21,654 sailings were cancelled and just 378 of them were caused by industrial action.[10] In the mid 1990s, though, the Interislander Line took a harder line and forced through substantial crew and remuneration cuts and put the service on a 24-hour basis.

Change on the Coast

The Cook Strait ferries literally railroaded the shipping lines and the coastal ports. Their impact became much clearer after the *Aranui* entered service. By then Railways had upgraded its bulk goods services and was working with commercial freight forwarders. These firms 'canvassed for traffic, set the rail rates and conditions, collected the goods, loaded them onto rail, received them at the other end of the run, delivered them, collected the money and the handled the complaints'.[11] It is, however, important to distinguish between liner (general cargo) and bulk shipping. Little liner shipping survived apart from the inter-island ferries and a few RO-ROs, but the quantity of coastal cargo carried in bulk held up well. Coastal cargo figures, 6.2 million in and six million out in 1970, slipped 20 per cent to 4.9 million and 5.1 million respectively in 1980, but had recovered to 6.6 million and 6.8 million tonnes in 1991.

For ports reliant on coastal general cargo, the figures were sobering. First to close were river ports such as Blenheim and Kaiapoi. For decades small ships had been crossing the hazardous Wairau Bar and threading their way up the Opawa River around bends named 'Tughard' or 'Waterwheel' to tie up at the Blenheim wharf. In 1939 James Cowan had described the Queen of the Opawa, Captain Thomas Eckford's hold scow *Echo*, in these affectionate terms:

> *She makes three trips a week between Wellington and Blenheim. The farmer on the bank of the Wairau exchanges greetings with the little ship working up the broad river under engine power. Out with the cargo and general merchandise and in with cheese and fruit, farm produce, bacon on the hoof and eggs for the Wellington breakfast table, and the* Echo *is off under power for the Wairau Bar and the sea; then up with the sails for Cook*

Strait and maybe a stormy night.

Her morning entry into Wellington harbour is often in company with the smart express ferry liner from Lyttelton; but our eyes are for the sturdy little maid-of-all-work of the Strait, pushed along by a robust "butt-end of a sou'-wester" or making a leading wind of a squally northerly, and rounding to take up sail when close up on the berth. A rough and toilsome life for the good old craft; this is no soft and summery Hauraki.[12]

In 1965, however, Eckford called it quits, blaming fast ferries and slow Wellington wharfies.[13]

One small, traditional-style company, the Karamea Shipping Company, limped on until 1976 when the *Te Aroha* closed the story of the Cook Strait 'mosquito fleet'. 'Ringbolt' recorded his impressions of one of the last round trips between the Petone Wharf and Mapua. His hosts aboard the 1909-vintage trader were master Bob Walling, engineer Alan Livingstone, able seaman Nick Nicholson and deck boy Dale Weeks. There should have been another hand but seafarers no longer wanted to stand for a ship like the *Te Aroha*. Perhaps it was not surprising. Who wanted to start work at four in the morning and struggle away until eight at night? The ship had radar, radio and the other essentials but none of the featherbedding that obsessed newspaper editors. 'My bunk was with Nick, Ian and Dale in what was the original cabin down several steps through the former scuttle from the forward end of the mess room,' 'Ringbolt' wrote. 'Now it contained six bunks with a twin tier on either side'.[15] He fell asleep to the sound of the

The *Tawanui*, seen here at Wellington in 1971, typifies the conventional general cargo carriers built between the late 1940s and the early 1960s. It was an engines-aft ship and, like so many of this last generation, was built by a Dutch yard, J Bodewes of Hoogezand. The 891-ton motor coaster began working for the Northern Company in 1959 as a general cargo carrier but by the time the ship was sold in 1973 was largely carrying bulk grain cargoes from east coast South Island ports such as Oamaru.

M Berthold Collection, Alexander Turnbull Library F-24994-1/4-

Mosquito Fleet Survivors

William Brown built the 125-ton hold scow *Echo* at historic Te Kopuru on the Kaipara in 1905. In the course of a long and very eventful trading career, the *Echo* was involved in six collisions, caught fire twice and stranded about 15 times; the ship's wartime exploits reputedly inspired the American movie *The Wackiest Ship in the Navy*. The *Echo* served several owners in many trades but is best known for its 40 years with the Eckfords on the Wellington–Blenheim run.

Legend has it that the famous Totara North shipyard T M Lane & Son built the *Te Aroha* in 1909 from a single large kauri log. In its early days the Wairoa & Mohaka Steam Ship Company and then Richardson & Company of Napier used the *Te Aroha* to transport frozen meat from outports to the region's export ports. The ship is better remembered, however, for the nearly 50 years that it spent running across Cook Strait and to the West Coast.

The Union Company met the rail ferry threat with its own coastal RO-RO service, using the *Hawea* (right, 1967) and *Wanaka* (1970). These 16.5-knot ships were built in Hong Kong and were designed to handle the company's 'seafreighters': collapsible units that could be stowed two-high in the hold by forklifts. The 15-tonne crane on the after deck could handle larger containers and special items. Unfortunately shippers preferred the ubiquitous ISO container to the seafreighters and the high cost of running dedicated sea cargo terminals only added to the company's woes. It sold both ships in 1976.

engine. Next morning one slight bump and then another told them that they had crossed the Mapua bar and were on their way to the little wharf. 'It was 7.15, and outside in the half light the rain continued to bucket down . . . For all the crew lay ahead, after the rain had cleared, a hard day's work handling cargo'. When 'Ringbolt' returned to the *Te Aroha* that afternoon discharge had been completed, 'with Nick driving the winch, Dale manning the bull rope, the skipper topping lift as required, and Alan doing the unskilled work together with a few shore-side hands'. The return cargo of timber and pallets of lime had been swung aboard and it was time to go catch the tide at the Pass.[16] The *Te Aroha*'s engines roared into life, taking the little coaster out into the lumpy sea at its arthritic best speed (eight knots). In more ways than one, it was sailing into history.

The bigger steel coasters had also fallen victim to the same changes. As more and more cargo vanished beneath railway tarpaulins the Northern and Canterbury companies switched some of their ships to the bulk grain trades and the Holm Company sent its ships chasing work up in the Pacific Islands. These modern 1000-tonners should have served until the 1980s but their business was going elsewhere, to the Railways and to the new bulk cement carriers. John Holm and Ian McKay tried to fight back. In 1967 they ran the *Holmpark* between Lyttelton and Onehunga as a 'container' ship, using small non-ISO (International Standards Organisation) containers. On its first voyage it loaded 800 tonnes of cargo in nine hours but stiff competition from the rail ferries and Northern and Union Company RO-ROs killed it within a year. By then Holm's bankers were panicking. In desperation, Union put the Richardson and Canterbury fleets under his management in 1969. Holm complained about

G T Radcliffe Collection, Alexander Turnbull Library, F-22439-¼

having 'to preside over its decline and final end perhaps in a rather ignoble manner' but the losses escalated. In 1972 the Union Company absorbed the Holm, Canterbury and Richardson ships into its fleet.[17] Three years later only the *Holmdale* survived, running a subsidised service to the Chathams. The Northern Company had sold its fleet a year earlier. Two Anchor Company coasters lasted slightly longer, servicing the isolated West Coast.

The coastal lines tried a few tricks to retain at least some of their liner business. The Northern Company built a 1600-ton RO-RO, but the Auckland Harbour Board turned its *Seaway Princess* into an uneconomic toad by not providing a terminal at Onehunga. The Union Company also tried to fight back with coastal RO-ROs, starting with its Lyttelton-Wellington ferries. Union converted the *Maori* to a RO-RO vessel in 1965 and built a new running mate, the *Wahine* (8944 tons) in 1966. Then it was the turn of the cargo vessels. In 1967 the RO-RO *Hawea* entered the run between Auckland and South Island ports. It had a service speed of 16.5 knots and, like all Union Company RO-ROs, worked from its own 'Seacargo' terminals. From 1970 the slightly larger *Wanaka* gave Dunedin a weekly link to Auckland and Wellington. But in general the company's general cargo services failed to compete, especially after the Labour government froze rail charges as a regional development incentive.

But it was not all gloom. No one seemed to notice the bulkers, but they carried enormous quantities of freight as quickly and

The Union Company's historic Lyttelton-Wellington 'steamer express' service was another of the casualties of the 1970s. The 9387-ton *Rangatira* replaced the ill-fated *Wahine* and could carry 733 passengers and 200 cars. Its quiet turbo-electric engines gave a very high maximum speed of 22.5 knots. To no avail. Air competition and the rail ferries had already eroded much of the traffic even before the *Rangatira* entered service in 1972. It lasted barely two years under the Union Company flag before being handed over to the government to run under charter. Even the government had to admit defeat and in 1976 the ship left New Zealand. Here we see the *Rangatira* up on the Wellington floating dock. The Wellington Harbour Board's Voith-Schneider tugs *Kupe* and *Toia* are to the left and behind the dock is the rail freight ferry *Arahanga*.

Out of Westport

Capt. D Barnes

Milburn New Zealand's shallow-draught bulk cement carriers operate from Westport's challenging harbour and make about 300 port calls a year around the country. The *Westport* (above, 1976) can carry about 3750 tonnes of cement. The bigger *Milburn Carrier II* (below 1987) can carry 7,800 tonnes. Specialist pneumatic cargo handling gear lets them discharge between 100 and 300 tonnes per hour.

Capt. D Barnes

efficiently as the more glamorous RO-ROs. Bagged cement had formed up to a quarter of some coasters' business and the lines felt the pain when the companies built their own bulk carriers. Their early ships looked like traditional coasters but from the early 1970s the cement companies built a new type of ship. New Zealand Cement Holdings' (now Milburn New Zealand) pair *Milburn Carrier* (1972) and *Westport* (1976) set the pattern: 2600-tons, 95 metres long, and able to carry about 4000 tonnes of cement in bulk. Oil tankers got bigger, too. After the Marsden Point oil refinery opened in 1965 the distribution chain changed completely. The 12,778-ton *Athelviscount*, as big as the foreign tankers that used to call direct at the ports, replaced the little 3000-ton coastal tankers *Maurea* and *Tanea*. Then came the *Hamilton*, *Erne*, the sisters *Kotuku* and *Kuaka* and the *Amokura*. By the time the Union Company's 21,187-ton *Taiko* entered service in 1984 four big black-hulled ships were shuttling black gold around the coast. That year, the coastal LPG tanker *Tarihiko* also entered service.

Union Company Short-Sea Routes

The Union Company's Pacific Islands services also faded out around this time. In 1973, nearly a century of Union Company Island passenger services ended when the *Tofua* berthed at Auckland for the last time. Travellers now preferred to fly. The Union Company chartered a small container/RO-RO ship, but it was fighting a losing battle. It was unpopular with island nations keen on crewing their own ships and, in any case, the small, seasonal cargo flows did not suit large, modern ships. Island traders, often old ships diverted from other trades, came and went but two lines now inherited most of the trade to the Islands: Sofrana Unilines, which had been trading from New Zealand since the late 1960s and the new regionally owned Pacific Forum Line, which started in 1978.[18]

By then the Union Company was finally free of P&O. It is hard not to see its long stewardship as dreary and limiting, with P&O acting like a Victorian parent, dosing its antipodean bairn with the entrepreneurial equivalent of laudanum. As the 1960s drew to a close, though, P&O's need to free up capital to reinvest in the new deepwater container trades produced a sale to Tasman Union Ltd, a 50:50 partnership between Australian and New Zealand interests. After taking over on 1 January 1972, the new owners rejuvenated the fleet, chartering in RO-ROs and Japanese-built mini bulk carriers to replace the obsolescent 'slow greens'. Ship buffs, usually employers, or at least their office wallahs, lamented the passing of the old ships, but Gerry Evans, a unionist, had little good to say about the last days of the conventional fleet. 'The low-paid conventional ships, referred to as "slow greens", were a different case,' he said. 'Very often they had a different crew every trip. Compo soared as men, sent from the roster, went on compo to get out of doing the voyage. There were enough drugs available on those ships to supply the

Livingstone Productions

In 1982 Brooke McKenzie's Pacifica Shipping Company revived the old Union Company Wellington–Lyttelton route. By 1983–84, in moves reminiscent of its early 20th century practices, Union had secretly acquired a controlling interest in Pacifica. Since 1985 the company has been owned by the Dunedin-based Skeggs Group. Pacifica operates other routes but since 1985 the 1599-ton, 1977-built RO-RO *Spirit of Competition* has linked Wellington and Lyttelton. This Lyttelton photo shows the stern door that characterises RO-RO vessels. The coastal tanker *Kakariki* is in the background.

needs of a rock-and-roll concert audience'.[19] To some observers, though, it seemed like a slaughter. In 1975, its centenary year, the Union Company and its subsidiaries disposed of an astonishing 19 ships. It was hard, though, not to notice their replacements. In 1976-77 Union introduced the mainstay of its new trans-Tasman service, the *Union Rotorua* and the *Union Rotoiti*. They were unlike anything that had worked the Tasman before. Huge — 23,000 tons gross and 204 metres long — and fast — 20 knots, from marine gas turbines — they had port-side quarter ramps and a (seldom-used) bow ramp.

Yet not even they could retain Union's market share. In 1978 Waitaki-NZR took control of Maritime Carriers New Zealand Ltd and entered the Tasman with a couple of mini bulk carriers, the *Dunedin* and *Waitaki*. The small, self-sustaining container ship *Totara* followed later but stiff competition and a recession drove Maritime Carriers to the wall in November 1982.[20] The Union Company really only had itself to blame for the creation of Forestry Shippers Ltd. Major customer Tasman Pulp & Paper had complained about newsprint stowage in its crane ships and eventually it commissioned two 8500 DWT specialist pulp and paper carriers, the *Tasman Enterprise* and *Tasman*

Venture, in 1977. The Union Company had to settle for managing them.

But the Union Company took its biggest drubbing in the trans-Tasman container trades, where the signing of a closer economic relations (CER) agreement between Australia and New Zealand heightened interest in the route. In 1983 the Australian National Line and the New Zealand Shipping Corporation started their new 'Tranztas' service.[21] Soon, though, they found themselves working with the Union Company against another box carrier, the Tasman Express Line. Owned jointly by three New Zealand companies (Geo H Scales, McKay Shipping and Refrigerated Freight Lines) and Australian firm Hetherington Kingsbury Ltd,[22] TEL chartered two small 200-TEU self-sustaining container ships, the *Auckland Express* and *Canterbury Express*. They made just 13 knots, but could bypass costly and congested Auckland for Onehunga. Big ships still offered economies of scale but TEL's regular 10-day schedule appealed to businesses making the change to 'just-in-time' purchasing. TEL captured a respectable share of the box trade by cutting rates, cutting corners and running a spirited advertising campaign.

Box Boats and Bulk Carriers

By the 1960s the conventional cargo ship had reached the end of its economic potential. Bulbous bows and fine lines gave them speeds of 20–21 knots, about the same as the passenger liners of a decade earlier. Data logging equipment, mechanically operated hatch covers and holds designed for forklift operations all increased their efficiency. So did faster, heavier capacity Stulcken or Hallen derricks. But the fundamental problem remained. Most cargo still went from the factory or freezing works into a harbour board shed. From there it was taken to the wharf, loaded into slings and then loaded, item by item, by watersiders. Bad weather could halt everything. Ironically, the latest generation of fast, expensive Conference Lines ships was tied up in port for just as long as their slower, simpler predecessors. Ships spent half of their time tied to a wharf, held there by unproductive work practices, poor management, bad weather, congested sheds or by shortages of rail wagons or trucks. 'It was a groddly inefficient and extraordinarily costly system.'[23]

It was the same everywhere. Using inflation-adjusted figures, the cost of loading a tonne of cargo in London, £100 in 1870, had risen from £468 in 1950, to £737 in 1960 and would soar to £1989 by 1970. In 100 years the time taken to turn around a cargo liner had not changed much, about four to six weeks. Better cranes and larger hatch openings helped, but even with them the real cost of loading and unloading a ship had risen 16-fold in a century and would treble in the inflationary 1960s alone. An American study showed that between 60 and 70 per cent of the sea transport costs of a ship accumulated in port.[24]

Containers

Containers soon spread from the cellular terminals, as these recent photos from Bluff show.

Southport Ltd

The solution came from thinking outside the square, although in this instance a steel rectangle provided the answer. The father of the modern container was American trucker Malcolm McLean, who loaded 58 trailer units onto the deck of a converted wartime freighter in 1956. McLean's containers were not the same size as today's all-conquering International Standards Organisation (ISO) box, but the sight of his shipping line, Sea-Land, running 236-container capacity ships fitted with their own cranes sparked interest. So, too, did the container enterprises of another American line, the Matson Navigation Co.[25]

McLean's trucking background was not coincidental, because that lightweight, cost-efficient container with a lift capacity of 10:1 poised to conquer the waves was born on the American freeways. The limits imposed on American road carriers of the day set the dimensions of the ISO box: a 20ft x 8ft x 8ft 6in (6.1 x 2.4 x 2.6 m) general purpose steel container, weighing about 2.3 tonnes and capable of carrying about 21.7 tonnes of freight. Joined by its longer companion, the 40-footer, the '20-footer' has become so ubiquitous that the shipping industry refers to a ship's earning power in terms of its container-carrying capacity as much as its gross tonnage or deadweight. TEU ('Twenty Equivalent Unit') and FEU ('Forty Equivalent Unit') entered the transport lexicon. The boxes have proved remarkably adaptable. The container range now also includes open-top boxes, hard-tops, ventilated, insulated and reefer (refrigerated) containers as well as bulk and tank containers (for liquid chemicals). The container's greatest virtue was its simplicity and universality, underlined by the term 'unitisation'. By housing mixes of different sized and shaped cargo, it could be packed and unpacked far from the ship's side, where both space and labour were expensive. LCLs ('Less than Container Load') are still packed and unpacked at portside terminals, but FCL ('Full Container Load') cargo can be processed anywhere.

These boxes also let naval architects rethink what a ship should look like. Until then the limit of ship growth had been economic rather than physical. Practical economic considerations restricted a conventional general cargo liner to about 14,000 DWT. So long as the handling of general cargo moved slowly, and each part of the varied cargo required its own handling, the cost of the time spent in port offset the economies of size made at sea. RO-RO and cellular container systems finally solved the problem that defeated the conventional stowage of cargo in large, multi-deck ships. Not all container ships are cellular, and containers are carried by a variety of ships, but in mature liner trades they predominate. In cellular ships container guide cells permit containers to be piled on top of each other. High-speed heavy lift cranes lift them on and off so rapidly that shipping lines can order general cargo carriers as big as bulk carriers. The cellular vessels built for the New Zealand run in the mid 1970s were about 42–45,000 grt, 248 metres long, 32 metres wide and drew about 12 metres.

The sheer scale of investment in ships, containers and associated support facilities exceeded the resources of most individual shipping lines. The British lines therefore formed consortia, of which Overseas Container Lines (OCL) and Associated Container Transportation (Australasia) Ltd (ACT) were the early leaders. OCL started in 1965, merging the resources of P&O (New Zealand Shipping and Federal's parent), Ocean Transport & Trading Ltd, British & Commonwealth Shipping Co. Ltd and Furness Withy & Co. Ltd (Shaw Savill's parent). They had about 60 per cent of the UK liner trades. ACT, uncharitably termed 'the odds and sods' of British shipping, drew on most of the remaining liner companies.[26] ACT's Australasian services combined the resources of the Blue Star Line, Cunard (Port Line) and Ellerman. OCL's first ships were the 'Encounter Bay'-class, *Encounter Bay*, *Botany Bay*, *Moreton Bay*, *Flinders Bay* and *Jervis Bay*, all about 27,000 tons. ACT chose to name its ships 'in the manner of suburban buses or railway wagons'.[27] The ACTs *1-3* entered service in 1969 and ACTs *4*, *5* and *6*, in 1971–72.

The container revolution washed over the ports. The Conference Lines had always said that New Zealand had too many for a country its size but just about every port with an overseas trade surveyed and lobbied. Northland dreamed of using coastal feeder ships to transport boxes to its deep-water berths.[28] In 1967, however, the British Conference Lines published the findings of the 'Molyneux Committee' on containerising the New Zealand trade. Reflecting a caution expressed by the committee members' belief that 'container cargo operation might look good, but so does the mini skirt', the committee recommended a four-ship service, to begin in 1973. Conventional ships would handle South Island exports through the all-weather mechanical meat loaders at Timaru and Bluff. The Auckland and Wellington harbour boards were building expensive new facilities to meet the Molyneux timetable when the Lines dropped a bombshell in May 1971. Perfidious Albion cancelled its container plans. Neither Shaw Savill nor the Port Line could afford to proceed, so the Lines decided to eke a few more years' profits from their conventional ships.

In fact, the Conference Lines could not put the genie back in the bottle. Others were moving in, led by the German Columbus Line, which sidestepped port politics by fitting gantry cranes to the three ships in its new service between Australian, New Zealand (Auckland, Wellington, Port Chalmers) and North American ports. In June 1971 the 19,145-ton *Columbus New Zealand* opened the container era for New Zealand. Ten thousand Wellingtonians went down to the wharf to watch. The ship had a large number of empty containers to deliver, but the statistics showed what container ships could do. In eight days the *Columbus New Zealand* worked 9775 tons of cargo, something a conventional ship would have taken 35 days to do.[29] ACT then announced that it would enter the New Zealand-United Kingdom trade in partnership with the Australian National Line. In September 1972 the *ACT 1* took the first containers 'Home'.

There now followed two unseemly scrambles, the first by the Conference Lines to containerise trade, and the second to become the South Island's sole container port. Lyttelton, Timaru, Otago and Southland all lobbied hard but in December 1974 the New Zealand Ports Authority — which controlled capital expenditure at the ports — announced that Lyttelton and Otago would split the calls between them. Otago appealed to Minister of Transport, Sir Basil Arthur. He dithered and the insults and statistics flew while Arthur wobbled nervously towards making his election-year decision. Port Chalmers (two cranes) would join Lyttelton (one crane) as a South Island container terminal.[30] They now had just 18 months to prepare for the full containerisation of the UK trade. The Conference Lines had just ordered six big 42–44,000-ton ships, supplemented by the earlier *Remuera* and calls from the *Encounter Bay ACT 1-6* and French, Italian, German and Japanese ships. A new 'Great Fleet' was bearing down on New Zealand.

Containers changed the entire transport system, making the sea and the land legs of every journey nearly seamless. At the ports themselves the harbour boards deepened navigation channels, widened swinging basins and created large areas of back-up space for cargo pre-assembly; container ships are too expensive to be kept waiting for cargo to dribble into the berth. Giant cranes capable of lifting 40–55-tonnes towered over the new heavy-duty berths. Elsewhere the Railways replaced conventional box wagons with flat-top container-class units, upgraded tracks, bridges and tunnels and built container-handling facilities at its depots. Road transport operators also invested heavily and container storage parks and washing facilities appeared. New customs procedures had to be devised and sophisticated computer systems developed to track container movements throughout the journey cycle.

Unitisation axed the Conference Lines' conventional ships, often long before the end of their working lives, and also extinguished the lines themselves. In 1971 P&O absorbed the historic New Zealand Shipping Company and Federal into its General Cargo Division. Blue Star, Port Line and Shaw Savill kept their identities a little longer, but only Blue Star retained any significant presence in New Zealand under its own identity. In just two short years, between 1977 and 1979, virtually all their conventional ships were scrapped, sold or diverted to other routes.

They did at least outlast the passenger liners. The Shipping Company withdrew its last *Rangi*s in 1968–69, beaten by air competition and strikes. Shaw Savill's pure-passenger liners *Southern Cross* and *Northern Star* were less affected by cargo-handling disputes and it even briefly added three ships, the *Akaroa*, *Aranda* and *Arawa*, but, almost overnight, the 80-year-old 'rite of passage', sailing to and from Britain in a British passenger liner, was over. No more crowds on the wharf, no bands playing 'Now is the Hour', no more parting streamers. A few European-flag ships hung on a little longer, but aircraft had won and the country's overseas passenger terminals languished for another decade until the cruising boom began to send ships to New Zealand over the summer months.

The other side of the transport revolution was the bulk carriage of cargo. Bulk carriers replaced conventional tramp ships and took many forms: general-purpose bulkers, log, chip and car carriers and even 'conbulkers', combination container ships and bulk carriers. The busiest bulkers were the ones used to carry away the products from the vast forests planted from the 1930s onwards. Mount Maunganui exported the greatest quantity of forest products, but Nelson, Southland, Otago and other ports soon found themselves handling logs, wood chips and other cargo. At first the ships were small, but, as the trade developed, they got bigger and more specialised. At Mount Maunganui, Nelson and Otago, monstrous wood-chip carriers could be seen sucking up chips from vast chip mountains. The 1980s closed with many ports planning for huge future throughputs.

In fact many secondary ports now accommodated ships the size of cellular container ships. The traditional UK–NZ liner trade had dominated the thinking of the Molyneux Committee and of the government planning teams. But that was changing as Britain's entry into the European Economic Community (EEC, later EC) became an inevitability. As trade diversification gathered pace from the late 1970s European lines such as Nedlloyd, Jebsen and

Wilhelmsen sent ever larger ships, creating welcome business for secondary ports still smarting from losing the European trade. Fortunately for Napier, Timaru and Southland, developing markets such as the Middle East and South East Asia still used conventional ships for meat, dairy and horticultural trade. The new multi-purpose ships came in two basic types. Jebsen, Gearbulk and New Zealand Unit Express used bulk-carrier-types carrying heavy deck or gantry cranes. Nedlloyd, Scancarriers and the Baltic Shipping Company favoured massive quarter-ramp RO-ROs.

Local Lines Try and Fail

These lines were all foreign-owned. New Zealand ships disappeared from the bluewater trades after the Union Company withdrew from the North American and South East Asian runs in the late 1960s. But from time to time local mavericks would try their hand. The most colourful was Robert Owens, the Tauranga shipping agent and all-round entrepreneur.[31] In 1969 he announced his plans to run a refrigerated cargo liner between New Zealand and Japan. His New Zealand Sea Transport Ltd renamed a 4670-ton freighter *Aotearoa* but although Owens also talked about a 24,000-ton bulk carrier, 'the *Aotearoa* saga' haemorrhaged money, caught between the Scylla of high costs and the Charybdis of a freight war. Owens withdrew the ship in late 1972.[32]

Owens was small beer compared to the rise and fall of the State-owned Shipping Corporation of New Zealand Ltd. Perhaps its sickly growth and early demise owed something to the incompatible gene pool from which it sprang. Farmers and maritime trade unions, two groups that seldom agreed on anything, had been calling for this national line for a long time. By the 1960s it was fashionable in the era of UNCTAD (United Nations Conference on Trade and Development) codes of conduct for conferences of 40-40-20 formulae for freight sharing between trading partners and cross-traders. The Labour government elected in 1972 bought two 12,200-ton conventional freighters, which became the *NZ Waitangi* and *NZ Aorangi*. The Corporation also ran in the coastal trans-Tasman, Island and Caribbean trades, but the European run was its priority and in 1978 it commissioned a giant container ship, the *New Zealand Pacific*, for the route. Nicknamed the 'Clockwork Orange' because of its bright orange hull, the 42,276-ton *New Zealand Pacific* was the largest ship yet registered in New Zealand. But from this highpoint it was all downhill. The Corporation's profitability suffered from its being undercapitalised and from being treated as an instrument of trade development rather than a straight business venture.[33] When a policy U-turn produced demands to sell the loss-making line, its new board started cost cutting to enhance its sale value. Most ships had gone already when the

Tugs Become Water Tractors

The flared bows and bulbous bows of the big bulk carriers and container ships forced every New Zealand port to re-equip its towage fleets. The British-built 502-ton tug *Otago* (above) typified the classic oceangoing salvage tug, with its tall masts and bulky superstructure. The Whangarei-built 304-ton Voith-Schneider 'water tractor' *Toia* (below, 1972), in contrast, had a stubby, compact hull and superstructure set back from the sides, permitting the *Toia* to get to grips with its customers. Powerful 2700 BHP English Electric engines worked a revolutionary Voith-Schneider unit that enabled the *Toia* to move in any direction, even backwards.

Corporation 'sold' the *New Zealand Pacific* and the *Forum New Zealand II* (renamed *Tui* and *Weka* briefly) at sea and imposed new crewing levels and conditions. The Labour Court called this 'a device or a sham or a façade',[34] but, while the Corporation removed the bogus names from its ships, it pushed the sale through. Early in 1989 it sold the national flag carrier to ACT New Zealand Ltd.

The British victory was more complete than many people thought. Some years earlier they had used the advent of the Shipping Corporation as the excuse to toss Geo H Scales out of the wool trade. Scales never really accepted this and in 1986 the 'shipping line without ships' entered a new consortium called NZ-Euro Line Ltd. The 6638-ton, slow *Geo H Scales* generated little support and NZ-Euro foundered when the established lines (which now included ABC Container Line, having entered the European trade in 1979, shaking but not quite breaking the Conference Lines' arrangements) slashed box rates. Scales withdrew it in October 1987 but threw good money after bad in a reconstituted venture, which also failed.[35] Now, as ever, the Conference did not welcome gatecrashers.

Harbour Craft and Shipbuilding

The big bulk carriers and container ships forced the harbour boards to upgrade their ship-handling services. Many had got away without full-size tugs. In 1965 even the major ports — Marsden Point excepted — had comparatively few large, modern vessels. The new tugs built from the late 1960s onwards were completely different. Above water they dispensed with tall masts, funnels and superstructures to get in right under the flared bows and sterns of the big freighters. But the biggest changes occurred below water. In the popular Voith-Schneider 'water tractor', four-bladed units mounted in a cage-like propeller guard directly beneath the bridge replaced propellers and rudders. At the stern a skeg keel replaced the rudder. Voiths such as Auckland's *Te Awhina* could turn in their own length and change the angle and direction of their pull effortlessly. Wellington office workers soon grew used seeing one of the port's 'big reds', *Toia*, *Kupe* and *Ngahue*, moving backwards behind a big box boat. Wheelhouses now offered nearly all-round visibility. Tugs' hulls still have a bow and stern, but in practice there is no 'front' and 'back' when working a ship this way. And, though they may have looked smaller than the conventional boats of the 1950s, the new tugs were very powerful. Otago's 205-ton Schottel tug *Rangi*, for example, had a bollard pull of 30 tonnes, compared to the 502-ton *Otago*'s 20 tonnes.

Local shipbuilders did well out of these tugs. Since the war they had built little more than small tugs, barges, fishing boats and yachts. They won few orders for trading vessels, although Auckland's Masons set a New Zealand record in 1961 with the 621-ton Stewart Island ferry *Wairua*. Later that decade, however, an injection of American capital turned the Whangarei Engineering and Construction Ltd (WECO) into the country's busiest shipyard.[36] WECO built many tugs, starting in 1967-68 with the Voith Schneiders *Rotorua*, *Te Awhina* and *Hauroko* for the Tauranga, Auckland and Southland Harbour Boards. Its more interesting jobs included the 916-ton Westport dredge *Kawatiri*, navy launches and a full-size replica of Captain Bligh's sailing ship, *HMS Bounty*, for a film company. Down in Otago, Sims Engineering Ltd bought the old Port Chalmers yards. At its peak in the mid 1980s, Sims built Taranaki's 283-ton tug *Rupe* and the 1056-ton dredge *New Era* for the Otago Harbour Board. Government tariff policies sheltered the yards, but, even so, they did not always get things their way. When the Otago Harbour Board rejected local prices for new tugs in the mid 1970s, it surprised everyone by building its own. It was 'a funny thing for a local body to take on', shipbuilder Ted Sims remarked, but the tug project worked. Board staff built the *Rangi* and *Karetai* upside down, turned over the completed hulls and launched them sideways from an improvised building berth.[37]

The Auckland mosquito fleet also provided a good base for local shipyards. Like the Cook Strait mosquito fleet, Auckland's had also been buffeted by competition from land transport and by the unit load revolution, but the northern trade proved more resilient. The last motorised scows bowed out, but several small fleets — McCallums, Parry Brothers and Winstones, supplemented by the Julian family enterprises — kept busy carting sand and gravel to feed Auckland's insatiable appetite for building materials.[38] As the old scows wore out, small tugs and purpose-built barges took their place. From the 1980s, Sea-Tow Ltd, Parrys' successor, would build bigger tugs and barges and branch out into coastal trading, hauling coal, timber and specialised equipment all around the coast. Passenger traffic also surged as lifestylers and tourists discovered the delights of the Hauraki Gulf islands. Both the newly renamed Gulf Ferries and the Subritzky Shipping Line put on new ships, Gulf Ferries concentrating on high-speed catamarans and Subritzky on ramped vehicular barges. The biggest and flashiest of all was the 33-metre, 33-knot *Quick Cat*, which began running in 1987. The fast catamarans now enabled Waiheke residents to commute across the water in 30 minutes, less time than many Auckland dwellers spent in their cars and buses.[39]

Sail Training and Recreation

Perhaps the most influential of all the craft launched during these years were the two *Spirit of New Zealand* sail training ships. In the 1970s several navies operated sail training craft but few countries could gave civilians the chance to experience life under sail. Auckland industrialist Lou Fisher admired the

Spirit of New Zealand

Since 1973 the Spirit of Adventure Trust's 'adventure voyaging ships' have become familiar sights in New Zealand ports. Although there are also special voyages, the mainstay of the Spirit of New Zealand's programmes are the 15–19-year-olds shown in the upper photograph talking to *Captain's Log* host Peter Elliott in 2001. The 184-ton barquentine *Spirit of New Zealand* can carry up to 12 crew and 42 trainees. The Gardner engine gives a speed of nine knots, five less than the vessel's best performance under sail

work being done by the new British schooners *Sir Winston Churchill* and *Malcolm Miller* and decided that New Zealand needed a ship of its own. He charmed, begged and cajoled successfully and the project grew from a maxi yacht to the graceful 84-ton topsail schooner *Spirit of Adventure* that slid down the ways at Vos & Brijs's Auckland yard in December 1973. Thirteen years later the Spirit of Adventure Trust took delivery of the bigger (184-ton), black-hulled barquentine *Spirit of New Zealand.* As the years went by the *Spirits* became familiar sights throughout the country as the Trust went about its task 'to provide equal opportunities for young persons to develop qualities of leadership and independence and to acquire a knowledge of ships and the sea, and to assist young persons to foster a community spirit and develop their responsibilities as junior citizens'.[40]

The big *Spirits* weaved their way in and out of a proliferation of yachts and launches. Boating had boomed from the late 1960s as New Zealanders rode the wave of an unprecedented period of prosperity. Although New Zealanders took to the water all around the country, the boating phenomenon was most obvious in Auckland, where the huge Westhaven Marina resembled a marine version of a supermarket car park, with hundreds of yachts crowding together in one of the world's biggest marinas. In the early 1970s it was said that a new boat more than eight metres long was being launched on the Waitemata every day. As fibreglass and then aluminium replaced traditional sheet ply, the proportion of home-built boats shrank.

Courtesy of Jim Gilpin

Of course, most young sailors got their sea legs in smaller, privately owned boats. One of the more popular was the 'Tauranga' or 'P' class, invented by Harry Highet at Whangarei and popularised by the Tauranga Yacht and Power Boat Club. Here Highet poses with Jim Gilpin, winner of the Tanner Cup three years in a row, 1951–53.

Professional boat builders stepped up their production lines, turning out large numbers of yachts from moulds, everything from the little P-class dinghies to large keelers. Although most messing about in boats was done in small P-class dinghies or Trailer Sailers, the bigger ocean-racing craft increasingly captured the public imagination. When Chris Bouzaid won the One Ton Cup in 1969 with the *Rainbow II*, the cup defence two years later in Auckland gave the city its first taste of hosting an international yachting event. In the heady days of the 1980s unprecedented numbers of New Zealanders followed the progress of skippers such as Peter Blake and Digby Taylor in the Whitbread Round the World Race. Yachtsmen were getting the kind of status normally reserved for All Black stars.

A Sea Change in Public Policy

After years of buying or borrowing Royal Navy ships, the RNZN built new from the early 1960s. The Type 12 'Rothesay'-class frigates were the first of its 'nuclear age' anti-submarine frigates. *Otago* and *Taranaki* commissioned in 1960–61. Of the latest British design, they mounted a twin 4.5 inch turret, carried two anti-submarine mortars and were fitted for the new 'Seacat' short-range anti-aircraft missile system. They served until the early 1980s. *Otago* became famous when the Labour government sent it to Mururoa Atoll to protest against French atmospheric bomb testing.

By the middle of the 1960s the Royal New Zealand Navy had replaced its last major war-built warships. The largest one, the cruiser HMNZS *Royalist*, broke down in the Pacific in 1965 under highly embarrassing circumstances. The navy bought new British frigates, the 'Rothesay'-class HMNZS *Otago* and *Taranaki* (1961–62) and the 'Leander'-class HMNZS *Waikato* (1966) and HMNZS *Canterbury* (1971). The 'Leanders' introduced helicopters into the navy, but by the time *Canterbury* joined the fleet, structural problems in the New Zealand economy were making themselves felt. In 1982–83 the 'Rothesays' had to be replaced by second-hand 'Leanders', one, HMNZS *Southland*, barely two years younger than *Otago*. Block obsolescence now loomed. It was the same with other ships. In the mid 1970s the navy got four fast patrol boats that were too small to do the job properly. For its new survey ship it spent a fortune on converting the government's redundant Cook Islands freighter *Moana Roa* into HMNZS *Monowai*. The one bright note was the new fleet tanker, HMNZS *Endeavour*, in 1988.

The navy did, however, become more visible as an instrument of State policy as New Zealand exerted its independence more strongly. The direction,

RNZN Official

it must be admitted, was not always consistent. New Zealand crewed a couple of British minesweepers in the Indonesian Confrontation during the 1960s, and 20 years later Prime Minister Robert Muldoon, alone of the Commonwealth leaders, sent a frigate into the Indian Ocean to release a Royal Navy ship for Falklands War service. But the trend was away from snuggling up against the superpowers and towards using the navy to support New Zealand's anti-nuclear policies. Ironically, New Zealand, which had earlier in the century been reluctant to follow Australia's example of creating an independent navy, was now pursuing a more independent foreign policy stance than its trans-Tasman neighbour.

In 1988 the RNZN received its first purpose-built replenishment oiler, the South Korean-built HMNZS *Endeavour*. The 12,390 (full-load) tanker restored an operational flexibility missing since the withdrawal of the last *Endeavour* in 1971. The new ship has a crew of 11 officers and 39 enlisted personnel, can carry two 20-mm AA and embarks a helicopter.

Yachties and small boat owners had been protesting against French nuclear testing in the Pacific, but in 1973 Prime Minister Norman Kirk sent HMNZS *Otago* to Mururoa Atoll to show our abhorrence of French testing.[41] In the 1990s HMNZS *Tui* also went there. The 1984 Labour government declared the country nuclear-free, delighting those who had been demonstrating against port visits by nuclear propelled or nuclear weapons-capable warships. Such displays of post-colonial wilfulness came at a price, though. The Americans stopped sharing some intelligence traffic but the French went further, sabotaging the Greenpeace protest ship, *Rainbow Warrior*. Just after midnight on 10 July 1985 underwater charges rocked the Auckland

RNZN Official

WECO built the inshore patrol craft *Wakakura*, *Hinau*, *Moa* and *Kiwi*. The Royal New Zealand Navy Volunteer Reserve uses them to undertake its two main tasks, mine countermeasures and the wartime direction of merchant shipping. The IPCs operate as 'Q-route' (cleared passage) mine survey boats at the main centres. Here is the Auckland launch, *Hinau*. They are 92 tons light, 26.8 metres long, make 12 knots and have a crew of five officers and 13 enlisted personnel.

waterfront, blasting two holes in the *Rainbow Warrior*'s hull. It sank alongside Marsden Wharf, killing a crewman.[42]

Labour was also rocking boats. In keeping with its leaders' libertarian beliefs, it rolled back the State, selling the Shipping Corporation and shaking up central and local government institutions. It dismembered the large Ministry of Transport into separate air, land and maritime transport agencies and separated policy provision from service delivery. In 1985 the Ministry's Stewart Island ferry *Wairua* made its last sailing, to be replaced by a privately run launch and an old oyster dredge.[43] In 1987 the Manukau Institute of Technology took over the Auckland navigation school and in 1988 the MOT stopped running the port of Westport. The Maritime Safety Authority inherited most of its remaining maritime services — ship inspection and registration, pollution prevention and lighthouses. There was a blaze of publicity in 1990 when the last lighthouse keepers moved out of their accommodation.[44] From Cape Reinga in the north to Puysegur Point in the south, New Zealand's 23 lighthouses and 73 light beacons are now all automated.

But the greatest changes occurred locally. Here the harbour boards, symbols of parochial pride since colonial days, were swept away in transport and labour market reforms. It began with an influential Ministry of Transport study of 'onshore costs', commissioned by National, which Transport Minister Richard Prebble released in 1984.[45] It recommended sweeping changes to port management and labour practices. Prebble preached the gospel of economic libertarianism with the fanaticism of a convert. Delegates to the Harbour Association's annual conference listened spell-bound while he set out the new dogma. Commercial port activity would be transferred to publicly owned port companies, which had to operate commercially. The new regional councils would keep broader harbour and waterways administration.

The Port Companies Act 1988 axed the New Zealand Ports Authority and harbour boards and replaced them with 13 port companies, which were told to make their own decisions.[46] At first the public noticed little change. The Otago Harbour Board, for example, became Port Otago Ltd and Auckland's company was Ports of Auckland Ltd. But behind the wharf gates things did happen. Prebble's reformation also stripped the lead from the abbey roofs, in this case the gold braid, rigidities and the overcapitalisation of the old regimes. Lyttelton and Wellington cut back heavily on tugs, dredges, floating cranes and launches. The new port companies made mistakes — Wellington's use of helicopters for pilot transfers and Ports of Auckland's placing an overweight crane on Bledisloe Wharf — but they could be corrected. Overall, cargo moved quicker and more cheaply.

Then, in 1989, the government reformed the waterfront labour system. Out went the Waterfront Industry Commission, which had overseen the labour pool system since the Second World War, and in came direct employment and enterprise bargaining. Shipowners and shippers were elated, trade unionists horrified. Thousands of harbour board and watersider jobs vanished. The Wellington Harbour Board, for example, had employed 490 people in 1987 but the Port of Wellington had just 125 in 1992. Watersider numbers had been falling because of unitisation, from about 7000 in 1970 to 5000 in 1984. Four years later there were just 1850.[47] As with any revolution, there were winners and losers. Port Nelson Ltd (fined, ironically, in 1996 for anti-competitive practices against Tasman Bay Maritime Pilots Ltd)[48] was a happy winner. Stevedoring charges for one cargo type fell by 75 per cent, it boasted, and in the new flexible environment, 'you will see our female office staff on ships' line gangs, tug crews, tally clerks on cargo work and even humping apples in the hold'.[49] Many of the workers given the hump were less ecstatic. The high unemployment figures of the 1980s and the 1990s proved that the theory that capital and labour freed up by structural change would find more productive uses elsewhere did not always work for the human side of the ledger. Picket lines appeared at the gates and 1990 began, as 1890 had, with unrest on the waterfront.

✸

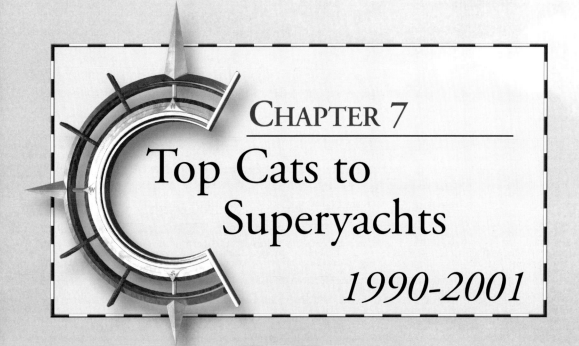

CHAPTER 7

Top Cats to Superyachts

1990-2001

Two things dominated the last decade of the 20th century at sea: speed and challenge. For most New Zealanders they were exemplified by the long campaign to take and then defend the America's Cup, and the Cook Strait 'fast ferry wars'. For five years the high-tech catamarans and wave-piercers enlivened things for shipping companies, travellers, Sounds residents and creditors alike. Crossing Cook Strait will never be the same again. More quietly behind the scenes, though, the new port companies started competing more aggressively for shipping business and building inland 'dry ports' to capture business from ports hundreds of miles away. As far as the shipping lines were concerned, it was all change on the short sea routes and a reassertion of traditional control in the deepwater ones. Without the protection afforded by the Tasman trade union accord, the Union Company, already losing market share to Australasian competitors, joined other New Zealand liner companies in selling out to foreign interests. On the historic European trade, now accounting for a diminishing but still significant share of the country's overseas trade, P&O, the old 'flag-bearer of imperialism' took an increased share of the business.

Fast Cats on Cook Strait

Preceding pages

Tugs and barges grew in size and numbers from the 1980s onwards. The biggest operator is Sea-Tow Ltd, which developed the old Parry Bros business into inter-island trading. This photograph shows its tug *Sea-Tow 21* and barge *Sea-Tow 17* bouncing their way across the Grey River bar on 20 November 1994. The barge took away 3000 tonnes of coal — as much as an old Union Company 'slow green'.

G Fergusson

Christmas should have come early that year for Pacifica founder Brooke McKenzie. On 8 December 1994 the capital city finally welcomed the first fast Cook Strait ferry. For years McKenzie had been pushing for something faster than the 17-knot conventional ships. 'Put yourself in the position,' he asked a public jaded with Railways' service, 'to travel on a high-speed ferry for an hour [or] one of their buckets for three and a half hours'.[1] Bucking the buckets was easier said than done, though. Fast ferries were expensive and Railways (Tranz Rail from 1995) was well entrenched. More importantly, it controlled all the rail freight, making it largely immune to competition. Rail had revamped its 'Searail' ferries as the 'Interisland Line' but its many critics complained that Railways still treated passengers like 'short-term prisoners', rather than customers.[2] By the early 1990s, however, a new generation of big, fast wavepiercing catamarans and monohulls had solved the technical problems for challengers.[3] Several consortia flirted with the Cook Strait fast option before McKenzie and his Argentinian partner, Buquebus International, chartered the 96-metre monohull *Albayzin*. Forced to compete, the Interisland Line hired the catamaran *Condor 10*.

Sea Shuttles NZ Ltd beat Railways into Wellington only to find that it had put up a dog to fight Rail's cat. The 3107-ton *Albayzin* limped, not roared, into Wellington, one engine down after a jet intake ingested a log off the Indonesian coast, then crunched into an unfendered part of Waterloo Wharf while

Fast Ferries Make Waves in Cook Strait

M H Pryce

Cook Strait became a crowded place in the mid 1990s when the 'ferry wars' peaked. This January 1995 photograph of Picton shows all the contestants. Strait Shipping's small livestock ferry *Straitsman* is in the foreground. At the main berth is Sea Shuttle's fast monohull *Albayzin*, with Interisland Line's conventional ferry *Aratika* towering behind it. In the background the Interisland Line's fast wavepiercing catamaran *Condor 10*, the first 'Lynx', is berthing.

Cook Strait can be hard on lightly constructed ships. On 16 March 1998 the *Condor 10* had just cleared the Wellington Harbour entrance and was doing 20 knots when it hit two swells in quick succession. The second swell, 'out of sequence', smashed the bow-door upwards, badly bending its beak-like bow. Welders flown up from Hillside Workshops in Dunedin had the ship back in service four days later.

M H Pryce

Top Cat to Taniwha

The business end of 'Top Cat', the *Incat 050*, the 26th vehicle-carrying wave-piercer built by Hobart shipbuilder Incat. The wavepiercer's catamaran hull reduces friction but speed is also gained by using aluminium and by bonding non-structural elements with adhesives instead of conventional welding. Brute power also helps. The four 18-cylinder Caterpillar engines each develop 7200 kW. The eyes and whiskers painted on the bow (snout?) are from its Australian trading name, 'Devil Cat'.

The 'Top Cat' became even stranger looking when it starred as the harbour taniwha for the Wellington millennium celebrations. The small wheelhouse was another weight-saving measure.

berthing.[4] The ship had already clipped the pilot launch on the way into port. Cracks discovered in the water jet units kept the ship from carrying paying passengers until 24 December. Even then triumph again turned to tragedy as strong winds prevented the *Albayzin* (which had inadequate astern power) from berthing.[5] For two and a half embarrassing hours, while TV cameras rolled, the *Albayzin*'s master tried and failed to berth. Finally he sent for a tug. Persistent engine problems scuttled the timetable as the 'Sea Shuttle' did an erratic sea shuffle across the Strait. The MSA banned the ship from using Tory Channel in darkness or in poor visibility, then suspended its seaworthiness certificate altogether. The *Albayzin* went to Nelson for repairs, sacrificing yet more peak season revenue. New managers took over and by mid February the *Albayzin* 'lay immobile at Waterloo Quay Wharf, a tattered and blackened Bahamas flag fluttering from the stern'.[6]

Interisland Line's *Condor 10* (trading as 'The Lynx') also had its moments, hitting a whale at 26 knots. 'I felt pretty sick,' Captain Andy Lowe told reporters, but not as bad as the whale, the remains of which were later scraped from the starboard T-foil strut stabiliser.[7] The *Condor 10* entered commercial service on 21 December, beating the *Albayzin* by a nose. In April 1995 an embarrassing engine failure grounded the ship about a kilometre from the Picton terminal with 386 passengers and crew aboard. Nevertheless, the *Condor 10* generally flew while the 'Sea Shuttle' floundered.[8] 'The Lynx' completed its season, returning each summer until 1999–2000 when the Interisland Line traded up to the 5007-ton *Condor Vitesse*. In 2000 it chartered the 6581-ton, 98-metre *Incat Tasmania* for the first year-round fast service. This latest 'Lynx' has a normal cruising speed of 42 knots,[9] much faster than the navy's newest frigates (about 28 knots).

Others followed in the *Albayzin*'s troubled wake. Two launched bids from Porirua, an improbably shallow inlet that restricted them to very small craft for one of the world's stormiest stretches of water. North by South Ferries started running the *Strait Runner* from improvised facilities at the 'port' late in 1995. Optimists to the bitter end, North by South even tried running to Nelson before the service closed down in May 1996. Incredibly, just two years later, Cook Strait Sea Cat Ferries stuck its head in the same Porirua noose. In February 1998, just in time to miss most of the crucial summer trade, the 208-ton *Te Hukatai* ('foaming water') foamed, and then fizzled out 15 months later.

Once again, though, Brooke McKenzie made the biggest waves. He roared back into the headlines in April 1999 with the new 96-metre *Incat 050*. Fast Cat Ferries' ship, branded as the 'Top Cat', looked like a refugee from a science fantasy movie, with its tiny wheelhouse peering out over a vast painted snout that later became a taniwha for Wellington's millennium celebrations. On trials the 5029-ton futuristic ship hit 49.3 knots with 550 tonnes aboard; light, it was expected to reach 50 knots. A reporter on an early *Albayzin* sailing had thrilled to the theatre of it all. 'The four water jets spew a huge amount of water per second,' he told readers. 'Standing on the engineers' deck at the rear of the vehicle deck is a phenomenal experience — similar to the noise and sight of the Huka Falls.'[10] And there was the rub. In 1994 the Wellington harbourmaster imposed a speed restriction in the harbour to reduce ferry wash and surge problems for ships berthed alongside Aotea Quay. The real problem, however, was at the other side of Cook Strait, where Sounds residents complained about shoreline damage, commissioned reports and lobbied hard. In May 2000 the Marlborough District imposed an 18-knot speed restriction between Picton and the Tory Channel entrance. This may have been the final blow for Top Cat Ferries. In November 2000 the company withdrew the ship, which had made 2334 commercial voyages in 17 months.

It was a Pyrrhic victory for the Interisland Line, which, with ill-judged timing, also withdrew the old freight ferry *Arahanga*. So, in just a few short weeks the Cook Strait Bridge fell from two fast and three slow ferries to one and two respectively, supplemented, as always, by Strait Shipping's two small ships. In words that it would soon eat, Interisland gushed that 'the new configuration provides a capacity mix that better matches today's market requirements'.[11] Quality fell along with quantity. In 1998 the Interisland Line had commissioned a replacement for the *Aratika*, the 12,596-ton *Arahere*, described as a $100 million technological marvel. One thing that was revolutionary and which did work smoothly was its unique set of 'Ironsailors'. These Lyttelton-designed devices replaced

Look closely and you will see that no lines tie the RO-RO ferry *Aratere* to its berth. Instead, a vacuum induced through the two 'Ironsailers' visible either side of the words 'The Interislander' on the hull keeps it in place.

M H Pryce

traditional mooring lines (and labour) with a vacuum pump system that mates the ship's port-side hydraulic arms to corresponding shore-mounted units that move up and down to allow for tidal and cargo displacement.[12] But it soon became clear that the 'Ironsailors' were not the only thing that sucked. The *Aratere*'s engines gave trouble on the voyage out and shipyard technicians were still tinkering when the ship reached Wellington. On 9 February 1999 its passenger certificate was withdrawn temporarily. Fifteen days later the *Aratere* lost all power in Wellington Harbour and had to be towed to the wharf, where the MSA detained it. The Interisland Line hastily recommissioned the old *Aratika* while it fixed the 'El Lemon' or 'Aradago', as many now called the *Aratere*. It resumed service but recurring problems produced another detention order and full-page apologies in national newspapers. After one engine failed completely late in 2000, the *Aratere* ran through the peak season at reduced speed, further exacerbating the space shortage problems. Perhaps the only chorus louder than the cicadas that hot, dry summer was that of the complaints coming from holidaymakers, truck-drivers, consumer groups and politicians.

'Open Coast' Closes Kiwi Shipping

The rest of the merchant marine fared no better once political ideologues had smashed cabotage (protected coastal shipping rights). In March 1994 a suspiciously new New Zealand Chamber of International Ship Operators popped up to back demands from Federated Farmers and others for an 'open coast' clause in reform legislation. The farmers described the old union accord that had reserved cargo on the Tasman for Australasian-crewed ships since the 1930s as 'the last bullying tactic of a bygone era'.[13] Overseas owners 'contribute nothing: no wages, no tax, no jobs', and the Seafarers' Union shot back, 'these shipowners are just parasites'.[14] Local shipowners argued that for competition to be fair, they needed the advantages enjoyed by the cross-traders: no New Zealand payroll, ACC and other taxes and in many cases subsidies and accelerated depreciation regimes. But appeals for a 'second register' incorporating these concessions fell on deaf ears. The minister's 'transit option' that permitted ships 'already here as part of their normal route, to move cargo between New Zealand ports', was, the *Shipping Gazette* said 'a sham'.[15] Ken Plowman from the New Zealand Shipping Federation blamed 'MPs within the National Government supported by revenge-seeking farmers'.[16] The Maritime Transport Act offered a shipping policy that the *New Zealand Yearbook* said 'considered that the country's interests were best served by being a ship-using, rather than a ship-operating nation. It sought to ensure for New Zealand exporters and shippers unrestricted access to the carrier of their choice, and to the benefits of fair competition between carriers.'[17] 'In layman's terms', the *Shipping Gazette* translated, 'that

Kakariki

Silver Fern Shipping

The 183-metre *Kakariki* entered service in 1999 and with a dead weight of 46,724 tonnes, shows how big some 'coasters' have become. Like most modern tankers, the *Kakariki* has a double-hull that allows the ballast tanks to protect the oil tanks in a grounding or collision. A large bow thruster, skewed propeller and a Schilling rudder let the *Kakariki* brake and turn simultaneously, turning in its own length. Despite appearances, the huge structure behind the wharf is not an oil tank — it is Wellington's WestpacTrust Stadium.

Livingstone Productions

The bridge of a modern ship is festooned with electronic navigation aids. The *Kakariki's* suite includes electronic charts and a Differential Global Positioning System, which can establish the ship's position to within 1.5 metres.

means that the New Zealand government considers the New Zealand merchant marine a dinosaur that should be laid to rest.'[18]

Perhaps less a dinosaur than the tuatara clinging so precariously to life on our island sanctuaries. Events gathered momentum in 1996 when the Howard government in Australia lipsynched the New Zealand-style reform mantra. To the delight of shippers and the dismay of local seafarers, in October 1996 the Maritime Union of Australia effectively dumped the trade union accord that prohibited non-Australian-crewed ships from the Tasman trade by permitting BHP Shipping to put foreign-crewed ships into the Tasman in return for certain benefits.[19] The unions had already accused international lines of surreptitious cross-trading, but the MUA put the torpedo into the accord's bulkheads.

Change soon swept through the shipping industry. Newcomer Searoad Ltd. lasted just months. By the end of 1998 Pacifica Shipping had reflagged its fleet. The previously profitable and innovative Tasman Express Line had to join a consortium with the cross-traders. Early in 1999 it had ceased trading, transferring its charters to P&O Nedlloyd. Even the bulk trades retrenched. By June 2001 the coastal fleet had shrunk to Interisland Line's three ferries, 'The Lynx', *Arahura* and *Aratere*, Strait Shipping's *Straitsman*, *Suilven* and *Kent*, Pacifica's *Spirit of Competition*, *Spirit of Resolution* and *Spirit of Enterprise*, coastal tankers *Kakariki* and *Taiko*, cement carriers *Golden Bay*, *Westport* and *Milburn Carrier II* and the little Chathams Islands freighter *Jenka*. The official statistics told the story. The gross tonnage on the New Zealand register fell from 482,180 tons in 1995 to 303,180 in 1998 and 253,739 in 1999.[20]

For New Zealand seafarers, the results have been mixed. Crewing levels fell on the surviving cargo carriers. The *Union Rotoiti*, which began running with 42 officers and crew in 1976, had been reduced to 22 by the late 1980s and had fallen to 17 in 2001 as it traded as the ANZDL-owned *Rotoiti*. On the positive side, the fishing and leisure sectors opened up new employment, some global traders such as Maersk-Sealand were offering New Zealanders cadetships, and officers at least could base themselves in New Zealand and work for the cross-traders. Women were also now finding their way aboard ship as officers and seafarers rather than as passengers or prostitutes. In 1974 Phillippa Reynolds became the first peacetime New Zealand ship's officer and later Sally Fodie became 'the first lady master on the Devonport ferry service', as a male colleague put it.[21] They faced strong opposition — as recently as the late 1980s the president of the Auckland branch of the Watersiders' Union declared that 'wharf work was definitely unsuitable for women' — but women formed a growing part of the maritime industry, especially in the agency business.[22] Nevertheless, the ageing workforce (on average 50 years old by 2000) and the long hours being worked by some officers on the Cook Strait RO-ROs posed serious problems. A Shipping Industry Review released early in 2001 found that 'there is a need for a sustainable domestic industry, with concessions to enable it to compete with foreigners' whose shipping is in effect a tax-free industry'.[23]

Gavin McLean Collection

Changing sovereignty with a pot of paint! As the *Spirit of Competition*'s stern shows, modern coasters can be registered anywhere. Paint is cheaper than raised steel lettering.

A stranger death was that of South Pacific Shipping Ltd. Since starting in Christchurch in 1992, SPS had quickly become New Zealand's largest shipping company. Like TEL, the line chartered so-called 'doctors' and 'dentists' ships: modern multipurpose ships built for investment under German taxation provisions. By 1995 SPS had 10 ships, bearing traditional names such as *Turakina*, *Rangitoto*, *Rangiora* and *Rangitata*. SPS was re-equipping with six larger ships when it collapsed in February 1998, taking down the jobs of 30 officers, 30 engineers and 44 ratings, shore staff and 300 employees of the New Zealand Stevedoring Services group. In fact the story was complicated, for the receiver's report showed that SPS had lost money every year since it started. Some argued that the European taxation provisions that benefited its majority shareholder had undermined local jobs by creating the overtonnaging that had driven down rates to uneconomic levels.[24] A notorious graph circulated within the industry pegged each collapse of cargo rates to the introduction of a new SPS ship or service.

The greatest casualty, however, was the Union Company. It had some profitable years in the early 1990s, but its trade share kept contracting, down from 92 per cent in 1980 to 60 per cent in 1987.[25] Bad though that was, the scuppering of the trans-Tasman accord was the company's undoing. In 1996 Brierley Investments Limited took over the Australian shares and it became as 'New Zealand-owned' as anything owned by a New Zealand-based multi-national could be. Next year, however, BIL sold Union's Bass Strait business. By 1998 the company was dead in the water. As the open-coast policy bit, Union chartered its three big RO-ROs to ANZDL and sold the tanker *Taiko*. The *Union Rotorua* went to the breakers in 1998 and in 1999 ANZDL bought the *Union Rotoiti* and *Union Rotoma*. A year later its last ships, Union Shipping Bulk's coal barge *Union Bulk 1* and the tugs *Karamea* and *Gawler* were laid up. For seafarers accustomed to seeing its red funnel for a century and a quarter, the company's disappearance was astonishing. In late 2000 one BIL employee was winding up the last vestiges of one of the world's great shipping lines. The 'Southern Octopus' was calamari.

The navy, too, lost ground. It was time to confront the looming block obsolescence of its four 'Leander'-class frigates. It was a hot political issue for a country with a struggling economy and many people questioned whether frigates

RNZN Official

were still needed. So, while New Zealand joined Australia's 'ANZAC Frigate' shipbuilding programme, it ordered just two. HMNZS *Te Kaha* was commissioned in 1997, followed by *Te Mana* in 1999. They are a German MEKO 200 variant, lightly armed with a five-inch gun, eight 'Seasparrow' point defence missile tubes, a 'Phalanx' close-in defence system, antisubmarine torpedo tubes and a Super Seasprite multi-purpose helicopter. The century closed with the RNZN downgraded to a three-frigate force, soon to become two as politicians suggested that *Canterbury*, due to retire about 2005, will be replaced by between two and four 75-metre ocean patrol vessels and some sort of multi-purpose logistics ship.

The navy's other force levels also declined as yard craft and inshore survey craft were discarded and one second-hand American ship (HMNZS *Resolution*) replaced the survey ship *Monowai* and the research ship *Tui*. The one new ship type, a RO-RO bought by the New Zealand Defence Force in 1994 for conversion to a logistics ship, fared badly. HMNZS *Charles Upham* ran briefly in naval colours but was such 'a chunder barge' in light conditions that it needed 500 tonnes of gravel ballast. In 1998 the navy chartered it to commercial operators and the 2001 Defence Review mandated its sale. While ship and personnel numbers fell, the outlook for gays and lesbians at least, improved. In 1998 the

The RNZN's four 'Leander'-class frigates all required replacement from the 1980s but the size of the bill worried politicians. Eventually the Labour government joined Australia in ordering the German-designed MEKO 200 ANZ, the so-called 'Anzac'- class. Many New Zealand businesses became subcontractors to the Australian shipyard but frigates remained an 'F'-word to many and the National government did not order a further pair. Here the newest 'Leander', HMNZS *Canterbury* (foreground) accompanies the first MEKO, HMNZS *Te Kaha*. *Canterbury* shows several improvements, notably the Vulcan Phalanx gatling gun atop the hangar enlarged to take the new Kaman Super Seasprite helicopter.

RNZN Official

RNZN Official

Since the late 1980s it has become increasingly common to scuttle redundant ships in coastal waters to form artificial reefs for marine life. The *Rainbow Warrior* was scuttled off the Cavalli Islands in 1987 and since then HMNZS *Tui* and HMNZS *Waikato* (seen here sinking in 2000) have also shared this fate. *Waikato*, a 'Leander'-class frigate, entered service in 1966 and was the first New Zealand warship to carry a helicopter.

RNZN's equal opportunities co-ordinator began issuing pink triangles as part of a programme to promote 'an awareness that the Royal New Zealand Navy is an organisation that will not allow homophobia in the workplace'.[26]

Box Boats and Chip Ships

The international lines, too, transformed themselves as they increased their penetration of the country's sealanes. New Zealand's trade routes kept diversifying as more exports went to Asia and South America and this inevitably brought a greater variety of shipping lines and ships to its ports. The secondary ports held on to their bulk trades and to the thriving developing trades better suited to multipurpose shipping. They also served conventional reefer trades. Some ports took advantage of the breakdown of the old rigidities to entice calls from cellular container ships. The number of boxes going through Tauranga climbed as it vigorously challenged Auckland, and in 1996, after channel development at Napier, the 238-metre cellular container ship *Ariake* set a port record. COSCO, the Chinese line and FESCO, a Russian one, all increased their services to New Zealand and by the late 1990s our ports were also being frequented by Swiss, Korean and Malaysian-owned container liners in addition to the traditional British, Dutch, French and Japanese operators.

The 1980s and 1990s brought a surprising reversal of the earlier trend towards consortia-building. In 1986 P&O bought out its partners in the OCL consortium. As we saw, three years later it bought the Shipping Corporation of New Zealand. In 1991, in a complicated deal, P&O took over the Cunard-Ellerman shipping interests, acquiring most of the ACT New Zealand trade ships. P&O now owned so much of the trade that it reined in outsider Contship Container Line to a conference that dropped the ANZECS title, to become simply P&O/Contship. By then container lines were suffering from overcapacity and even established market leaders were struggling. In 1996, in the biggest shake-up in decades, the P&O and Nedlloyd container empires

Resolution Charts Cook Strait

The RNZN continues to honour Cook's memory by naming its ships after his vessels. This is HMNZS *Resolution*, a seven-year-old surveillance ship bought from the USA in 1996 for conversion into a hydrographic vessel. The 68-metre, 11-knot ship has outstanding endurance and crew facilities. It can use its mapping sonar in waters up to 5000 metres deep.

The technology carried aboard the *Resolution* enables surveyors to create views of our submarine landscape that are as clear as anything above water. This 3D digital terrain model of 50 sq nautical miles of Cook Strait was developed from multibeam echo sounder data gathered by the ship.

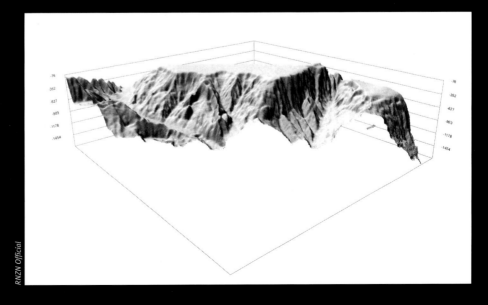

C E Corkill

Trading vessels only rarely encounter problems in New Zealand waters these days. Here is the bulk carrier *Prince of Tokyo* being refloated from the North Mole at the entrance to Otago Harbour on 14 February 1999. It took the combined efforts of the Timaru tug *Te Maru*, Otago's tugs *Rangi*, *Karetai* and *Kapu* (all at the bow) and the dredge *New Era* (far side) to extract the *Prince of Tokyo*. The ship suffered a small hole in the bow bulb, dented hull plating and damaged floors.

merged, bringing together a fleet of 112 owned and chartered vessels. Two years later they took over Blue Star's 15 owned and chartered container ships.[27] In 1996 Danish global container giant Maersk-Sealand had added New Zealand to its 80-ship worldwide service. These two global carriers, P&O Nedlloyd and Maersk-Sealand, now dominate the country's liner services, although P&O, with many other investments in New Zealand, entered the 21st century with a stronger stake in the country's economy than ever.

The ships now visiting New Zealand were developments of the new types introduced during the 1960s and the 1970s — container ships, roll-on, roll-off vessels and bulk carriers. They tended to get larger and uglier, at least in the opinion of the traditionalists. Specialist craft such as oilfield support vessels were one thing, they argued, but the new cruise ships and the slab-sided, square funnelled container ships and bulk carriers were quite another. The car carriers, which called more frequently after the rundown of the domestic car assembly industry, were particularly derided. Their romantic ballet and opera names belied their lumpish lines — Madame Butterflies that looked more like Falstaffs. If the new ships' lines did not offend, their livery could. Just when people were getting used to Columbus ships' red hulls and the Shipping Corporation's orange ones, Contship threw caution (and the paint chart) to the winds by giving its *Contship Italy* a turquoise hull and superstructure, painting the *Contship Singapore* all yellow and turning the *Contship Germany* into 'The Pink Lady'. Names, too, tested the traditionalists' patience. Branded names had become fashionable in the 1970s, with the Union Company's 'Union' names or Forestry Shippers' 'Tasman'. The P&O Nedlloyd merger produced new jawbreakers by prefixing the words P&O Nedlloyd to port names but the prize went to a caller to Auckland in 2000 that sounded like a dropped Scrabble board, the *CMA CGM Matisse*. Inevitably, ship schedulers developed their own shorthand names. They abbreviated TEL's *Auckland Express* and *Canterbury Express* to AEX and CEX, and, oh so inevitably, *Sydney Express* to SEX!

Sealords of the Sunrise?

It was not all gloom and doom. A growing deep-sea fishing fleet did much to offset the tumbling tonnages on the New Zealand register. Their crews call them 'boats' but these steel leviathans dwarf the little wooden day boats of old. For most of the 20th century a big trawler or two worked out of Auckland, Napier, Wellington or Otago but until Sanford, Watties and JBL bought bigger boats in the 1960s, they were rare. In 1965 New Zealand Sea Products Export Ltd ordered two big 43-metre Norwegian stern trawlers. The unimaginatively named *Sea Harvester I* and *Sea Harvester II* arrived in 1966–67 but the Nelson company sank faster than its nets. The *Sea Harvester II* became the government research vessel *James Cook* and the other went back to Norway.[28] The industry's real growth had to wait until the late 1970s, when it could build on one of the world's largest Exclusive Economic Zones (EEZ) and improved research from vessels such as the *James Cook* and the *W J Scott*, which identified the potential of previously unexploited species such as orange roughy. With the one of the largest coastlines on the globe (thanks to its outlying islands) New Zealand was well placed to share in this new bounty. Soon Sanford, Sealord, Skeggs and Fletcher Fishing were buying large trawlers and chartering Soviet, Korean and Japanese vessels.

At times in the 1970s the squid jiggers lit up the sea off our coast so brightly that it seemed as if new cities had sprouted up out there. When the jiggers streamed into Wellington for registration at the rate of 20 a day the stream looked like a mini Tokyo Bay. In 1986 the government introduced a quota management system to manage and conserve the country's major commercial fish species. This divided the EEZ into 10 areas. Thirty-two species or groupings are managed as 181 separate fish stocks. Each year the Ministry of Fisheries assesses the Total Allowable Commercial Catch for each species by area and sets new levels. These can fluctuate significantly. Quota owners can fish up to the limits for which they own or lease quota. Since quota is held on an annual basis and cannot be carried over, there is much shuffling about between fishers each October after the season is over. This hugely sophisticated marine version of a car boot sale benefits everyone. Companies that have exceeded their quota can avoid facing stiff fines (and in some cases vessel confiscation) by selling their overcatch. Similarly, quota owners who do not have the catch power to land the fish for which they hold quota can buy product, thereby maintaining their standing in the system. The trade of 'overs' and 'unders' has become an important feature of a complicated management system.[29]

New Zealand companies moved into the deepwater business cautiously, beginning with joint ventures and by chartering foreign vessels. In the 1980s many Soviet, Japanese and Korean fishing boats worked for them inside the EEZ, and even ports such as Wanganui got in on the act. It was not all smooth sailing. Several boats caught fire or sank. Korean fishers developed a particularly bad reputation for their navigational skills. In 1986 the *Oyang No 85* ran at full speed onto the beach near Wanganui. Two men were on the bridge at the time, but one was asleep on duty and the other was catching up on his paper work in an enclosed chartroom, oblivious to what was going on. The financial side could be as tricky as the navigational and, like the prey they hunted, several ventures went belly-up. This was exacerbated by the collapse of the Soviet Union, which bequeathed Russia and the Ukraine too many fishing boats and too little expertise in fishing capitalist-style. In the mid 1990s stories of chartered Russian trawlers under arrest at New Zealand ports flooded the news, their crews stranded and reduced in some cases to begging. The *Ivan Korobkin* spent 15 months in Timaru in 1995–96. At one stage in mid 1996 four detained Russian trawlers were rusting away in Dunedin. In fact, the *Mys Chaykovskogo* and the *Novopskov* spent so long there that port agent Tapley Swift had to bring in portable toilets.[30]

Gradually, though, New Zealand companies such as Talleys, Amaltal, Skeggs and Sanford took charge. The best known is Sealord, which became partially Maori-owned during the Treaty claims settlement process. Indeed, Maori have taken such a remarkable stake in fishing that Sir Peter Buck's 'Vikings of the Sunrise' have become 'Sealords of the Sunrise'. By 1997 Sealord's trawlers and processing plants employed over 1600 people and the company had nearly a quarter of the country's fishing quota. Like some of its competitors, Sealord's biggest trawlers are almost as big as the Union Company's 'slow greens' of 50 years earlier. The flagship, the 67.5-metre factory stern trawler *Aoraki*, for example, has a gross tonnage of 2966. The *Aoraki* and the 66-metre *Rehua* and *Aorere* can spend six or seven weeks at sea, processing and freezing fillets. Shipboard fishmeal plants ensure that nothing is wasted or dumped. The industry has created thousands of new jobs. The big Norwegian-designed factory freezer boats employ about 80 men and women, who work six hours on and six hours off. For every seagoing job there are several shore-based ones in processing factories, cool stores and support businesses such as shipyards and provedores. Port companies know that the fish trade is big business. In 2001 the Port of Nelson and — increasingly — Dunedin's Upper Harbour earned a sizeable portion of their income from these big craft.

Undoubtedly, though, the big boats have hammered the inshore fisheries.

Sealord Group Ltd

The 66-metre *Rehua* powers towards the camera as it works its way up to 15 knots. The 2483-ton factory trawler can stay at sea for weeks at a time as it catches and processes up to 1000 tonnes of fish.

'There's a dark storm moving in from out on the horizon and it's headed for the small-time fisherman,' Kirk Hargreaves warned in his 1998 tribute to the small operators. 'The end of an era is looming for many fishing families; the next generation will no longer have birthright to an income in taking on the family boat'.[31] Even so, the familiar little white-hulled boats still bob about in odd corners of most New Zealand harbours. And, despite some toxic algal blooms, there has also been a healthy interest in marine farming. Oysters are farmed in the Bay of Islands and in the Hauraki Gulf. Mussel farming prospers, especially in the Marlborough Sounds, and the old coastal timber port of

Gavin McLean Collection

Home for the day. The veteran launch *Rakiura* passes the Oamaru breakwater. In recent years such craft have declined in numbers as the inshore fishery has come under heavy pressure from bigger craft.

Havelock now serves as a base for a fleet of servicing barges as impressive as anything seen in the days of the old Cook Strait 'mosquito fleet'.

Dry Ports and Gritty Survivors

As we saw, the port reforms of 1989 produced winners and losers. There were many redundancies and waterfront workers lost many of the gains of previous decades as casualisation crept back in. No new ports were built, for all Tranz Rail's talk about a new terminal at Clifford Bay or West Coast plans for a deepwater jetty. But existing port companies did build major deepwater facilities at Shakespeare Bay (Picton) and at Marsden Point. Port company shares were now traded on the stock exchange, but public pressure, especially in Auckland, prevented full privatisation. With the breakdown of rigid divisions between workforces and between the cellular container terminals and the other facilities, the ports made better use of precious back-up space. Ports of Auckland redeveloped its container and general cargo facilities around 'Axis Bledisloe', 'Axis Jellicoe' and 'Axis Fergusson' and in 1996 it cut up its last conventional cranes: five survivors of 90. That year retiring CEO Robert Cooper claimed that, since reform, cargo volumes had doubled and profitability had increased 245 per cent, all on increased revenues of just 19 per cent.[32]

But, as shipowners complained, real competition between ports was limited. Low-value cargoes, too bulky to move cheaply by road or rail, are effectively 'captive' to the nearest port. High-value, low-bulk goods in containers are less so, as the late 1990s showed. Auckland and Tauranga competed vigorously and in 1999 Port of Tauranga, now the country's second busiest container port, set up an inland port, 'Metroport', in South Auckland to siphon off Ports of Auckland's box traffic. In 2001 Ports of Auckland's 'Axis Intermodal' contracted with Tranz Rail to feed boxes from its new 'dry' port in the Manawatu up to its wharves. With ports preparing for the new 4100-TEU replacements for the 2700-TEU 1970s-era ships from 2002 onward, commentators speculated about how smaller ports such as New Plymouth, Napier and even Wellington (now Centreport) would fare.[33] Even marine servicing contracts became competitive. In 1999 the Ports of Auckland Ltd beat Northland Port Corporation for the towage contract at the Marsden Point oil refinery, right on Northland Port's doorstep. POA's subsidiary, North Tugz Ltd, ordered three new tugs from Northport Engineering.

Nevertheless, the survival of the smaller ports has been remarkable. Oamaru and Raglan never reopened to commercial shipping, but Gisborne benefited from the region's physical isolation. It lost its coastal tanker service in 2000 but Port Gisborne handles squash, conventional refrigerated cargoes and forest products, and looks forward to a future timber bonanza. Wanganui, managed by Ocean Terminals Ltd, has had a tougher struggle, existing on scraps of business from Korean trawlers, tugs and barges and the odd cement carrier. Those barges have had their adventures. On 5 May 1996 the tug *Wybia* was towing two barges into Wanganui in strong northerlies and a large swell, when the *Dixie III* over-rode, holing the second barge, *Dixie II*, which broke its tow. Waterlogged, it drifted ashore.[34] Five months later the dancing *Dixie*s were in trouble again off the entrance. First the inward-bound *Dixie III* broke loose and grounded. Salvage agents were still recovering its sodden grain a week later when someone set the timber-laden *Dixie II* loose from the Castlecliff wharf. The barge swept out the entrance to ground a kilometre south of the *Dixie III*. The pilot launch *Strathallan* raced out to rescue it but fouled its propeller on a towline and also went ashore. Its three crew scrambled ashore from their badly strained boat.[35] Already in port was the damaged *Seatrader 2*, detained by the Maritime Safety Authority after capsizing off the entrance in April. Castlecliff's wharves and sheds have a melancholy, beaten-up look to them, but some ships continue to thread their way up and down the historic channel.

LOVE YA, PALMY.
WE'LL BE DOWN AS
SOON AS...
...WE FIND YOU ON THE
MAP.

Ports of Auckland is reversing the national trend – it has begun a southward drift.

The Aucklanders have a plan – they want to implement a "vision of how the freight dynamics of New Zealand should be configured".

At CentrePort, Wellington, we welcome the challenge Ports of Auckland is laying

down. And we'd certainly be glad to help them get their bearings.

It's no fun losing your way in unfamiliar territory.

CentrePort
Wellington

Centreport Ltd

But no survivors were grittier than the West Coast bar harbours. Many people had written them off in the late 1970s after the Union Company sold its 'slow greens' and the coal market shrivelled up. In fact Greymouth did not see a single freighter between 1978 and 1982 and was just a fishing port. Far from writing its obituary, however, the little port ended the century by setting new records as a new generation of tug and barge operators, led by Sea-Tow Ltd, revived coal carriage by sea. In 1997 a record load of 8020 tonnes of coal left aboard the 3565-ton barge *Sea-Tow 4*. Westport had its cement works and from 1988 the cement company subsidiary, Buller Port Services, managed the port. Since then the cement carriers *Westport* and *Milburn Carrier II* have been joined by coal barges, trawlers and even the occasional cruise liner. In January 2001 102 camera-toting tourists traipsed across a red carpeted section of the old wharf and up a 'tree-lined boulevard' of 300 potted trees as Westport hosted the small cruise liner *Clipper Odyssey*.[36] Watching a ship surge across either West Coast bar harbour can still be a breath-taking experience under certain sea conditions, but modern sounding gear has reduced many of the risks.

In the 21st century competition between ports has intensified, especially for the high-value container traffic. When the Ports of Auckland set up an inland 'port' in the Manawatu to draw cargo away from Wellington and Napier early in 2001, Centreport (formerly Port of Wellington Ltd) responded with a jibe at the stereotypical Aucklander. In fact, the longest-running battle has been between Tauranga and Auckland, with the Bay of Plenty port enticing several lines away from Auckland.

Strandings at Wanganui

Tugs and barges are now widely used but they require careful handling, especially off the West Coast of both Islands. In 1996 Network Shipping's barges had a run of bad luck near the entrance to Wanganui Harbour. The top photograph shows the grain being salvaged from the barge *Dixie III* just outside Wanganui (see entrance training walls in the top right). The lower photo shows the *Dixie II* and the Wanganui pilot boat *Strathallan* ashore about a kilometre south of the *Dixie III*. All three were salvaged.

Capt. D Barnes

The West Coast bar harbours staged an unexpected revival at the end of the 20th century. Bulk cargoes of cement and coal were their mainstay, but even passenger ships started calling. The expanding cruise ship industry, which developed smaller vessels for specialist markets, made this possible. In January 1999 Westport's first cruise ship, the 5218-ton *Oceanic Odyssey*, put ashore its eco-friendly passengers for whale watching, coastal walking and other attractions. It returned in 2001 under the name *Clipper Odyssey*.

From Ship to Shop, Scow to Superyacht

It was an odd sight, pot plants greeting *Clipper Odyssey* passengers where 40 years earlier sweating, swearing wharfies and seafarers would have been working clanking, dusty coal grabs. The arrival ceremony had an appropriately rough and ready, low-key West Coast look about it, but it merely reflected a wider trend. As commercial shipping retreated behind fenced-off, flood-lit, 24-hour-a-day bulk facilities and container terminals, it left the old conventional wharves available for other uses — museums, marinas, bars, restaurants and apartments. The 'from ship to shop' phenomenon has swept around the developed, post-industrial world as communities have found new uses for decaying urban waterfronts. Here, as elsewhere, the hiss from the espresso machines drowns out the sound of the gulls.

Wellington and Auckland have turned parts of their waterfronts into urban playgrounds, although not without controversy. In Wellington the recession of the late 1980s toppled some of the more Albert Speerian plans of Lambton Harbour Management Ltd. In 2000 public outcry forced the city council to water down its Variation 17 plans that would have had 'wharves islandised: buildings eviscerated to create viewing shafts and humble cargo sheds sledded to and fro to stock tourist gewgaws'.[37] Nevertheless, the incremental development that has occurred has produced a new city museum, apartments, restaurants, shops, park space, recreational facilities, a new national museum of questionable architectural merit and an events centre without any. Small cruise liners and visiting warships now share Queens Wharf with international yachts or other special visitors. At other times the waterfront becomes the setting for public spectacle on a grand scale: colourful, high-energy dragon boating or spectacular Guy Fawke's Night and New Year's Eve fireworks displays. The wheel has turned full circle. Like the 1840s 'loungers' that killjoy Port Nicholson residents criticised for lying about 'The Beach', 21st century idlers and revellers can now walk, watch, gossip and drink at their city's water's edge.

Auckland had less land to play with but Hobson Wharf, the 'New Zealand Maritime Museum', opened east of the Viaduct Basin in 1993 to great acclaim. It has a large fleet of small watercraft, the replica scow *Ted Ashby* and innovative displays. Several old waterfront buildings had already been turned into bars and restaurants but the real spur came when the yacht *Black Magic* won the America's Cup off San Diego in 1995. The quixotic quest for the Cup had not always been popular with people who jibbed at jibing. Tessa Duder recalls that 'the very idea of New Zealand — in effect, Auckland — challenging for the America's Cup was treated with some derision when it first surfaced in 1983'.[38] That was certainly so in 1988 when banker Michael Fay challenged with the enormous 41-metre *KZ1 New Zealand*.[39] American Dennis Conner wiped it out with 'an equally silly catamaran in a series that did little for New Zealand's reputation and even less for the 137-year history of the America's Cup'.[40] But New Zealand's *KZ-7* had come within a hair's breadth of challenging for the Cup in the summer of 1986–87 and victory in 1995 ensured the Basin's redevelopment. In 1999–2000 'Team New Zealand' made the first successful non-American defence of the 'Auld Mug' from a transformed waterfront. There Auckland went as Black Boat crazy as George Weller's folk who had gone Black Whaling mad in 1837 and it is tempting to compare the planting of a designer Cup Village in the old Viaduct to the pre-colonial whaling stations plonked down in alien pre-colonial landscapes. It is also tempting to wonder how long the good times will last.

One thing that the Cup challenges did help was shipbuilding and servicing. Steel shipbuilding had remained centred on Whangarei (where Ship Constructors, now Northport Engineering, succeeded WECO, and built numerous tugs and barges, including six 48-metre barges for the Clyde Dam project) and Dunedin (where Sims Engineering built some ships and serviced rail ferries and coastal tankers). However, a few barges, harbour ferries and other craft were also built elsewhere. Right from the days of Logan and Bailey, New Zealand yacht designers had been generating business for local boat yards. While backyard builders had worked with plywood and ferro-cement, Bruce Farr, Ron Holland and others worked creatively with plywood and fibreglass. The America's Cup challenges and defence really lifted their international profile further.

The first 'superyachts' appeared in the late 1980s. In 1986 Sensation Yachts Ltd launched the 37-metre luxury yacht *Aquel II*, the world's largest single-masted yacht. More followed as Sensation and Alloy Yachts International built luxuriously appointed yachts in the 30–45-metre range for wealthy overseas clients. By the late 1990s northern shipyards were being flooded with orders for superyachts, some almost as big as small Cook Strait ferries. In 2001 major superyacht building facilities were being planned for Whangarei (where New Zealand Yachts opened the first stage of a $100 million yard in April 2001, with seven ships on its order book, including a 33-metre wavepiercer) and at Hobsonville (where Sovereign Yachts signed a deal to build a $18 million shipyard.)[41] About 15 were under construction in Auckland alone in March 2001 when Sensation Yachts delivered the $50 million, 47-metre *Aria* to its American owner.

Few people can enjoy the comforts of an *Aria* of their own but the vigorously growing leisure sector has created many jobs for seafarers as well as shipbuilders. Northland's fast catamarans tout for business alongside traditional craft such as the old auxiliary ketch *Te Aroha*, offering eco-tours, or the replica schooner *R. Tucker Thompson*. In Auckland, increasing numbers of city workers have taken to the sea to avoid the congested Harbour Bridge. They take the ferry *Kea* as it shuttles between Devonport and the city by the restored historic Ferry Building. If they are in a party mood, they can book one of the traditional *Kestrel*'s charter cruises. Commuters, lifestylers and tourists crowd aboard high-speed catamarans such as the 578-ton *Superflyte*, the *Quickcat*, the fast monohull *Jet Raider* and the many other small craft that crisscross the Gulf and the Waitemata for Fullers

In the 1980s and 1990s Sims Engineering refitted several big ferries and coasters in the Dunedin Steamer Basin. As this photograph shows, it did not let the absence of a dry dock deter it! The ship in the undignified position is the coastal tanker *Kotuku*. The *Kotuku* and *Kuaka* were twin 16,221-ton tankers built for the New Zealand trade in 1975; they ran until the mid 1990s. Between January 1976 and March 1996 it was estimated that the *Kuaka* carried about 25 million tonnes of oil, making 750 coastal voyages, 40 across the Tasman and loading 250 feedstock cargoes from Marsden Point.

C E Corkill

Alloy Yachts — Ivor Wilkins

The *Georgia* epitomises the new superyacht boom. When launched by Alloy Yachts in 1999 for a wealthy American owner, the *Georgia* was the largest sloop-rigged yacht in the world. The ship displaces 338 metric tonnes, making it longer, faster and just about as heavy as Cook's *Endeavour*.

Group.[42] At the more sedate, 8.25-knot end of the market, Subritzky Shipping Line Group runs eight powered barges and vehicular ferries.[43] Even Wellington has a harbour ferry again. In 1989 a former Bay of Islands tourism catamaran began running between Queen's Wharf and Days Bay. Its cascade of trading names — *Government Print 1*, *East by West*, *Trust Bank Ferry* and finally *WestpacTrust Ferry* — reflected the ups and downs of the commercial sector but the service itself survived and in 2000 the newer *Evening Post Ferry* took over.

The *Evening Post Ferry* also combines its commuter run with calls to the Department of Conservation's sanctuary on the former quarantine station Matiu/Somes Island. Throughout New Zealand eco-tourism and a growing appreciation of natural and historic heritage produced a new breed of men and women to follow in the whalers' wake. Two centuries earlier Europeans and Maori worked together killing seals and whales but now Otago Harbour's *Monarch* shows tourists the seals and albatrosses at Taiaroa Head and tribal venture Whale Watch takes tourists out in small boats to view whales off Kaikoura. There was high unemployment in Kaikoura when Whale Watch began in 1987 but, despite early difficulties, the venture prospered. In 1995 Whale Watch carried 40,000 tourists and employed up to 70 people, mainly Maori, during the peak season.[44]

Further south in the lakes and fiords of Fiordland, the circle has turned fully. From Te Anau, Fiordland Travel Ltd, formed in the 1950s, runs a large fleet of modern tourism vessels.[45] Its large, sail-assisted motor vessels, the 40–metre *Milford Mariner* and the 30–metre *Milford Wanderer*, are inspired — loosely, it must be said — by the old coastal scows. They offer tourists the opportunity to 'follow in the steps of iwi Maori or European explorers in an area that has seen few changes since Captain Cook first entered Dusky Sound in 1773'.[46] Lured by the opportunity to explore deserted shorelines and rainforest, kayak among

Fiordland Travel Ltd

The leisure sector's growth has made it a significant employer of seafaring labour. One of the largest tourist fleets is that of Fiordland Travel Ltd. Several of the company's specially designed craft cruise Cook's old southern stamping grounds. The 30-metre *Milford Wanderer* is shown in Dusky Sound.

sheltered bays or 'simply relax on deck and soak it all in', tourists from all over the world are now taken on Cook's Tours through James Cook's old stamping ground. Tourist attire being what it is, were Cook to return he would probably be as puzzled by the sight of chardonnay-sipping *Milford Wanderer* passengers as were Maori over 200 years ago when they first set eyes on 'goblins from the sea'.

❂

Notes

Introduction

1   Frank Broeze, *Island Nation: a History of Australians and the Sea*, Allen & Unwin, St. Leonards, 1998, p. 38.

2   Geoffrey Blainey, *The Tyranny of Distance: How Distance Shaped Australia's History*, Revised edition, Sun Books, Sydney, 1983.

Chapter 1

1   J C Beaglehole (ed.), *The Journals of Captain James Cook: the Voyage of the Endeavour*, 1768–1771, Cambridge University Press for the Hakluyt Society, Cambridge, revised edition, 1968, p. 167.

2   Midshipman John Bootie's journal, quoted in Anne Salmond, *Two Worlds: First Meetings Between Maori and Europeans 1642–1772*, Viking, Auckland, 1991, p. 122.

3   Salmond, *Two Worlds*, p. 138.

4   Three useful introductions to the subject are Geoffrey Irwin, *The Prehistoric Exploration and Colonisation of the Pacific*, Cambridge University Press, Cambridge, 1992; Janet Davidson, *The Prehistory of New Zealand*, Longman Paul, Auckland, 1984; and Douglas G Sutton (ed.), *The Origins of the First New Zealanders*, Auckland University Press, Auckland, 1994.

5   Geoffrey Blainey, *A Short History of the World*, Viking, Ringwood, 2000, p. 234.

6   Ranginui Walker offers a useful interpretation of canoe traditions in the third chapter of *Ka Whawhai Tonu Matou: Struggle Without End*, Penguin, Auckland, 1990. For a listing, see Jeff Evens *Nga Waka O Nehea*, Reed Books, Auckland, 1997.

7   Walker, *Ka Whawhai Tonu Matou*, p. 48.

8   James Belich, *Making Peoples: a History of the New Zealanders from Polynesian Settlement to the End of the Nineteenth Century*, Allen Lane, Auckland, 1996, p. 31.

9   Geoffrey Irwin, 'Exploring the Pacific, Strategies and Motives', in *Bearings*, Vol. 5, No. 2, 1993, p. 44.

10 For a fuller explanation of these techniques, see Irwin, as well as Jeff Evans, *The Discovery of Aotearoa*, Reed Books, Auckland, 1998.

11 It should be noted, however, that European seafarers also knew how to 'read' the sea; Cook's journal shows that they also took heed of currents, driftwood and birdlife.

12 Alan Grey, *Aotearoa and New Zealand: a Historical Geography*, Canterbury University Press, Christchurch, 1994, p. 97.

13 David Johnson, *New Zealand's Maritime Heritage*, William Collins in association with David Bateman, Auckland, 1987, p. 20.

14 Michael King, *Moriori—A People Rediscovered*, Viking, Auckland, 1989, pp. 32–33.

15 James Watson, *Links—A History of Transport in New Zealand*, GP Books, Wellington, 1996, p. 3.

16 Watson, *Links*, p. 13.

17 See Philip Bosscher (ed.), *The Heyday of Sail: the Merchant Sailing Ship 1650–1830*, and Conway's History of the Ship series, Conway Maritime Press, London, 1995, pp. 47–51.

18 Joel Mokyr, *The Lever of Riches: Technological Creativity and Economic Progress*, Oxford University Press, Oxford, 1990, p. 47.

19 See Dava Sobel, *Longitude; the True Story of a Lone Genius Who Solved the Greatest Scientific Problem of His Time*, Fourth Estate, London, 1995.

20 See Miriam Estensen, *Discovery: the Quest for the Great South Land*, Allen & Unwin, St. Leonards, 1998.

21 Salmond, *Two Worlds*, pp. 63–84.

22 Peter Whitfield, *Mapping the World: a History of Exploration*, Folio Society, London, 2000, p. 144.

23 See Grahame Anderson, *The Merchant of the Zeehaen: Isaac Gilsemans and the Voyages of Abel Tasman*, Te Papa Press, Wellington, 2001.

24 David Mackay, 'James Cook', in W H Oliver (ed.), *The Dictionary of New Zealand Biography*, Volume 1 1769–1869, Allen & Unwin in association with the Department of Internal Affairs, Wellington, 1990, p. 92

25 J C Beaglehole (ed.), *The Journals of Captain James Cook: the Voyage of the Endeavour*, p. 185. 'I have caused it to be boild with Portable Soup and Oatmeal every morning for the Peoples breakfast, and this I design to continue as long as it will last or any is to be got, because I look upon it to be very wholesome and a great Antiscorbutick'.

Chapter 2

1   David Landes, *The Wealth and Poverty of Nations*, Norton, New York, 1998, p. 89.

2   G R Hawke, *The Making of New Zealand: An Economic History*, Cambridge University Press, Cambridge, 1985.

3   Alan Grey, *Aotearoa and New Zealand: a Historical Geography*, Canterbury University Press, Christchurch, 1994 and Belich, *Making Peoples*, Allen Lane, Auckland, 1996.

4   Salmond, *Between Two Worlds*, p. 194.

5   See Brian Duggan, *Incidental History of Australasia 1792–1796*, author, Taradale, 1997 and Robert McNab, *Historical Records of New Zealand*, Vol. II, Government Printer, Wellington, 1914.

6   McNab, *Historical Records*, p. 529.

7   See Margaret Steven, *Trade, Tactics and Territory*, Melbourne University Press, Melbourne, 1983.

8   A Charles Begg and Neil C Begg, *The World of John Boultbee*, Whitcoulls Publishers, Christchurch, 1978, p. 164.

9   John Hall-Jones, Thomas Chaseland in *The Dictionary of New Zealand Biography*, Volume I, p. 80

10 Quoted in Erik Olssen, *A History of Otago*, John McIndoe, Dunedin, 1984, p. 13.

11 Olssen, p. 13.

12 Commercial seal killing was made illegal in 1916, although many animals were killed in one disastrous open season in 1946.

13 Atholl Anderson, *The Welcome of Strangers: an Ethnohistory of Southern Maori AD 1650–1850*, University of Otago Press in Association with Dunedin City Council, Dunedin, 1998, p. 207.

14 Michael Roche, *History of Forestry*, New Zealand Forestry Corporation Ltd. in association with GP Books, Wellington, 1990, p. 17.

15 Duncan Mackay, *Frontier New Zealand: the Search for Eldorado (1800–1920)*, Auckland, 1992, p. 19.

16 Judith Binney, Judith Bassett and Erik Olssen, *The People and the Land, Te Tangata me Te Whenua: an Illustrated History of New Zealand 1820–1920*, Allen & Unwin, Wellington, 1990, p. 19.

17 Quoted in Jack Lee, *Hokianga*, Reed Books, Auckland, 1987, p. 48.

18 Grey, *Aotearoa and New Zealand*, p. 126.

19 Belich, *Making Peoples*, p. 137.

20 The best general account of South-West Pacific whaling is Harry Morton's *The Whale's Wake*, University of Otago Press, Dunedin, 1982. Also useful are A Charles Begg and Neil C Begg, *The World of John Boultbee*; Angela Caughey, *The Interpreter: the Biography of Richard 'Dicky' Barrett*, David Bateman, Auckland, 1998; Joan Druett, *Petticoat Whalers: Whaling Wives at Sea 1820–1920*, Collins, Auckland, 1991; Don Grady, *Guards of the Sea*, Whitcoulls Publishing, Christchurch, 1978; *The Perano Whalers of Cook Strait 1911–1964*, A H & A W Reed, Wellington, 1982, and *Sealers & Whalers in New Zealand Waters*, Reed Methuen, Auckland, 1986; Granville Allen Mawer, *Ahab's Trade: the Saga of South Seas Whaling*, Allen & Unwin, St. Leonards, 1999; J P C Watt, *Stewart Island's Kaipipi Shipyard and Ross Sea Whalers*, author, Havelock North, 1989. Two classic accounts, often reprinted, are Frank Bullen's *The Cruise of the 'Cachalot'* (1899) and Robert McNab's *The Old Whaling Days: a History of Southern New Zealand from 1830 to 1840* (1913).

21 Morton, *The Whale's Wake*, p. 82.

22 Morton, p. 83.

23 Morton, p. 50.

24 Rhys Richards, *The Foveaux Yarns of Yankee Jack*, Otago Heritage Books, Dunedin, 1995, p.14.

25 Rhys Richards and Jocelyn Chisholm, *Bay of Islands Shipping Arrivals and Departures 1803–1840*, Paremata Press, Paremata, 1992 (not paginated).

26 Quoted in Don Grady, *Sealers and Whalers in New Zealand Waters*, p. 131.

27 Belich, *Making Peoples*, p. 153.

28 Quoted in Richards and Chisholm.

29 See Wade Doak, *The Burning of the Boyd: a Saga of Culture Clash*, Hodder & Stoughton, Auckland, 1984; Tony Simpson, *Art & Massacre: Documentary Racism in the Burning of the Boyd*, The Cultural Construction Company, Wellington, 1993; Louise Callan, *Shipwreck: Tales of Survival, Courage & Calamity at Sea*, Hodder Moa Beckett, Auckland, 2000 and the accompanying Greenstone TV series, 'Shipwreck'.

30 Don Grady, 'Elizabeth Guard', in W H Oliver (ed.), *The Dictionary of New Zealand Biography*, pp. 164–65.

31 Frank Tod, *Whaling in Southern Waters*, author, Dunedin, 1982, p. 125.

32 Morton, p. 247.

33 Anderson, p. 214.

34 Anderson, p. 214.

35 Quoted in Mackay, p. 21.

36 Gavin McLean, *Wellington: the First Years of European Settlement 1840–1850*, Penguin, Auckland, 2000, p. 14.

37 Belich, *Making Peoples*, p. 280.

38 Belich, *Making Peoples*, p. 189.

39 See Les Drew, *On the Move: Christchurch Transport Through the Years, 6. 'The Tidal Travellers: the Small Ships of Canterbury'*, A & M Publishers, Christchurch, 1991.

40 A H McLintock, *The Port of Otago*, Whitcombe and Tombs, Christchurch, 1951, p. 29.

41 Clifford Hawkins, 'The Waka in Trade and Transport', in *New Zealand Marine News*, Vol. 49, 1, 2000, pp. 12–14.

42 Paul Monin, 'The Maori Economy of Hauraki 1840–1880', in *New Zealand Journal of History*, Vol. 29,2, October 1995, p. 198.

43 Atholl Anderson, *The Welcome of Strangers: an Ethnohistory of Southern Maori A.D. 1650–1850*, University of Otago Press in Association with the Dunedin City Council, Dunedin, 1998, p. 210.

44 Anderson, p. 214.

45 Harry C Evison, *Te Wai Pounamu, The Greenstone Land*, Aoraki Press, Wellington and Christchurch, 1993.

46 Paul Monin, 'The Maori Economy of Hauraki 1840–1880', pp. 197–210.

47 Appendix A of M N Watt, *Index to the New Zealand Section of the Register of All British Ships*, New Zealand Ship & Marine Society, Wellington, 1961, pp. 163–65, contains a useful list of Maori ship ownership.

48 James Watson, *Links*, p. 65.

49 Examples drawn from M N Watt.

50 Obituary, *Marine News*, Vol. 46, No. 1, 1997, p. 6.

51 See 'Palinurus', 'The Shipbuilders of Dusky Bay', in *Marine News*, Vol. 42, No.2, 1993, pp. 67–71.

52 Salmond, *Between Two Worlds*, p. 290.

53 Salmond, *Between Two Worlds*, p. 289.

54 McNab, *Historical Records*, p. 523.

55 Duncan Mackay, *Working the Kauri*, Random Century, Auckland, 1991, p. 5.

56 Claudia Orange, *The Treaty of Waitangi*, Allen & Unwin/Port Nicholson Press, Wellington, 1987.

57 Una Platts, *The Lively Capital*, Avon Fine Art Prints, Christchurch, 1971, p. 62.

58 W W Stewart, *Steam on the Waitemata*, A H & A W Reed, Wellington, 1972, p. 9.

59 Gordon Ogilvie, *Banks Peninsula, Cradle of Canterbury*, GP Books, Wellington, 1990, p. 87.

60 C W N Ingram, *New Zealand Shipwrecks*, 7th edn, Beckett Publishing,

Auckland, 1990, p. 39.

61 See Ian Church (ed.), 'Coastal Voyaging in Otago 1858', in *Marine News*, Vol. 37, Nos 2 and 3, 1987, pp. 71–74 and 117–22.

62 See Sheila Natusch, *The Cruise of the Acheron*, Whitcoulls Publishers, Christchurch, 1978.

63 Malcolm McKinnon (ed.), *New Zealand Historical Atlas*, David Bateman in association with Historical Branch, Department of Internal Affairs, Auckland, 1997, Plate 35.

64 J D Wilkinson, *Early New Zealand Steamers*, Maritime Historical Productions, Lower Hutt, 1966, p. 50.

Chapter 3

1 McKinnon (ed.), *New Zealand Historical Atlas*, Plate 49.

2 Alan Grey, *Aotearoa and New Zealand*, p. 127.

3 Gavin McLean, *Otago Harbour: Currents of Controversy*, Otago Harbour Board, Dunedin, 1985, p. 46.

4 Judith Bassett, 'A Paradise for Working Men' in Judith Binney, Judith Bassett and Erik Olssen, *The People and the Land, Te Tangata me Te Whenua: an Illustrated History of New Zealand 1820–1920*, Allen & Unwin in association with the Port Nicholson Press, Wellington, 1990, p. 165.

5 Alan Grey, p. 227.

6 Many family histories record the journeys of loved forbears. The best general studies are: Tony Simpson, *The Immigrants*, Godwit, Auckland, 1997; Charlotte Macdonald, *A Woman of Good Character*, Allen & Unwin in association with the Historical Branch, Wellington, 1990, and Rollo Arnold, *The Farthest Promised Land*, VUP with Price Milburn, Wellington, 1981. Sir Henry Brett's two-volume *White Wings*, Brett Publishing Company, Auckland, 1924 and 1928 remains a seminal work. The best guides to the ships themselves are Alan Bott, *The Sailing Ships of the New Zealand Shipping Company 1873–1900*, BT Batsford, London, 1972 and David Savill, *Sail to New Zealand: the Story of Shaw Savill & Co. 1858–82*, Robert Hale, London, 1986.

7 Macdonald, *A Woman of Good Character*, p. 75.

8 Simpson, *The Immigrants*, p. 137.

9 Macdonald, *A Woman of Good Character*, p. 76.

10 Simpson, *The Immigrants*, p. 191.

11 Belich, *Making Peoples*, p. 286.

12 Simpson, *The Immigrants*, p. 195

13 Belich, *Making Peoples*, p. 287.

14 Brett, *White Wings*, Vol. 1, p.78.

15 Brett, *White Wings*, Vol. 1, p. 62.

16 Macdonald, *A Woman of Good Character*, p. 100.

17 Quoted in Erik Olssen and Marcia Stenson, *A Century of Change, New Zealand 1800–1900*, Longman Paul, Auckland, 1989, p. 235.

18 See Bruce E Collins, *The Wreck of the Surat*, Otago Heritage Books, Dunedin, 1991. Chasland's Mistake (note the spelling) was named after the sealer and whaler Tommy Chaselands, whom we met in the previous chapter. It got its name not because he hit the promontory but because he passed by a promising seal rookery there.

19 Ingram, *New Zealand Shipwrecks*, p. 76.

20 See Thayer Fairburn, *The Wreck of HMS Orpheus*, Whakatane Historical Society, Whakatane, 1987.

21 See Joan McIntosh, *The Wreck of the Tararua*, A H & A W Reed, Wellington, 1970.

22 John O'C Ross, *Pride in Their Ports*, Dunmore Press, Palmerston North, 1977, p. 14.

23 Alan Grey, p. 261.

24 *Instructions to Lightkeepers*, 1886, quoted in Grant Sheehan and Anna Gibbons, *Leading Lights*, Hazard Press, Christchurch, 1991, p. xii.

25 James Belich, 'The Governors and the Maori', in Keith Sinclair (ed.), *The Oxford Illustrated History of New Zealand*, 2nd edn, Auckland, 1996, p. 84.

26 R J McDougall, *New Zealand Naval Vessels*, GP Books, Wellington, 1989, pp. 161–63.

27 Richard Taylor, 'Colonial Naval Activities' in Ian McGibbon (ed.), *The*

Oxford Companion to New Zealand Military History, Oxford University Press, Auckland, 2000, p. 104.

28 Two former scow men have written about the scow, P A Eaddy, *'Neath Swaying Spars*, Whitcombe & Tombs, Christchurch, 1939, and Ted Ashby, *Phantom Fleet: the Scows and Scowmen of Auckland*, A H & A W Reed, 1975. Cliff Hawkins has written about their construction in *A Maritime Heritage, the Lore of Sail In New Zealand*, Collins, 1978. See also three articles from *Bearings*: two by Hawkins, 'An Introduction to the Scow' in Vol. 2, No. 1, and 'A Further Look at the Scow' in Vol. 2, No.4, and Rodney Wilson, 'What's in a Name: Or the Ultimate Origins of the New Zealand Scow', in Vol. 3, No. 4; also Hawkins, 'The Scow' in *Marine News*, Vol.18, No. 3, Summer 1966–67, pp. 68–73, 'The Scow in the Shape of a Punt', in *Marine News* Vol. 47, No. 3, 1998, pp. 119–128.

29 *Southern Cross*, 26 June 1873.

30 Eaddy, *'Neath Swaying Spars*, p. 40.

31 Johnson, *New Zealand's Maritime Heritage*, p. 115.

32 *Hawke's Bay Herald*, 14 Oct 1874.

33 See T J Hearn and R P Hargreaves, *The Speculators' Dream: Gold Dredging in Southern New Zealand*, Allied Press, Dunedin, 1985.

34 See John Ingram, *Gold, Quartz and Cyanide: the Story of the Barewood Reef*, Otago Heritage Books, Dunedin, 1980.

35 W H S Scotter, *A History of Port Lyttelton*, Lyttelton Harbour Board, Christchurch, 1968, p. 137.

36 See Anthony G Flude, *Henderson & Macfarlane's Circular Saw Line*, author, Auckland, 1993.

37 Simon Ville, 'The Coastal Trade of New Zealand Prior to World War One', in *New Zealand Journal of History*, Vol. 27, No. 1, April 1993, p. 78.

38 Johnson, *Wellington Harbour*, p. 99.

39 See Gavin McLean, *The Southern Octopus: the Rise of a Shipping Empire*, New Zealand Ship & Marine Society and the Wellington Harbour Board Maritime Museum, Wellington, 1990.

40 McLean, *The Southern Octopus*, pp. 32–33. The NZSSCo. held on to a few smaller vessels and muddled along until it sold the last ones in 1882.

41 McKinnon (ed.), *New Zealand Historical Atlas*, Plate 52.

42 Rollo Arnold, *New Zealand's Burning*, Victoria University Press, Wellington, 1994, p. 194

43 Arnold, *New Zealand's Burning*, p. 213.

Chapter 4

1 Felipe Fernandez-Armesto, *Millennium*, Bantam Press, London, 1995, p. 391.

2 Figures from the *New Zealand Official Year-Book*, various years.

3 Simon Ville, 'The Transition to Iron and Steel Construction' in Robert Gardiner (ed.), *Sail's Last Century: The Merchant Sailing Ship 1830–1930*, London, 1993, p. 54.

4 Watson, *Links*, p.109.

5 Martine E Cuff, *Totara Estate*, New Zealand Historic Places Trust, Wellington, 1982, p. 31.

6 Cuff, p. 35.

7 Brett, *White Wings*, Vol. 1, p. 149.

8 K C McDonald, *White Stone Country*, Oamaru Borough Council, Oamaru, 1960, p. 185.

9 McKinnon (ed.), *New Zealand Historical Atlas*, Plate 61.

10 McDonald, *White Stone Country*, p. 197.

11 S D Waters, *Clipper Ship to Motor Liner*, New Zealand Shipping Company, London, 1939, p. 31.

12 Mrs Robert Wilson, *My Journal in New Zealand*, Sampson Low, Marston, Searle & Rivington, London, 1894, pp. 59–60.

13 Quoted in Waters, p. 43.

14 W A Laxon, I J Farquhar, N J Kirby and F W Perry, *Crossed Flags*, World Ship Society, Gravesend, 1997, p.16.

15 Holdsworth to Mills, 21 Apr 1915, C. Holdsworth Letterbook, 8.7.14–29.8.15, Union Steam Ship Company Archives, Hocken Library.

16 J M Ritchie to J W Temple, 22 Dec 1896, J M Ritchie Private Letterbook 1895–97, Hocken Library.

17 T G Coveney, *A Venture Into Shipping: A Success Story*, Geo H Scales, Wellington, 1972, p. 37.

18 McLean, *The Southern Octopus*, p. 94.

19 Wanderer, *Antipodean Notes Collected on a Nine Months Tour Round the World*, Sampson Low, Marston, Searle and Rivington, London, 1888, pp. 194—95.

20 Quoted in McLean, *The Southern Octopus: the Rise and Demise of the Union Steam Ship Company 1875–2000, an Essay*, Museum of Wellington City & Sea, Wellington, 2001, p.10.

21 See Gavin McLean, *Canterbury Coasters*, New Zealand Ship & Marine Society, Wellington, 1987.

22 See Gavin McLean, *Richardsons of Napier*, New Zealand Ship & Marine Society, Wellington, 1989.

23 See Gavin McLean, 'The Maoriland Steamship Company', *Bearings*, Vol. 2, No. 2, pp. 11–13, 1990.

24 See Barbara Mountier, 'Pehr Ferdinand Holm', in Claudia Orange (ed.), *The Dictionary of New Zealand Biography*, Vol. 2, Bridget Williams Books & Department of Internal Affairs, Wellington, 1993, p. 226.

25 N S Falla to Sydney Holm, 11 Feb 1935, Holm Shipping Company Papers, Union Steam Ship Company Archives, MOWCAS.

26 Johnson, *New Zealand's Maritime Heritage*, p. 76.

27 Erik Olssen, 'The Seamen's Union and Industrial Militancy 1908–13', *New Zealand Journal of History*, Vol. 19, No. 1, p. 17.

28 Belich, p. 428.

29 *Evening Post*, 15 Dec 1898.

30 Neill Atkinson, 'Against the Tide: the Auckland Seamen's Union 1880-1914', in Pat Walsh (ed.), *Trade Unions, Work and Society: the Centenary of the Arbitration System*, Dunmore Press, Palmerston North, 1994, p. 70.

31 A McNab, 'Westport in the Not So Olden Days', in *Marine News*, Vol. 26, No. 4, 1975, p. 150.

32 S D Waters, *Richardsons of Napier*, Whitcombe & Tombs/Richardsons, 1959, p. 64.

33 McLean, *The Southern Octopus*, p. 99.

34 *New Zealand Times*, 23 Nov 1905.

35 See Conrad Bollinger, *Against the Wind: the Story of the New Zealand Seamen's Union*, New Zealand Seamen's Union, Wellington, 1968. Also Neill Atkinson, 'Against the Tide' and John Walsh, 'The Seamen on Strike, 1922–1923', in Pat Walsh (ed.), *Trade Unions, Work and Society*, 1994 and Erik Olssen, 'The Seamen's Union and Industrial Militancy 1908–13'.

36 Olssen, 'The Seamen's Union and Industrial Militancy', p. 15.

37 Atkinson, p. 72.

38 McLean, *Southern Octopus*, pp. 103–5.

39 Gordon McLauchlan (ed.), *The Line That Dared: a History of the Union Steam Ship Company*, Four Star Books, Auckland, 1987, p. 62.

40 Christopher J Napier, 'Secret Accounting in New Zealand: P&O and the Union Steam Ship Company, 1917–1936', in Atsuo Tsuji and Paul Garner, *Studies in Accounting History: Tradition and Innovation for the Twenty-First Century*, Greenwood Press, Westport, 1995, p. 138

41 Gordon Boyce, *Information, Mediation and Institutional Development: the Rise of Large-Scale Enterprise in British Shipping, 1870-1919*, Manchester University Press, Manchester, 1995, p. 105.

42 G D G Jensen, 'First Voyage', in *Marine News*, Vol. 47, 2, 1998, p. 75.

43 Frank Broeze, 'Distance Tamed: Steam Navigation to Australia and New Zealand from its Beginnings to the Outbreak of the Great War', in *The Journal of Transport History*, Third Series, Vol. 10/1 Mar 1989, p. 14.

44 Johnson, *New Zealand's Maritime Heritage*, p. 125.

45 Gavin McLean, 'New Zealand Division of the Royal Navy', in Ian McGibbon (ed.), *The Oxford Companion to New Zealand Military History*, pp. 362–4.

Chapter 5

1 James Belich, 'Colonisation and History in New Zealand', in Robin W Tonks (ed.), *The Oxford History of the British Empire*, Vol. V, Oxford, 1999, pp. 183–84.

2 John Darwin, 'The Dominion Idea in Imperial Politics', in Judith Brown and Wm Roger Louis, *The Oxford History of the British Empire*, Vol. IV,

The Twentieth Century, Oxford, 1999, p. 72.

3   *Marine News*, editorial, Vol. 23, No. 2, 1971, p. 35.

4   Gordon Boyce, *Information, Mediation and Institutional Development: the Rise of Large-Scale Enterprise in British Shipping, 1870–1919*, Manchester University Press, Manchester, 1995, p. 160.

5   Quoted in Anna Green, *British Capital, Antipodean Labour: Working the New Zealand Waterfront, 1915–1951*, University of Otago Press, Dunedin, 2001, p. 17.

6   Gordon Boyce, *Information, Mediation and Institutional Development*, p. 161.

7   Quoted in Green, *British Capital*, p. 19.

8   Green, *British Capital*, p. 19.

9   Gavin McLean, *Rocking the Boat?*, p. 212.

10 Geo H Scales annual reports, Scales Corporation Archives, Christchurch.

11 Christopher J Napier, 'Secret Accounting in New Zealand'.

12 Christopher J Napier, 'Allies or Subsidiaries? Inter-Company Relations in the P&O Group, 1914–39', in *Business History*, Vol. 239, No. 2, 1997, p. 85.

13 Napier, 'Secret Accounting in New Zealand', p. 155.

14 Geoffrey Blainey, *The Tyranny of Distance: How Distance Shaped Australia's History*, Revised edn., Sydney, 1983, p. 286.

15 Gordon Boyce, 'Union Steam Ship Company of New Zealand and the Adoption of Oil Propulsion: Learning-by-Using Effects', in *Journal of Transport History*, third series, Vol.18, No. 2, Sep 1997, p. 136.

16 Mike Richards, *Workhorses in Australian Waters: A History of Marine Engineering in Australia*, Turton & Armstrong, Wahroonga, 1987, p. 157.

17 Richards, *Workhorses in Australian Waters*, p. 161.

18 G A Ricketts, 'RRMS 'Aorangi' 1924–1953', in *New Zealand Marine News*, Vol. 30, No. 2, 1980, p. 56.

19 See W A Laxon, *Davey and the Awatea*, Dunmore Press, Palmerston North, 1997.

20 M H Pryce, 'Shell Tankers of New Zealand', *Marine News* Vol. 27, No. 2, 1976, p. 61. and Pryce 'New Zealand's Coastal Tankers', *Marine News* Vol. 49, No. 4, 2000, pp.164–77.

21 I G Stewart, *Ships that Serve New Zealand*, p. 19.

22 Abrose Greenway, 'Passenger Liners', Ambrose Greenway (ed.), *The Golden Age of Shipping*, Conway Maritime Press, London, 1994, p. 20.

23 Scotter, *A History of Port Lyttelton*, p. 193.

24 See Jeff Maynard, *Niagara's Gold*, Kangaroo Press, Kenthurst, 1996.

25 See K R Cassells, *Fairmile Flotillas of the Royal New Zealand Navy*, New Zealand Ship & Marine Society, Wellington, 1993.

26 Johnson, *New Zealand's Maritime Heritage*, p. 133. Nancy M Taylor, *The Home Front Vol. II*, Government Printer, Wellington, 1986, p. 741, gives slightly different figures: 50 small wooden tugs, 22 steel seagoing tugs, and 15 powered lighters; later wooden barges, oil barges, five small general purpose vessels for servicing Pacific Islands and more wooden tugs for the British.

27 Taylor, *The Home Front*, p. 741.

28 *Marine News*, Vol.1, No.5, 1949, 1999 souvenir reprint, p. 86.

29 Stewart, *Ships That Serve New Zealand*, p. 95.

30 Megan Hutching, *Long Journey for Sevenpence: Assisted Immigration to New Zealand from the United Kingdom 1947–1975*, VUP, Wellington, 1999, p. 10.

31 ibid., p. 110.

32 Hank Schouten, *Tasman's Legacy: the New Zealand-Dutch Connection*, New Zealand-Netherlands Foundation, Wellington, 1992, p. 100.

33 These were Southern Cross Shipping, which ran the small coasters *Gael* and *Koau* between 1948 and 1964 and the Tasman Shipping Company, whose story is told by Captain Clough Blair in the aptly-named *Shoestring Shipping Line*, A H & A W Reed, Wellington, 1967.

34 *Marine News*, Vol. 1, Nos.1–6, 1999, souvenir reprint, pp. 13–14.

35 Quoted in McLean, *Richardsons of Napier*, pp. 65–67.

36 John O'C Ross, *Pride in Their Ports*, Dunmore Press, Palmerston North, 1977, p. 84.

37 See Ian Church, *Little Ships of Patea*, Dunmore Press, Palmerston North, 1977.

38 Figures from Canterbury Shipping Company records, quoted in McLean, *Canterbury Coasters*, New Zealand Ship & Marine Society, 1987, p. 57.

39 *New Zealand Herald*, 30 Jun 1951.

40 *Auckland Star*, 5 Jul 1956.

41 McLean, *Richardsons of Napier*, p. 80.

42 Robert Chapman, 'From Labour to National' in W H Oliver and B R Williams (eds), *The Oxford History of New Zealand*, OUP, Wellington, 1981, p. 154.

43 Green, *British Capital*, p. 22.

44 McLean, *Rocking the Boat?*, pp. 251–60.

45 Green, *British Capital*, pp. 9–10.

46 Green, *British Capital*, p. 82.

47 Bert Roth, *Wharfie: 'From Hand Barrows to Straddles', Unionism on the Auckland Waterfront*, Auckland Branch New Zealand Watersiders' Union, Auckland, 1993, p. 87.

48 Roth, *Wharfie*, p. 70.

49 Gavin McLean, *Masters or Servants?*, p. 55.

50 Barry Gustafson, 'The National Governments and Social Change', in Keith Sinclair (ed.), *The Oxford Illustrated History of New Zealand*, Oxford University Press, Auckland, 1990, p. 277.

51 For accounts of the 1951 strike, see Michael Bassett, *Confrontation '51: the 1951 Waterfront Dispute*, A H & A W Reed, Wellington, 1972 and Dick Scott, *151 Days*, commemorative edition, Reed Books, Auckland, 2001.

52 I M McGibbon (ed.), *The Oxford Companion to New Zealand Military History*, p. 239.

53 Robert Chapman, 'From Labour to National', in Geoffrey W Rice, *The Oxford History of New Zealand*, 2nd edn, Oxford University Press, Auckland, 1992, p. 375.

54 Quoted in Green, *British Capital*, p. 148.

55 Green, *British Capital*, p. 91

56 See John Hall-Jones, *Bluff Harbour*, Southland Harbour Board, Bluff, 1986.

57 W H Scotter, *A History of Port Lyttelton*, Lyttelton Harbour Board, Christchurch, pp. 302–7.

58 Graham Vercoe, *Bow Waves on the Waikato*, Reed Books, Auckland, 1997, p. 79.

Chapter 6

1   Emmanuel Makarios, 'Pathway Over the Seas', *Marine News*, Vol. 41, No. 1, 1991, p. 6.

2   These numbers were later increased. The description of the *Aramoana* is based on two small booklets issued by the NZR Printing and Publicity Department in 1964; A T Gandell, *The Cook Strait Rail-Ferry* and H Z Purchase, *Mechanical Features of the Aramoana*. See also Bob Stott, *The Cook Strait Ferry Story*, Southern Press Ltd., Porirua, 1981.

3   David Lyon (compiler), *The Denny List, Part IV*, National Maritime Museum, Greenwich, 1975, p. 1005.

4   Johnson, *Wellington Harbour*, p. 358.

5   Alan A Kirk, *Express Steamers of Cook Strait*, A H & A W Reed, Wellington, 1968, p. 164.

6   Stott, *The Cook Strait Ferry Story*, p. 16.

7   Quoted in Johnson, *Wellington Harbour*, p. 354.

8   Ted Caldwell, *Strikebound*, Caxton Press, Christchurch, 1994, p. 161.

9   Johnson, *Wellington Harbour*, p. 447.

10 Johnson, *Wellington Harbour*, p. 448.

11 David Leitch and Bob Stott, *New Zealand Railways: The First 125 Years*, Heinemann Reed, Auckland, 1988, p. 124.

12 James Cowan, foreword in Eaddy, *'Neath Swaying Spars*.

13 H S Eckford, *History of the Eckford Shipping Company & Blenheim River Traders 1881–1965*, author, Blenheim, 1995, p. 79.

14 See Pauline Wood, *Kaiapoi: a Search for Identity*, Waimakariri District Council, Rangiora, 1993.

15 'Ringbolt', 'One Ship-One Trip', in *Marine News*, Vol. 21, No. 3, 1976, p. 83.

16 'Ringbolt', 'One Ship-One Trip', in *Marine News*, Vol. 21, No. 3, 1976, p. 87.

17 J F Holm to F K Macfarlane, Holm Shipping Papers, Wellington Museum, City & Sea.

18 See Tony Nightingale, *The Pacific Forum Line: a Commitment to Regional Shipping*, Clerestory Press, Christchurch, 1998.

19 Gerry Evans, *Where Giants Dwell: a Sailor's Tale*, David Ling, Auckland, 2000, pp. 96–97.

20 *Marine News*, Vol. 33, No. 1, 1983, p. 132.

21 The *New Zealand Trader* entered service in February 1984.

22 In 1995 TEL produced a small, spiral-bound company history, *Making Waves: the First Decade of History 1985–1995*.

23 Johnson, *Wellington Harbour*, p. 371.

24 Sidney Gilman, 'Container Shipping', in Alistair Couper (ed.), *The Shipping Revolution: the Modern Merchant Ship*, Conway Maritime Press, London, 1992, p. 42.

25 Gilman, 'Container Shipping', p. 45.

26 For a history of ACT, see I J Farquhar, 'Introduction, ACTS 1 to 12 and Finale', in *Marine News*, Vol. 47, No. 4, 1998, pp. 178–208.

27 Johnson, *Wellington Harbour*, p. 385.

28 See Northland Harbours Board, 'The Farmer and the Container Age: Will the Farmer Gain Anything?: If So, How?', Northland Harbours Board, Whangarei, 1969.

29 McLean, *Otago Harbour*, p. 199.

30 McLean, *Otago Harbour*, p. 208.

31 See John McCrystal, *The Owens Story: the Life and Businesses of Sir Robert Owens*, Four Star Books, Auckland, 1999.

32 *Marine News*, Vol. 36, No. 2, 1986, pp. 66–68.

33 For a history of SCONZ, see Ian Farquhar, *Jack of All Trades, Master of None: the Shipping Corporation of New Zealand Limited 1973–1989*, New Zealand Ship & Marine Society, Wellington, 1996.

34 McLean, *Masters or Servants?*, Wellington, New Zealand Merchant Service Guild, 1990, p. 78,

35 McLean, *Rocking the Boat?*, p. 163.

36 For WECO, see P J Leahy, 'Whangarei Engineering and Construction Limited', *Marine News*, Vol. 28, No.2, 1977, pp. 48–53 and R J McDougall, 'Whangarei Engineering and Construction Limited', *Marine News*, Vol. 35, No. 4, 1985, pp. 131–2 and 135. For Otago shipbuilding, see Gavin McLean, *Otago Harbour*.

37 McLean, *Otago Harbour*.

38 See Harry Julian, *Sea in My Blood*, author, Auckland, 1999.

39 See David Balderston, *The Waiheke Ferries of Auckland*, Grantham House, Wellington, 1991.

40 Tessa Duder, Barry Thompson and Clifford Hawkins, *Spirit of Adventure*, Century Hutchinson, Auckland, 1985, p. 29.

41 HMNZS *Canterbury* followed later.

42 See Michael King, *Death of the Rainbow Warrior*, Penguin, Auckland, 1985; David Robie, *Eyes of Fire: the Last Voyage of the Rainbow Warrior*, Lindon Publishing, Auckland, 1986 and Shears, Richard and Isobelle Gridley, *The Rainbow Warrior Affair*, Unwin Paperbacks, Sydney, 1985.

43 *Marine News*, Vol. 36, No. 2, 1986, p. 73.

44 For a modern survey of some of the country's lighthouses, see Grant Sheehan and Anna Gibbons, *Leading Lights: Lighthouses of New Zealand*, Hazard Press, Christchurch, 1991.

45 'Onshore Costs – The Transport, Handling and Related Costs of Goods Carried by Sea', Wellington, 1984.

46 A few minor commercial ports were transferred direct to local authorities.

47 Johnson, *Wellington*, p. 438.

48 *Shipping Gazette*, 13 Jul 1996.

49 Doug Green, 'Port Reform in New Zealand, One Port's Perspective', http://www.hrnichols.com.au/nicholls/nichvol17/volxv0io.htm

Chapter 7

1 *Dominion*, 13 July 1989, quoted in Johnson, *Wellington Harbour*, p. 449.

2 Johnson, *Wellington Harbour*, p. 447

3 See Robert Clifford with Kim Lowrie, *Incat – the First 40 Years*, Baird Publications, Southbank, 1998.

4 *New Zealand Shipping Gazette,* 3 Dec 1994.

5 *Marine News*, Vol. 44, No. 1, 1995, p. 43.

6 *Marine News*, Vol. 44, No. 2, 1995, p. 99.

7 *Evening Post*, 15 Dec 1994.

8 *Marine News*, Vol. 44, No. 2, 1995, p. 100.

9 *Marine News*, Vol. 49, No. 3, 2000, p. 141.

10 *Evening Post*, 7 Dec 1994.

11 *Marine News*, Vol. 49, No. 3, 2000, p. 142.

12 *Shipping Gazette*, 18 Jul 1998.

13 *Shipping Gazette*, 29 Jun 1996.

14 *Shipping Gazette*, 29 Jun 1996.

15 *Shipping Gazette*, 2 Apr 1994.

16 *Shipping Gazette*, 20 Jan 1996.

17 *New Zealand Official Yearbook 2000*, Wellington, 2000, p. 479.

18 *Shipping Gazette*, 4 Apr 1996.

19 *Shipping Gazette*, 5 Oct 1996.

20 *New Zealand Official Yearbook*, various years.

21 Balderston, p. 84. New Zealand's first female ship's officer was Gladys Yorke, who worked on the ferry *Tamahine* during the war. For interview with Phillipa Reynolds, see Roy Sinclair, *Journeying with Seafarers in New Zealand*, Random House, Auckland, 1999. Sally Fodie's reminiscences were published in *Waitemata Ferry Tales*, Collins, Auckland, 1991.

22 Roth, *Wharfie*, p. 191.

23 *Dominion*, 16 Mar 2001.

24 *Shipping Gazette*, 16 May 1998.

25 Keith Trace, 'A Most Vexatious Business: Union Shipping and the trans-Tasman Liner Trade', in the *Australian Economic History Review* XXXII: 2, 1992, p. 93.

26 *New Zealand Herald*, 23 Oct 1998.

27 P&O Nedlloyd kept the Blue Star names.

28 W H Parr, *Port Nelson – Gateway to the Sea*, Nelson Harbour Board, Nelson, 1979, p. 204.

29 This summary is based on the article 'The Fish Quota Management System', which appeared in *Scales News*, Issue 2, September 1996, p. 4.

30 *Shipping Gazette*, 17 Aug 1996, p. 3.

31 Kirk Hargreaves, *On the Next Tide*, Canterbury University Press, Christchurch, 1998, p. 12.

32 *Shipping Gazette*, 11 May, p. 1996.

33 Rachel Body, 'Ports Risk Drowning as Battle of Big Boys Intensifies', *Dominion*, 31 Mar 2001.

34 *Marine News*, Vol. 45, No. 2, 1996, p. 110.

35 *Shipping Gazette*, 19 Oct 1996 and *Marine News*, Vol. 45, No. 4, 1996, pp. 195–7.

36 *Press*, 23 Jan 2001.

37 Gavin McLean, editorial, *Marine News*, Vol. 46, No. 4, 1997, p. 168.

38 Tessa Duder, *Waitemata, Auckland's City of Sails*, Century Hutchinson, Auckland, 1989, p. 111.

39 See Rodney Wilson, 'The Birth of the Big Boat', *Bearings*, Vol. 2, No. 2, 1990, pp. 4–9.

40 Harold Kidd, Robin Elliott and David Pardon, *Southern Breeze*, Viking, Auckland, 1999, p. 201.

41 *Otago Daily Times*, 5 Feb 2001.

42 For histories of the Devonport and Gulf Ferries, see David Balderston, *The Harbour Ferries of Auckland* and *The Waiheke Ferries of Auckland*, Grantham House, Wellington, 1986 and 1991. An update can be found in *Marine News* Vol. 49, No. 2, 2000, pp. 90–95.

43 See M R G Subritzky, *Subritzky Shipping (A Heritage of Sail) 1843—1993*, and *Marine News,* Vol. 49, No.3, 2000, pp. 133–37.

44 Whale Watch website, http://www.whalewatch.co.nz/the.htm

45 For a history of Fiordland Travel, see Les Hutchins, *Making Waves*, author, Queenstown, 1998.

46 Milford Travel website, http://www.fiordlandtravel.co.nz/Fiordland

Index